"Millions have sought ̇ Williams has hunted dow̲   d distilled their inspiring stories into lessons that we can all put to use. It's an engaging, actionable read for anyone looking to gain fans, followers, or customers in the digital age."

—Adam Grant, Wharton professor and *New York Times* bestselling author of *Originals* and *Give and Take*

"*Full of actionable insights, this book is pure gold for anyone wanting to make it in the Influencer Economy.*"

—Nir Eyal, author of *Hooked: How to Build Habit-Forming Products*

"*If you've ever thought about monetizing your passion, Ryan Williams delivers an insiders guide to prospering from the Influencer Economy.*"

—Jay Samit, bestselling author of *DisruptYou! Master Personal Transformation, Seize Opportunity*, and *Thrive in the Era of Endless Innovation*

"In an age when a big idea can be launched—and a big industry shaken up—with nothing more than a laptop, The Influencer Economy *offers a blueprint for how to do it. If you want to understand the way the world works now, this is a must read."*

—Willie Geist, host NBC's *TODAY* and MSNBC's *Morning Joe*

To Katherine, who was the original lightning in a bottle.

To Julia and Libby, who have kept me enjoying life as this book was completed.

Contents

Preface

The Influencer Economy is a movement and book to help you to launch your idea, share it with the world and thrive in the digital age. What I realized early in the process of writing this book and creating my podcast, is that in order to thrive in the digital age, you don't need to go to business school. You don't need an Ivy League degree. You don't need to know celebrities. And you don't need to have a lot of money. You just need to learn the new rules of success from the emerging leaders of the Influencer Economy.

I wrote this book from my own perspective as a creative entrepreneur, bootstrapping my ideas and vision without any large budget. I'm imagining you're in a similar boat—it's you and maybe a co-founder out there working on your idea, and it's a lonely slog. I want this book to move your journey along and help you build a community and platform around your idea, even if your idea has yet to launch.

When I began attending VidCon, Comic-Con, South by Southwest (SXSW), TechCrunch Disrupt and other tech and fan-geek conferences, I noticed two remarkable things: these events were celebrating geeks, technology, and modern social media; and no one was telling the stories of the awesome people embracing this new form of influence and the wildly successful businesses they were creating. I was on the front lines of what I called the Influencer Economy, and this movement was permeating all technology and media-based businesses, from California to New York to London to Mumbai.

I was inspired and went on to launch a podcast dedicated to interviewing the Influencer Economy pioneers. After speaking to more than a hundred artists, experts, and entrepreneurs—from world-famous YouTubers to *New York Times* best-selling authors to the most creative start-up founders and investors on the planet—I reverse engineered their careers, to understand the stories behind their success, and now present everything I learned in *The Influencer Economy: How to Launch Your Idea, Share It with the World and Thrive in the Digital Age.* You can listen to the podcast here:

www.influencereconomy.com

This is the book I wish I had when I launched my podcast and started writing this book. The three primary steps to success in the Influencer Economy—launch, share and thrive—can be applied to both business and life. I wrote about the fascinating stories of more than a dozen people who turned their visions, ideas, and hobbies into influential and profitable digital media empires. In each chapter I also provide the "Influencer School Lessons" derived from each of these individuals' journeys for everyone to learn from. I aim for you to understand lessons from influencers, that will help you to launch your idea. I also wrote-out specific actions readers can take to launch their own ideas into the online universe.

The Influencer Economy features 10 key principles that are the building blocks of the Influencer Economy—with elements such as crafting your big vision, picking a platform, community collaboration, and opening doors for others.

I wrote this book for you—people with a business idea or product launch who are interested in how they might become part of this fast-moving phenomenon. If you have a curious personality and an idea that you'd like to explore, or an itch that you want to scratch around building a business or a creative idea whether it's a hobby or passion project, this book was made for you to serve as a guidebook to get your idea out to the world. Whether you have a day job working on a side passion project, or have gone full-time with your idea, the lessons and actions of this book will give you a business launch framework for the digital age. The book comes with an action-guidebook for you to take the next steps with your idea.

For the entire *Influencer Economy Lesson and Action Guidebook*, go here:

http://www.influencereconomy.com/influencers

Learning from the Influencer Economy

Years ago I was performing stand-up comedy onstage at the world-renowned DC Improv. With bright lights shining in my eyes, I was in front of a packed house of 300 people who were drinking watered-down lite beers and ready to laugh. I was eyeing my set list of seven well-rehearsed jokes that I had practiced at open-mic nights for years. I gazed into the bright spotlights looking me straight in the eye, feeling the anticipation of the crowd, waiting for the moment to tell my opening joke.

I wanted to puke.

In the early 2000s I had battled through nerves, smoky clubs, and hecklers in an effort to tell jokes for a living. Audiences called me every name in the book. When I did do well, and "kill it" as my fellow comedians would say, it felt amazing. But after performing stand-up for many years, I quickly learned the lesson that in comedy you get rejected, a lot. This insight helped me later in life when I turned to a career in tech entrepreneurship, but at the time the rejection was much more palpable. Ultimately I realized to become the next Louis C.K., Patton Oswalt, or Amy Schumer, you need 510 years of honing your craft to get really good.

I also spent part of my mid-twenties battling chronic depression, even while I was regularly performing stand-up. There were days where I never left my one-bedroom studio except to drive to comedy gigs and go to my day job. My entire life outlook was negative and self-defeating, I didn't completely understand my dark mood, and I knew something was off.

Dealing with Rejection

Around this time, I had met an amazing and beautiful woman who eventually became my wife, and she helped me to realize that I should "drop the mic" on my comedy career and retire. She was right. At the same time, I learned to manage my depression and dark moods, I was better, and I started to fire on more cylinders.

Stand-up comedy taught me that rejection is a part of life, and anything worth pursuing will make you work hard for it. This was an important lesson to learn. During that period, from meeting my awesome wife, it was a turning point in my life. I realized that in pursuing a passion project, there is no guarantee you can turn it into a successful business, or even a way to earn part-time income. With stand-up I faced rejection nearly every night that I performed. Even now when I get rejected I look back at my stand-up comedy career for motivation.

Relationships Are Key to Your Success

After "dropping the mic" on comedy career, I worked a job at a DC-based nonprofit, the Pension Rights Center. While feeling that I was helping the world at this advocacy group, it also helped to pay my bills, but as a curious person by nature I had another creative itch to scratch. I started making short films on the weekend with friends and amateur filmmakers. I was a hobbyist filmmaker, which helped me grow my network in the industry, and I eventually got my foot in the door of the entertainment business working as an assistant on TV shows shot on location like *The Wire* and movies like *Evan Almighty* and *Breach*. After a year and a half of working in film and TV in DC, I took a risk. My girlfriend

Katherine and I moved to Los Angeles to chase a career in Hollywood.

In the film industry the old adage is true: It's not what you know but who you know." If stand-up taught me how to deal with rejection, the film industry taught me that relationships were paramount to one's success in business and life. By getting my foot in the door of the DC/Baltimore film scene, it helped me to cultivate a professional network across the country in Los Angeles. By working film gigs and as a location scout and personal assistant, I had built meaningful friendships & business relationships that I could tap into to help my career in Hollywood. I got work in LA because I knew the right people.

My first jobs in LA were once again working as an assistant on TV shows like *Ugly Betty* and as a coordinator on National Geographic films. It was fun working on the front lines of the entertainment business. My bosses were some of the more brilliant writers and producers in the field. But it didn't take long to realize that the TV and film industry is controlled by gatekeepers and people who are determined to make you "pay your dues." Many smart people end up eating dirt for years before having even the possibility of getting their work seen. A lot creative people move to LA with ambitions to "make it" but 10 years later they are still waiting tables waiting for their big break.

Playing the Long Game in Life

A second learning from my Hollywood entertainment work was that business and life is very much a "long term game," where you need to put in the hours and even years to make it your respective field. A friend had given me great advice that Hollywood was "all about attrition," and that every year, people move back home and quit pursuing their entertainment careers. When people return home whom you are competing with, you move up one more spot to get your opportunity. There's a military phrase, "only the strong survive," which rings true here. In my life's endeavors, I find that if you keep pursuing your goals while others quit, you will find success in the long run.

These Hollywood experiences made me stronger. Often in life lessons, you need to cross things off your list for what you want to do. You are better for having made the effort, rather than avoiding it entirely. I'd rather fail and learn than miss the failure entirely because I didn't take the risk. After pursuing my entertainment career, I began accepting the risk-taking nature of my personality. I loved that chance I created to move to Hollywood, and was ready to move onto the next challenge.

That's when I segued my career into tech and media start-ups.

Entering Technology Entrepreneurship

In 2006, I started working full-time at cutting edge social media marketing firms and full-scale YouTube video networks. I networked a way into a start-up, job at a startup, DigiSynd, and it was a great move. Disney acquired the company and we focused launching the social media for major Disney brands like Pixar and Disney Parks. We were on the front lines of Facebook, Twitter, and YouTube to market major Disney properties to the world. The job at Disney was awesome experience and truly valuable.

But I was laid off a year and half after the acquisition. I had dealt with rejection before as a comedian, and after accepting the fall-out of not having a job anymore my instincts took over. I relied on my entertainment relationship-building skills and I tapped into my professional network. After sending out a few e-mails, I was only laid off for one week. After I reached out to a friend at a startup Machinima.com, that at the time was a

YouTube video network focused on the video game generation, I got a job at Machinima in no time, and even negotiated myself a raise at the new job. It was an exciting time.

While working at Machinima in 2009, I oversaw the network marketing for our YouTube channels and was promoted to Director of Marketing. At that time, we were serving over four billion views a month on YouTube videos. Yes, four *billion* views a month! I was in the middle of a digital revolution, where a new class of creators was emerging and our company was valued at $200 million by investors around that time. This is when I first saw the Influencer Economy at work.

Influencers Are Transforming Media and Technology Industries

When I attended the global video conference VidCon for the first time in 2010, I witnessed another amazing thing: YouTube personalities were their own businesses, and it was all centered on their videos. Creators were getting checks of $60,000 to $100,000 on a quarterly basis for playing video games like *Minecraft* and posting their videos on YouTube for millions to see. Many of these gamers were still in high school or living in their college dorm room. Confused parents would call our office demanding to understand how their child was making so much money playing games like *World of Warcraft*. At Machinima, these young creators were not only driving massive YouTube video channels, they were also becoming successful entrepreneurs.

This all inspired me. In 2014, with an amazing and supportive wife and a newborn baby, and years of marketing knowledge in my brain, I decided to bet on myself. I wanted to shine a light on the incredible ways these new influencers were shaping society on several levels—economically, technologically, and socially. In the end I decided to write a book, something I'd never done before. I also had to create something from nothing. But where would I start?

I set out to write a book and called this phenomenon the Influencer Economy. Then I created a podcast. I spoke to over a hundred people who are experts in this exploding new form of influence, from world-famous YouTubers to *New York Times* best-selling authors, to the most creative start-up founders and investors on the planet. (You can hear these interviews at www.influencereconomy.com)

After years of living and breathing this stuff, I then reverse-engineered the careers of geeks, creators, and entrepreneurs across all emergent media industries and distilled their success stories into three steps and ten principles. With some variance, every one of these people has followed this Influencer Economy framework. Every single one.

Sharing Influencer School Lessons

Each chapter in this book is centered on a philosophy that anyone with an idea in the digital age can apply to their area of focus. The philosophies are presented and discussed in three steps that serve as the book's overview and backbone. The three steps are 1) Launch 2) Share 3) Thrive. Each chapter opens with a brief playbook outlining the guiding philosophy and goals for the chapter. Then comes a featured story that highlights the inspiring narratives of some of today's leading influencers. At the end of each chapter, I provide Influencer Economy lessons and actions. There are key takeaways from all the narrative stories, making this book not simply an entertaining collection of profiles but a lesson plan to help you learn from these influencers, and an action guide for you to make moves in the Influencer Economy that will have a positive and fulfilling impact in your own life.

I have been extremely lucky and am grateful for the collaborative experience of writing this book. Many people have given me their time, insights, and feedback to make the final product, and it all started with my podcast guests. I am a curious person by nature and created the podcast to provide a forum to get to know this new class of influencers. I treated the podcast like a laboratory, where each guest could share with my audience their ideas, work, and passion behind how they built amazing things in the digital age. I was incredibly fortunate, because with each episode I could explore the worlds of amazing thinkers, pioneering creators, and world-renowned entrepreneurs and learn as much as possible for my listeners.

But the collaboration didn't end there. As the podcast picked up steam week by week, month by month, and year by year, I discovered the most amazing thing about the entire book-writing process: the people who joined the community around the book. It has been awesome teaming up with the podcast community, and luckily some very smart listeners volunteered to crowd-edit my early drafts. They 100 percent made this book much better than I could have if I went at the writing process on my own. I thank each of these editors in the acknowledgments.

I found inspiration in telling the stories of more than a dozen people who turned their visions, ideas, or hobbies into influential and profitable digital media empires. I have included YouTube sensations who crowdfunded millions of dollars for film projects, founders of large conferences like VidCon, and comedians who have built media empires off a podcast. Additionally I profile the stories of music industry and tech magnates, journalists who pioneered online column writing, and many others who have define the movement and culture of the Influencer Economy. I look forward to sharing this book with you.

Here's the basic framework of *The Influencer Economy*. We'll spend the rest of the book discussing each one of these areas in detail.

Step 1: Launch

Chapter 1: Craft a Big Vision

Chapter 2: Pick Your Platform

Chapter 3: Book Your Own Gigs—The Jay Z Effect

Chapter 4: Adopt New Technology Early and Often

Step 2: Share

Chapter 5: Strive for Authenticity

Chapter 6: Collaborate

Chapter 7: Capture Lightning in a Bottle

Step 3: Thrive

Chapter 8: Open Doors for Others

Chapter 9: Meet People In Real Life (IRL)

Chapter 10: Give Your Community Ownership

Step 1: Launch

ONE OF THE BIGGEST TAKEAWAYS from my conversations with leaders in the Influencer Economy is that they all just started and launched their ideas. As a creative entrepreneur, you'd rather make mistakes when no one is watching rather than when the bright lights on the big stage are focused on you and your work. You need to get your practice now before you get famous or well known in your field. Why? Because as Flula Borg, the subject of chapter 7, has said, unless you are famous like Kanye West, no one cares if you make mistakes.

So just start. Hone your craft. Start making, creating, and producing. Be inspired. And launch.

When I performed stand-up comedy, the single most common piece of advice that I received was to "get on stage as much as you can." Super-successful comedians like Mitch Hedberg always advised me to practice in front of crowds as much as possible. You can't simulate stand-up comedy crowds, and the same goes for launching your ideas—you won't know how they'll be received until you put them in front of people. When I started recording my podcast in 2013, I followed a similar philosophy by launching it after interviewing influencers whom I respected. When I wanted to write my book, I just started writing and now, years later, you're reading my work. When you start launching, you can focus on the important principles that encompass taking those first four steps of the Launch phase: Crafting a big vision, Picking a platform, Booking your own gigs, and Embracing technology early.

I recommend that you find something you believe in, make it while you go, and launch your idea. Remember that in the Influencer Economy, often the journey is just as important as the end result. Again, until you are famous, no one will care if you make mistakes. The guests on my podcast taught me to not worry about perfection; they focused on creating their idea and then launching it into the world. Like most of these influencers, you will get rejected. A lot. But you must wear rejection like a badge of honor, realizing it's a temporary roadblock. You have to in order to survive in the Influencer Economy.

Chapter 1

Craft Your Big Vision

"It's the little details that are vital. Little things make big things happen."

—John Wooden

Chapter Playbook

If you are reading this book, you probably have one thing that you geek out about more than anyone else you know. It's that one topic that really excites you that you chat endlessly about when grabbing a beer at the pub with friends. Or it's that business idea that drives your coworkers crazy because you can't stop chatting about it over an afternoon coffee. It may even be something that you understand more than anyone else, and you are eager to share your knowledge with everyone else.

My geek passions have been stand-up comedy, filmmaking, tech start-ups and now *The Influencer Economy*. From all these passions, I've enjoyed the most success with tech start-ups. Why? I crafted a big vision around my passions. Looking back, I had no such vision around stand-up comedy and filmmaking, which is why they never panned out as viable career options. When I worked closely with tech founders helping to market their ideas and products, I learned the value of having a big vision. I saw first hand that people love to respond to big ideas. If you have a big idea that starts small, with tangible projects and actions, then you can thrive in the Influencer Economy. I have learned when presenting an idea to influencers, investors and collaborators, people are responsive to the challenge of helping you fulfill your big vision with smaller projects along the way.

With my podcast, I knew that I wanted to write *The Influencer Economy* book, and the podcast helped me to reach that larger goal. I had wanted to launch a podcast for years, and it was finally time to stop talking about doing it and to just start making it. The podcast and book were symbiotic in their relationship. The book was the big vision to help launch my podcast. The podcast was the smaller project to help me write my book. Without the weekly work I put into the podcast, the larger vision of the book would have died. Without the larger vision of the book, the podcast would have lost purpose.

In this chapter, we will help you transform your geek passion into a bigger vision, and we'll look at conceiving and launching projects to help you along the way. Forming a big vision can sound intimidating, but I have learned that you can truly hone your vision if you follow the actions that we will detail in this chapter. The lessons you will learn are how to: find what drives you, determine your values, hone your big vision, forget perfection, start small with your big ideas when starting the launch phase.

There are two brothers who crafted a big vision over time, first starting by chatting with each other via online videos for one year. By creating video blogs, aka "vlogs," they built an amazing community to help them launch a lot of big ideas and inspiring projects along the way

The Vlogbrothers

There is an underground walkway in the Century City neighborhood in Los Angeles that connects the Hyatt Regency Hotel with the Hollywood talent representatives of the Creative Artists Agency, one of the biggest companies of its kind in the entertainment industry. On July 10, 2010, YouTube video creators of every genre met at that Hyatt Regency for the first annual VidCon video conference. I'm willing to bet that no talent agents from CAA or any entertainment agency were among the 1,200 attendees of the first VidCon, despite the close proximity of this conference to Hollywood. At this kickoff event, the pop culture vlogger, Mike Buckley, was appearing in videos with fans of his *What the Buck?!* vlog. Dan Brown, iJustine, Shay Carl, and a mix of other creators visited with their devoted YouTube subscribers and met fellow YouTubers like them. The Vlogbrothers themselves, Hank and John Green, were on hand because VidCon was their idea, born of the desire to spend time in real life (IRL) with their community and bring YouTubers together with industry leaders to discuss and celebrate online video.

It felt like a three-day party, with nightly performances by Mystery Guitar Man and other musicians who had built huge followings through YouTube. I've been back to each VidCon since that first summer and have watched the party get bigger. Now over 20,000 people went to the Anaheim Convention Center, VidCon's home since 2012. When you walk through the Convention Center it's as if Justin Timberlake has entered the building. Teenage girls shriek in fandom when they see their favorite stars, leaving their parents who are often in tow, awestruck at the passion for these video creators.

Over the past five years, I've heard the keynotes and fireside chats at VidCon push way beyond YouTube. Everyone from Vine and Vimeo to Snapchat and video companies you've never heard of are part of the conversation now that smartphones and digital video apps are more available than ever. These developments are all to the good as far as VidCon's founders are concerned. But dating back to 2006, when Hank and John Green first started to collaborate, YouTube was the dominant platform.

Who are the Greens? Apart from their online accomplishments, John is known for best-selling young adult novels and movies such as *The Fault Is in Our Stars*. Hank is John's visionary and entrepreneurial younger brother who has the leadership role on many of their co-ventures and has launched several of his own innovative charitable and education-based projects. But going back to 2006, when Hank and John Green first started to collaborate, YouTube was the dominant platform. And that's where they first emerged as pioneers in the Influencer Economy.

"It was 2007, YouTube had been around culturally and people had known of it for about a year," Hank said of his origins on the platform. "It just seemed really interesting, particularly Ze Frank who is now running BuzzFeed Videos. He was doing a really cool project that was fascinating and weird and not even on YouTube, but it was online video. So we thought we would try to do a thing like Ze." That thing became Brotherhood 2.0, a year during which the Green brothers communicated daily with each other by video instead of by phone, e-mail, or text messages. "A fun, jokey, trying-to-one-up-each-other brother project" is how Hank explained it.

One of his vlogs to John, a musical tribute to *Harry Potter and the Deathly Hallows*, made the front page of YouTube. Many fans attribute their discovery of the Greens' yearlong experiment to that "Accio Deathly Hallows" song—coming across the video and then binging on the rest of the vlogs.[1] The time frame and other elements of Brotherhood 2.0 were indeed inspired by *the show with zefrank*, a daily collection of social commentary, comedy, and original songs.

Finding Your Nerdfighters

Hank and John Green saw something that they loved in Ze Frank's pioneering vlog and then used YouTube, only a year old in 2006, to reach a wide audience of their own. After their successful year of

Brotherhood 2.0, the Greens honed their vision and created their new Vlogbrothers YouTube channel with similar content and shared it with a growing community that they called "Nerdfighters." This online community of Vlogbrothers' supporters joined forces with Hank and John, and their vision evolved over time.

Here's how Hank explained what Nerdfighters are fighting for: "I do like the idea that a goal of humans is to decrease suck and increase awesome. That was a saying from early Vlogbrothers. But those are two different things. It's so objectively better to decrease suck. You know, people have awful lives. People die of preventable diseases, hunger, wars . . . These are problems we can solve. The only reason we aren't solving them is because we haven't applied the right amount of resources, both cognitive and monetary. And that's messed up. But you can't go through life just playing defense. You also have to do interesting things. You have to send a rover to Mars and have the World Series. These things are good. They help us lead full lives and allow us to apply ourselves to other goals."

Crafting your big vision helps you make your ideas that you care about for an audience equally excited to claim you for their own. Nerdfighting is a powerful example of this kind of vision because the battle against "world suck" is actually a charitable venture. If you look at how Hank and John have deployed their talents and the resources of their fans, you'd have to say that their larger vision is to make the world a better place.

Creating Big Ideas That Start Small

I first knew Hank and John as the creators of VidCon, the largest conference for the online video world, bringing together over 20,000 video content creators, the web video online community, and industry executives to an annual conference in Anaheim, California. It's my favorite conference in the world because it's the only one where the community, creators, and companies all hang out under one roof. I have attended VidCon since its inception, when it was just a couple hundred people hanging out at a hotel bar and ballroom in the Century City neighborhood of Los Angeles.

Even before VidCon, the Vlogbrothers understood how You-Tube-wide collaborations could help to improve lives. Since 2007, their Project for Awesome (P4A) has been an annual call for videos from fellow YouTubers and Nerdfighters that highlight charitable causes in everything from education and health care to food insecurity.[2] In December of each year, thousands of people post videos across YouTube, where both influencers and the community promote and raise funds for these charities. Video creators are instructed to tag the videos with "P4A" in the descriptions in order to help the Vlogbrothers and others discover each video, empowering people to both watch and share the videos to gain visibility for the causes they promote. The videos reach a large audience due to this coming together of the YouTube community. The project is part of the larger mission of the Foundation to Decrease World Suck, Inc., a nonprofit organization that Hank started in his home state of Montana. Joining forces with the crowdsourcing website Indiegogo, the 2014 and 2015 Project for Awesome managed to raise over a million dollars.[3]

"Basically, this is a very new way to have an audience," Hank said of the work that he and other early YouTubers put out in general. "The systems of distribution are so flat now that all of the models break down and have to be rebuilt. And so our story has been [to] take yourself out of [a project] for a second and look at what it is, and what's interesting about it. What does it need? What are the new models going to be and what should you try out? Some of the things work and some of them don't. The number one thing is that we have this community that is very supportive of the stuff that we do . . . If they like an idea, they will be the

initial activation energy. If they don't like it, they won't hate us forever. And that's really nice."

Another idea that the Vlogbrothers' community apparently
liked a lot is DFTBA.com (Don't Forget To Be Awesome), the
website that Hank and his friend, Alan Lastufka, launched in
2010. Similar to VidCon, which began the same year, Hank felt
that the site would be a way for YouTuber musicians to become
more empowered and self-sufficient—in this case, by improving
the quality and accessibility of the merchandise that they sell. The
goal has been to raise money that helps the creative community
make videos on a full-time basis while ensuring that their fans
can buy "cool stuff without any hassle or confusion."⁴ Centralizing
the "merch" on DFTBA.com has also benefited fan-art creators
who voluntarily design products and have received over $400,000
in revenue over the early years.

Keep in mind, Hank Green didn't make an e-commerce site
for himself and some YouTube friends the moment he realized
that his Vlogbrothers channel could be monetized. He didn't pass
the hat among his fans at the earliest opportunity. Instead he
waited, because crafting a vision first is smarter than figuring out
where to put a shopping cart on your website—at least in the early
days when nurturing your ideas should be your priority. Giving
the Nerdfighters great, relevant videos and developing a sincere
bond with them made much more sense than quickly hitting up
people for revenue. Yes, the Vlogbrothers did launch the Project
for Awesome in the winter of 2007, but that was for charity. Hank
and John have always been more interested in getting to know
their fans rather than profiting from them.

Honing the Big Vision

"That's one of the reasons why I thought VidCon was necessary
and important in 2010 when YouTube was starting to be a big

deal. We had done a little tour that was all free stuff, like library tours. That was around the release of John's best-selling book *Paper Towns*. We had experience with that." Hank figured somebody should create an industry conference regarding online video but also make it fan focused. "I wanted to do both of those things in the same place. Penny Arcade does that at PAX, which I really like, and PAX was a big inspiration to me in terms of how they've built their community and the business around their community. I wanted to do that for online video."

For all of Hank and John's successes, the growth of VidCon and its inclusive vibe makes it a uniquely powerful achievement. "There are a ton of underserved communities. That is a really interesting thing about YouTube and I was always fascinated by that," Hank said. "Like the English-speaking Indian community has recently become a big deal on YouTube and there are a bunch of new Indian creators who have become popular and are fantastic." Similarly, people of color, gay and lesbian communities, and many other video fans who aren't part of the "dominant culture," as Hank puts it, regard VidCon as an amazing opportunity to meet YouTube stars such as the Canadian-Indian comedian Lilly Singh, and LGBT youth advocate Tyler Oakley.

There is plenty to support this theory beyond VidCon. Project for Awesome and DFTBA.com are early examples of Hank and John's desire to help others. But more recently, the brothers have collaborated on a video-based education project called Crash Course that was initially funded by YouTube and now relies on contributions from viewers. Animation and tons of humor help to bring biology, world history, and other subjects to life for high school–age learners as well as teachers who need classroom tools designed for this age group. Hank is also justifiably proud of how the cool concepts and science news on his SciShow YouTube channel have caught on with "a much stronger female demographic than science programming usually draws," he wrote on his website. "This is really exciting for me, because it's exactly the sort of people that our world needs taking an interest in science."[5]

By 2013, Crash Course and SciShow had both outlived the start-up money provided by YouTube. But Hank had another project in mind. He was thinking that it was time to roll out a voluntary subscription service that enabled fans to fund his education programming and the work of other online creators. "It's tied into this idea that we want to help creators create professionally. We want to do that for ourselves and for other people because it's a great job." He and his brother launched the crowdfunding website Subbable, which was enormously helpful to more than 20 artists and creators, as well as the fans who love their work. Patreon, the San Francisco–based crowdsourcing company, acquired the website two years after it went live. Hank said both companies started at about the same time and have obvious similarities. "When Patreon launched, we were like 'Whaaat?!' because, of course, we had been working on it for six months. I called [Jack Conte, the founder] because I had known Jack before then and said, 'Just so you know, I'm about to launch the exact same thing, but we've spent so much money on it that we can't not do it.'"

Crowdsourcing on any platform is reliable if a community has reached the point that it considers itself in partnership with a creator. Of course it's only an implied contract, but the Influencer Economy principle that recommends giving your community ownership of your brand and identity empowers an audience to be your top marketers and supporters. The Vlogbrothers give their "Nerdfighters" a branded term that inspires participation in their charitable work and makes the audience feel included and needed. With the success of Hank's other projects, like his award-winning nature and technology blog, *EcoGeek*, it's clear that geek culture and Nerdfighting can be energized around environmental issues, too. "Brains can save our planet," is how Hank puts it in one of his posts. Giving a community ownership of concepts like this and reminding it to be awesome has done much more than add up video views and subscribers across the Vlogbrothers channel. Their real pride centers on the continual support they received for the wonderful causes that they champion, and on the many ways that they enable online creators to make cool stuff.

It's hard to say if Hank and John will also end up saving the planet. After all, this is still the early days of the Nerdfighters' fight. But just from the vibe at VidCon alone, it already looks like the world sucks a little less. For Hank personally, the conference and his other enterprises have at least become rewarding in ways that he never anticipated. "Running a business is a creative thing, like dealing with people and getting the best work out of them. Understanding their motivations aren't the same as your motivations. It's all a bunch of moving parts, a piece of artwork in its own way. The fact that I get to do 20 different things, and that Monday looks nothing like Tuesday, is just really satisfying to me. It's allowed me to build up a toolkit of both personal skills and, you know, having all of these great people who work with me—it allows for creativity on a level that I never believed I could have access to."

Influencer School Lessons: What the Vlogbrothers Can Teach You About Crafting Your Big Vision

Lesson 1: Find What Drives You

To succeed in any endeavor, you need to find what drives you. There are certain parts of our lives that fire up our bellies in the morning. These things drive us and keep us going throughout the day. These are the ideas and motivations that we geek out about. And that geekery can drive us to build something special online.

John and Hank Green were driven to communicate for an entire year via online videos. They geeked out over the idea that they could video message one another during the Brotherhood 2.0 phase of their lives. Rather than communicate through a text, phone call, or online chat, they chose the nascent medium of "vlogging." Vlogging wasn't much of a thing back then, but they geeked out about it. And then they just started and launched their idea.

When putting yourself out there to start creating, don't get hung up on details around thoughts like, "How can I make money from my idea?," "What if no one likes my work?," or "What if I embarrass myself by failing?" I understand these anxieties as well as anyone, but you need to find your vision without judging yourself. Find that thing that you speak about with unwavering passion and transform that geekiness into a larger vision.

We are focusing on how to transform your passion into a vision because passions alone won't make you successful. If you're hoping to launch a business from your geekiness, unfortunately a "passion business" isn't a guaranteed path to success. Passions are important when thinking about any idea; however, the market has to dictate if your passion can be turned into a business. If you're looking for a career change or aim to turn a hobby into a business, a passion isn't going to pay the bills. However, skillfully crafting a vision will help you reach your goals, even if they are monetary.

At this stage you need to find out who your Nerdfighters are. John and Hank's community were inspiring and awesome to help the Vlogbrothers grow vision. Think of it as enlisting your fellow nerds to follow and even collaborate with you on your big vision. You need to pinpoint that community of folks who will get behind your work. John and Hank inspired their community to find their inner "awesome" and the community in turn inspired them to develop their vision. It was a symbiotic relationship.

Again, Nerdfighting is a powerful example of this kind of community building because the battle against "world suck" is actually helping to make the world a better place. Who doesn't want to make the world suck less?

Here's another thing: when launching any idea on the web, it's always smart to look for inspiration from those who came before you. Ze Frank inspired John and Hank to start vlogging, and they continue to pay homage to Ze in their videos. Studying the pioneers in your field of interest will guide you in your journey. And it will only make your work better.

So who inspires you? You can accelerate your growth by learning from the experiences of others in your field. Whether it's studying the format or style of your heroes, or learning from their successes or mistakes, it's to your advantage to learn from the best. You need to understand the market for your idea and acquire the necessary knowledge to succeed.

You also need to assess whether or not you can build influence in your geekiness. For example, if your geek passion is deep-sea fishing, can you build an audience around fishing? What if your geek passion is helping brands market their social media? Can you reach followers around that? If you want to write about basketball data and analytics, can you build an audience in that field? Unfortunately, passion doesn't always translate to influence. Building influence in a specific area comes when you can address an actual need in the market. And sometimes the markets are overcrowded with people who have already launched ideas like yours. Hank and John's crowdfunding company Subbable, for example, was similar to another company, Patreon. And they were willing to give up their business and sell it to Patreon, which allowed them to focus their attention on other projects. Building influence comes from finding your own Nerdfighters, and if you can't join or contribute value to your Nerdfighters, then you'll have trouble building influence.

You need to consider the reality of the answer to this question: "Can I build an audience in this area?" You can't shortcut your way to becoming influential. And you need to get involved with the communities of anywhere you want to be influential. It sounds simple, but it's not always obvious. For example, if you have worked a job in finance for 10 years and suddenly want to become influential in the artisanal cheese world, you need to join the artisanal cheese community ASAP. You can't fake being a part of the community. And it's never too early or too late to join communities online. When I started writing my book and launching my podcast, I was lucky enough to be part of the YouTube community from my early days at Machinima.com. It's always fun to join a community related to something that you are passionate about, so don't wait—just do it!

Actions to Find What Drives You

1. Determine who inspires you in your category or business. Identify at least three of these influencers, then write three traits for each person and why those traits inspire you.

2. Determine how you can mirror role models and follow their lead. Write out how they succeeded and what paths you can take to replicate their success. Make sure you respect their work and pay homage when appropriate.

3. Determine who you believe your Nerdfighters can be. Write out who the geeks are that will follow you along your journey and help you craft your vision. This is a two-part process:

   a. *Find your inside track.* List three current communities you are a part of that would support your big vision. Determine what you value in these relationships and how you already help them, and write out how you think they would equally support you.

b. *Find your outside track.* List three potential communities that you would like to collaborate with for your big vision. Determine the path to engage these communities. Write out how you think you can help them, and write your strategy for how you will enlist this group into a collaboration.

4. Determine if you can actually build a community around your big vision. List three reasons why you feel it's realistically possible to build a community around your idea. Be certain and confident that this will happen.

Lesson 2: Determine Your Values

Whether you just want to develop an idea or community, or you want to build a sustainable business, you need to ask yourself, "What values do I represent?" It sounds like a deep way to think, but it's really simple to write down your values. You can think of values as a personal mission statement—they are what you stand for, what you believe in, and ultimately what you need to create your mission based on what drives you.

It helps to realize that your values may evolve over time, but I always recommend writing out your values early on in the process. This is important because writing out your mission makes your ideas feel more alive. And it also gives you a line in the sand for what you are trying to create.

The Vlogbrothers' values were simple:

❖ Decrease world suck.

❖ Increase awesome.

The Vlogbrothers' values came to be a year *after* their Brotherhood 2.0 project began. By making vlogs for each other over the course of 365 days, their community formed and helped shaped these values over time. Their community was a partner. Oftentimes in life, we do not know what our endgame is going to be. When our businesses or ideas grow, so do our values. We can sometimes create values that surpass even our own expectations. That is what I find inspiring about this phase of the "Craft Your Big Vision" principle. It's exciting to discover and evolve your values.

Using *The Influencer Economy* as an example, my goal was to tell the stories of people doing what they loved, sharing their work, and thriving in the digital age. I also wanted to help creators and entrepreneurs learn how to launch their ideas into the world. I aimed to create a business framework for the digital age. Those were my values, which aligned perfectly with my vision to write a business book about creative people in the DIY economy, and then share what I learned with a larger audience.

Sometimes if you have trouble defining your values, it can help to think what you are *not*, and then your values of what you *are* will come into focus more easily. As another example with *The Influencer Economy*, I checked off a lot of boxes stating what I didn't want it to be. I didn't want this book to be a "Get Rich" guidebook, nor did I aim to write a "10 Steps to Wealth" book. The market is oversaturated with those types of books, and I don't like them. They aren't for me and are not what I represent. Instead, I aim to teach people philosophies and principles for the modern age, and to help people take action in their life and careers. Those are my values, and they are reflected in the subtitle of my book: *How to Launch Your Idea, Share It with the World, and Thrive in the Digital Age.*

It took time for me to identify my true values, so don't feel stressed if your values aren't set in stone yet. They will crystallize and become stronger over time. They may even change, and that's okay, too.

If you don't have a list of values in mind already, just start working on your idea and don't get overly hung up on pinning them down. It doesn't have to be hard, I promise. I know thinking about values can be intimidating but, like the Vlogbrothers, it can be helpful to work backwards. It took creating Brotherhood 2.0 for them to really start defining theirs.

The same principle applies to crafting your vision. Successful people often recommend crafting your vision before doing anything else. I believe that it's important to just start with a geek passion and assess the opportunity to build community around that passion. Once you do that, your values and vision for your geek passion will begin to define themselves. Your vision will be more authentic if you follow these steps.

Actions to Determine Your Values

1. Write down the initial values for your idea, and realize they may change over time. They should correlate to your vision, which is something that you believe in deeply. Keep your values simple.

2. You need to decide whether your idea is linked to a larger career opportunity. If you want to build a business around your idea, start thinking now about how your values tie into your business goals. List some specific connections. But if you don't want to build a business around it, that's fine too. The Influencer Economy is not about just making money. In other words, it's okay to geek out about something for fun.

3. Map out your longer-term goals for your values. If you think your values can kick-start into a bigger idea, then you're on your way to forming your big vision. Start exploring what the vision looks like.

Lesson 3: Hone Your Big Vision

Most leaders of the Influencer Economy launched an idea and then formulated their big vision over time. The Vlogbrothers pursued their vlogs, and amazing things came from their passion. When Hank's Harry Potter video was featured on the front page of YouTube, their video channel really started taking off. They became leaders in the early days of the YouTube community. As this happened, they began transforming their values into a larger vision, which ultimately led them to create groundbreaking conferences like VidCon, fascinating businesses like DFTBA that help creators sell merchandise to their audience, and fund-raisers like Project for Awesome.

To put it simply, your big vision is your end goal. To get there, make your vision simple and stick to it. Don't let anyone or anything get in the way of this vision. The Vlogbrothers spent an entire year learning the ropes of YouTube and video creation, experimenting with the medium. Then came their values and ultimately their vision.

Don't be afraid to make your vision big. People respond well to big visions. We love big ideas, and people need to love yours. And like the Vlogbrothers, keep growing your vision along the way.

Actions to Hone Your Big Vision

1. Write down the big vision behind your idea. Consider how your passion, values, and ideas will ultimately come together to accomplish something big. Be bold in your thinking, and realize that you can adjust and adapt your vision over time. It's not permanent.

2. Determine how your vision will be fulfilled. Map out how you want to change the world. Include smaller steps

that you can take to fulfill your vision. Visions need actions that can take you to your endgame.

Experimenting to Find Your Goals

This book is a strategy, a philosophy, and a method for navigating the new digital landscape. And you need to be patient when working in this new economy. You can't quit pursuing your geek passion until you have exhausted all avenues. It may take years to build out your big vision, and you have to be okay with that. It's all part of a greater process that you'll learn about in chapter 2, "Pick Your Platform."

When pursuing something that you geek out about, sometimes it is best not to have a defined goal when starting out. Oftentimes, just scratching that creative itch or pursuing something you care about will lead you into surprising and thriving environments.

I learned a lot about this when I spoke with investor Brad Feld of the tech venture-capital firm Foundry Group and the start-up accelerator Techstars. Brad is based in Colorado, has long, shaggy hair, and wears white-framed glasses not often seen on a 50-year-old tech investor. He has invested in over a thousand start-up companies and has written numerous best-selling books, including *Startup Communities*, *Do More Faster*, and *Venture Deals*. Many start-up accelerators, like TechStars, are known for providing start-ups with mentorship, a supportive entrepreneurial community, and resources to help entrepreneurs and their companies reach their full potential. TechStars is an elite group, as less than 1 percent of all companies that apply are accepted, and they have programs from Boulder to Boston to Berlin. Brad backs up his advice with a proven track record of success.

In our discussion, Brad said that when starting a project, "you don't need to have to have your outcome or goal clearly articulated at the beginning, especially when you're trying things that have very low barriers to try." We talked about how having specific goals can cause you to miss much more important goals and "can get in the way of the process." Experimenting in one direction can often cause you to find more specific and significant goals along the way. When Brad started Techstars with his co-founders David Cohen and David Brown, he said "they actually had no idea if [Techstars] was a good idea or bad idea . . . We had this premise that it might be interesting. And our worst case was that we make some new friends." And when Brad started blogging in 2005 ahead of many investors on the Internet, he told me, "With the blog I didn't have any idea whether it was going to turn into something useful . . . I just figured out this is interesting. And if it's interesting I'll keep doing it and if it stops being interesting or I don't find a value I'll stop doing it."

In other words, don't get bogged down if you struggle with pursuing what you geek out about. And don't worry if there is or is not a defined goal at the end for you. Moreover, don't be afraid to reshape your idea as you go along. Sometimes starting with your ideas can build new friendships, help you gain a new skill, or completely open up new opportunities. It can be better to launch and be fueled by your own curiosity to see where the opportunities take you.

Curiosity is a powerful tool in the Influencer Economy. Don't sweat the time it takes to find that vision.

Lesson 4: Forget Perfection

When you find that big vision, the only reason it matters to the world is because you believe in it. At first, people may not get your idea, or they may think you are weird because you care about it so much. You may even obsess about your big vision, and your friends may question why you're so invested in your idea. Don't worry about it. Keep going along in your journey and accept that not everyone will understand what you're doing. Moreover, don't let other people's judgment or criticism affect your vision.

Also, don't worry if you're not perfect. You'll need to hone your craft as you go along because, to use a basketball metaphor, no one becomes Stephen Curry hitting three pointers the first time they step on the court. You need to practice and get better every single day in order to start sinking three pointers. Mark Zuckerberg put it well when he said "done is better than perfect," and in the case of visions, you need to start creating as soon as you can. Once you create, you are well ahead of everyone else. (More about this in the next chapter.) So don't worry about nailing everything on the first try.

The pace of the Internet is quick. Ideas come and go at rapid speed. In the culture of the Internet, people forgive and forget quickly when you make mistakes. Were all the Vlogbrothers' Brotherhood 2.0 videos perfect? Of course not. In fact, they could not afford to be perfect because they didn't have the time to create that much content flawlessly. They got their stuff up on the Internet because they knew it's better to complete your work than to never release it.

I spoke with Burnie Burns about this. Burnie founded Rooster Teeth, an online video studio that, among many successful projects, created the pioneering *Red vs. Blue*, a web series of animated comedy short videos told in the world of the video game *Halo*. Rooster Teeth has worked in online video since 2003 and has served many billions of views worldwide. In the process, their gaming and entertainment videos have earned a loyal and passionate following. (Burnie and his team's story is featured more in chapter 8, "Open Doors for Others.")

When chatting with Burnie, I asked him what advice he'd give younger creators aspiring to thrive like he and the Vlogbrothers have. He subscribes to the "don't wait" theory. He told me, "No matter what you're doing, honing your craft is time well spent. Even if you spend three years and no one sees it, you're three years ahead of everyone else that just started." That sage advice can be applied to any creative idea in the Influencer Economy. And it's coming from Burnie Burns, whose YouTube channels have over 10 million subscribers, which is no small feat.

When empowering yourself to create a big vision, the Internet is your friend and can help you find a home for your vision. In the digital age, every idea has a home on the Internet, and you need to find that home. I get a lot of e-mails from students who ask for advice on how to "build community" for their projects. I always suggest to start building community now, ahead of any project launch. Whether you are set to launch a mobile app, book, video game, or e-commerce website, your community is firepower for your success. We'll cover building community much more in step 2 of the Influencer Economy, but you need begin thinking about it now.

I highly recommend a *New York Times* best-selling book, *The Lean Startup*, by start-up entrepreneur and investor Eric Ries. Eric talks about building a "minimum viable product" in the book. The MVP, as it's called, is "a version of a new product which allows a team to collect the maximum amount of validated learning about customers with the least effort." In other words, it's like piloting an idea and testing the market to see if there's a demand for what you are building. In the Lean Startup methodology, an entrepreneur finds a problem to solve and builds an idea around that problem. The term *minimum* refers to "bad products that no one wants to use" and *product* refers to "bigger ideas that companies can afford to build." So the MVP is the intersection of these two worlds, where your idea needs to sit.

When launching, think about the bare essential of your idea and what you need to create in order to start getting feedback. Remember, "Done is better than perfect." Whether it's a digital song download, alpha version of a mobile app, or storyboards for your film, you'll need to think about the most basic element of your idea. In writing my book, the MVP was my podcast. I knew if I could build an audience around my podcast, get feedback, and make it better, then there would be a larger demand for my book. And I could test out the market for the book ahead of its launch. In fact, getting a weekly podcast up was a big challenge for me. In posting a weekly show, believe me, done was always better than perfect!

Actions to Forget Perfection

1. Write out potential roadblocks getting in the way of starting to launch your idea. Include everything that is keeping you from honing your craft. Add things that you even love to do (like be with your family) that may get in the way. If you need to maintain full-time employment to pay your bills, include that as well. All of these diversions can get in your way, even if they're things you really enjoy or obligations you have to meet.

2. Determine what is "done" for your project. Write out the minimum viable product for your idea, or the most basic version of what you want to create. This is about defining the bare essential for you to launch your idea.

Lesson 5: Create Projects That Help Fulfill Your Vision

The vision of the Vlogbrothers was sustained in their various projects. For example, VidCon was an idea that came from Hank and John's meet-ups around the country. When the brothers went on tour to promote John's book *Paper Towns* in 2008, they met with fans throughout the Midwest and were astounded by the number of real people who came out to the book events after following the Vlogbrothers on YouTube. Their community of the "online space" (or hyperspace) transitioned into the "meet space" (or meetspace). Realizing they had an amazing community they barely knew existed, they wanted other YouTube and video creators to have the opportunity to meet their own audiences IRL (in real life) . . . and VidCon was born.

All of John and Hank's many projects are tied to their vision:

❖ VidCon: A place for deep and multifaceted discussions of community-based online video as well as a celebration of the YouTube community with performances, parties, and face-to-face interaction with YouTubers.

❖ DFTBA: A website that helps online music creators connect with their audience to directly sell items like albums, merchandise, T-shirts, accessories, and posters.

❖ Project for Awesome: A community-driven charitable movement on YouTube, founded and still overseen by the Nerdfighter community.

❖ Subbable: A crowdfunding website that supported community-generated funding for various web series and other online projects, and continues to do so through its parent company, Patreon.

❖ SciShow: A series of science-related videos on YouTube hosted by Hank Green and several other YouTube creators.

❖ Crash Course: An educational channel focusing on humanities and science courses taught by Jon and Hank, as well as a few guest educators.

What is interesting about these projects is they are platform agnostic, meaning the projects all have their own platforms (the products), but the inputs are always consistent with the Vlogbrothers' vision. When I spoke with Scott Belsky, founder of the creative online community Behance and its spinoff 99u Conference and author of the book *Making Ideas Happen*, he told me that oftentimes creative people are "mission-centric and medium agnostic" and that "the message is the same" in all their projects because people's values don't change, but the projects do.

The common threads in the Vlogbrothers' projects are inclusiveness, community involvement, and educational value. Their products and businesses are on a variety of platforms but are based on the same vision. When you want to execute your vision, everything you create needs to have the same philosophy.

We discussed that when you define your vision, it helps to have a big idea that helps get people hooked on your vision and thus follow your ideas. Then you need to create projects that encourage people to return to your work on a regular basis. To achieve this, leaders in the Influencer Economy focus on projects that support their vision. When you do that, great opportunities can knock on your door, and you will thrive.

People respond to big visions that are simple to understand. And in those visions you need to think longer term about projects that you want to create. If you have an idea for a bigger book, tech product, video game, music download, film, or anything that you will charge people for, you need to connect that with your vision.

The Vlogbrothers had their YouTube platform and are fortunate to have many projects built around their communities. As Scott Belsky said, they have a lot of ideas that are similar in mission but executed as different projects. If I didn't plan on writing *The Influencer Economy*, then my podcast might never have started. Equally, without the podcast, I might never have written this book. They formed a symbiotic relationship—the book was my project, and my podcast was my platform to gather material for it.

There are two general ways to work with your ideas: 1) you have your idea and you launch it, and a big vision develops from your experimenting or 2) you have a big vision and then create projects around that vision. There's no right or wrong way. Either works. With *The Influencer Economy*, I had the big vision to write the book and then started creating around it. With the Vlogbrothers, they just started creating and larger ideas came from it. Either way, you need to create something on a platform, while also having your big vision. I wasn't a journalist, but the book was intriguing to folks. That was my endgame. But the podcast was my entry point into getting interesting and successful people to be profiled in the book.

Actions to Create Projects That Help Fulfill Your Vision

1. Brainstorm a list of project ideas. It could be a tech product, e-book, film, e-commerce company, live event, etc. Write out how these projects tie back to your big vision.

2. Determine which of these projects best aligns with your big vision. I recommend picking just one to start in order to stay focused. Write the goals of the project and determine how you can build an audience around your idea, in advance of the project launch.

3. List smaller projects that can help fulfill your big vision. I knew a book was a big idea, and the podcast was a smaller project to get me to write/publish a book. Think about small actions you can take to help you fulfill your vision.

MY INFLUENCER ECONOMY STORY

Finding the Influencer Economy Big Vision

Throughout the book, I'll be sharing my own experiences and journey acting on the Influencer Economy steps and principles. I have practiced them as a student, after learning from the great minds that I interviewed on the podcast, and I have succeeded and made mistakes along the way. I hope you can learn from my experiences.

When I set out to write *The Influencer Economy*, I was incredibly passionate about the subcategory of creators called influencers. I attended global tech and media conferences like VidCon, SXSW, and TechCrunch Disrupt and saw this new class of people with amazing stories to share. And much to my surprise, no one was documenting their thriving role in the digital age. They weren't entertainers, they weren't technologists, and they weren't traditional entrepreneurs. These creators were a mash-up of those three archetypes. It was fascinating.

My big vision was telling me that I had to tell these Influencer Economy stories to the world. I wanted to learn from these creators and entrepreneurs, and I thought there was a larger group out there who would also love to learn the steps that these new media makers took to succeed. I had always been curious about writing a book and thought this was the right time to pursue a new phase of my life after working as a start-up entrepreneur for years in tech and media.

So I created a big idea, and set-out to write a book. I didn't know where to start, and I saw a book as a longer-term project that would take years to write. I had never written a book, so I needed smaller projects and milestones to help launch this new and exciting project. I knew I was passionate about these creators and entrepreneurs, and my vision became focused on putting in the time to write a book about them to share their lessons and stories to the world.

So how did I make it happen?

I knew writing a book would be a labor of love that would take years. I also knew that I wasn't a journalist who had natural instincts to find "sources" and "interviews" to profile in the book. I realized that I had to be creative if I was going to land the types of high-profile subjects that would make my book relevant, interesting, and successful. So that's when I launched the podcast and I learned awesome new skills along the way as I had to produce, edit, and record each episode on my own.

And to follow the advice of "done is better than perfect," I published my podcasts on schedule, even when I didn't think they were good enough. Even if they weren't perfect, I made sure to get the episodes up for my listeners to hear. It wasn't easy. I was not a trained producer, editor, or even podcast host. And even after reading books and online articles about it, I knew the only way to get better in a craft like podcasting was to launch it.

Looking back now, what I realize is that no one has judged me for those early episodes, whether they were perfect or not. All that mattered was that they were posted online. And that Burnie Burns, Flula Borg, Freddie Wong, Taryn Southern, Shira Lazar, and other YouTube creators were my early guests and we had awesome conversations. I did well booking fascinating guests, getting smart conversations, and uploading regular episodes for people to hear.

I started recording podcast episodes in late 2013. I wanted to profile and tell the stories of "makers, creators, and entrepreneurs revolutionizing media." In fact, that was my first podcast tagline. I'll get more into the mechanics of how I executed my vision in chapter 2, "Pick Your Platform," but this is how I jumped into the world of creating my vision. And after launching my podcast and building an amazing community that I love, my big vision was honed and the book started to write itself.

Chapter 2

Pick Your Platform

"The pain of not doing it is much worse than the pain of doing it."

—Steven Pressfield

Chapter Playbook

Once you hone in on your big vision, you need to take the next step to pick a platform to express yourself. Even if it's well ahead of your launch, building a platform is critical in the digital age. It's never too early to pick your platform. It's important to pursue one platform where you can find an edge for your idea. Your edge on that platform makes you unique and the best in the world at what you are pursuing.

I recommend focusing your efforts on platforms where you can build subscribers rather than worrying about superficial stats like followers. You will want to create on-demand content for people to understand your POV (point of view), so you will need to find the best platform—whether it's e-mail, YouTube, podcasting, blogging, Instagram, Snapchat, or some other network—to deliver the goods.

In my journey, the big vision was writing *The Influencer Economy* and the platform to help me get there was podcasting. Hosting a weekly podcast helped me on multiple levels—it allowed me to reach A+ podcast guests that would be featured in the book, build an awesome community of listeners, and find an outlet to create something I enjoyed. It's a lot of hard work to build a platform, but remember to have fun while you're doing it. Otherwise, what's the point? Remember that the journey is more important than the end result in the Influencer Economy. Enjoy the process on the way up.

Within your platform, you want to become a go-to person in your niche for people to look to for answers. If people can read your blog, test your product, view your video series, listen to your podcast, hear you speak, take your course, read your e-book, and find you on the web, it'll open doors. Consider that Google is everyone's home page, and when people search your name, you need to supply them with awesome search results to help them understand your level of amazingness.

There was one guy who felt that embracing his inner nerd would help him find work that fed his soul, while also advancing his career. And when he launched his podcast around this nerd and geek culture, from that platform, this podcaster built a thriving media company, paving the way for many other personality-driven media networks that followed.

Chris Hardwick

For some guys, hosting an MTV show in which dozens of attractive, single adults hang out like they're at a college frat party would be a pretty fun gig. Having Jenny McCarthy, a former *Playboy* playmate, as your co-host might also sweeten the deal. Even though hosting dating shows like *Singled Out* and later Spike TV's *Shipmates* helped give Chris Hardwick steady paychecks, they weren't a great fit for Chris's creativity and mental well-being. In fact, making a great living as a TV host was sucking at Chris's soul. In his book, *The Nerdist Way: How to Reach the Next Level (In Real Life)*, Chris admits that a postmillennial lull in his career led to a drinking problem. He was up to about 15 beers a day and, according to Chris, he was looking like "death puked on a turd."[1] *Singled Out* had actually depressed the hell out of him, especially after it was cancelled in 1998, and yet it dogged his reputation as he looked for more satisfying work. Also a talented comedian, Chris went on to do stand-up at various Los Angeles clubs where audiences would sometimes heckle him as that "MTV kid" trying to be funny.

Today Chris wears many hats, including podcaster, actor, and CEO of Nerdist Industries, a network of digital entertainment and news that has become a phenomenal success in geek and pop culture. But before all that, he had reached a breaking point, got sober cold turkey, and lost 20 pounds. He saw a therapist, and after his girlfriend broke up with him, Chris kept trying to put things in the proper perspective.

"The first half of my career, the first two-thirds of my career, weren't really spent on pursuing things that I was passionate about," he wrote. "It was more just surviving and getting jobs. And then at a certain point I was like, 'Oh, wait—maybe I should just work on things that make me happy.'"[2] It's a deceptively simple realization. Many of us are stuck in jobs that have long ago stopped being fulfilling, if they ever were. Or we somehow have gotten caught up in a career track that has more to do with our last job title than the new role we envision for ourselves. But if you've been busy for years pleasing your boss and making nice with your co-workers, it's possible to lose touch with that vision we honed in chapter 1. And it's a shame because that vision—the thing that personally inspires you—can actually become your life's gratifying work. Back in 2003, Chris Hardwick looked to the past in order to figure out what really motivated him.

Your Personality Is Your Competitive Advantage

"It occurred to me," Chris writes in *The Nerdist Way*, "that I had arrogantly banished all the nerd qualities that defined me as a youth. I distinctly remembered that I once had the ability to focus intensely on many things. Programming computers, winning chess tournaments, playing video games, collecting action figures, Dungeons & Dragon-ing, ruining the bell curve in Latin class. I needed to reconnect with that past and find a way to harness those nerd powers to turn my life around."[3]

While he didn't always find what he was looking for, some of his subsequent acting roles and TV hosting jobs began to reflect his true interests. He successfully lobbied the Los Angeles affiliate of PBS for hosting duties on *Wired Science*, a 2007 weekly television series that delved into technology and science topics. He also began to research the Internet's most popular blogs and websites to learn how and why they were connecting with their audiences. Perez Hilton, for instance, had a big entertainment blog in which he ripped on celebrities and occasionally drew penises on their faces. Maybe not the branding Chris Hardwick had in mind for himself, but he was discovering that personality-driven websites were a huge draw online.

Even if your niche or big vision isn't about high-tech stuff, the methodical way that Chris experimented with growing his platform early on is valuable to anyone learning the ropes of the Influencer Economy. In 2008, he joined Twitter and also purchased the Nerdist.com domain as his own personal blog. Rather than posting self-promotional content, Chris wrote about the topics he grew up loving and stuff that was happening in the media and tech world at that time. His point of view was inspired by sites like Gizmodo and Lifehacker, where nerds sounded forth on pop culture, gaming, and other topics of interest in ways that were catching on with mainstream audiences. Using his connections and visibility on *Wired Science*, Chris also landed a job writing for *Wired* magazine and a subsequent hosting gig on G4 TV's *Attack of the Show!*, where he reviewed cool tech gadgets of the day.

Pick the Platform That's Right for You

Nerdist.com was Chris Hardwick's main hub, and on this website he defined the term that reinvented his career. "There are nerds, and then there are Nerdists. A Nerdist is, more specifically, an artful nerd. He or she doesn't just consume, he or she creates and innovates."[4] This all played well at a time when people no longer apologized for geeking out on video games, or the latest *Star Wars* movie or smartphone. Events like Comic-Con were a fine place to dress in cosplay as your favorite superhero, but they also informed the world's conversations about tent-pole movie releases and other aspects of pop culture. On February 7, 2010, while most of us were gathered around our televisions to watch that year's Super Bowl, Chris Hardwick and a couple of friends were recording their first podcast—innovating as Nerdists do with this relatively new format.

Those early episodes of *The Nerdist Podcast* featured people Chris knew from the comedy and stand-up scene, as well as well-known Internet creators. Drew Carey was guest number two on *Nerdist*. Famed podcaster and radio host Adam Carolla came on the show, as did Conan O'Brien's sidekick, Andy Richter. Fans of Felicia Day from the online video series *The Guild,* and now the YouTube channel Geek & Sundry, tuned in to hear Chris interview her. There was even Stan Lee from Marvel Comics, Weird Al Yankovic, and the actor Wil Wheaton, who discussed his turn on *Star Trek: The Next Generation* and other adventures. This guest list kept growing and growing.

Adam Rymer, president of Nerdist Industries, spoke to me about another reason the company's flagship podcast attracts so many interesting guests. "I think Chris is a phenomenal interviewer. When you listen to a Nerdist podcast, you really feel like you're getting inside the head of the person that he's talking to. Their conversation might seem to be about promoting something that [the guest] is about to be part of, whether it's a movie or a TV show, but it's actually more about them in life, and what they're interested in. I think you come away from almost all the podcasts feeling like you actually just experienced a very personal moment with these people."

Podcasting is an intimate earbud experience, and listening to your favorite show on your car stereo can be just as binge-worthy as watching a Netflix series. *The Nerdist Podcast* only took a year to reach 75,000 downloads per episode and 1.4 million followers on Twitter.[5] Those and other numbers have since shot up, but along with comedians like Scott Aukerman and Marc Maron, Chris Hardwick found a voice that connected with listeners fairly early in the history of this medium. Positive and supportive, *Nerdist* interviews underscore the show's respect for guests and are never confrontational or sensationalist. Instead, Chris channels the curiosity of his listeners so that an appreciative Nerdist curiosity seems to guide the discussion.

"What you find on the podcasts is that the follow-up question is the question that you would want to ask yourself," Adam Rymer explained. "If I got Ian McKellen in a room, and I had a chance to talk to him, and we started the conversation talking about X, I would then want to ask this follow-up. That's where these podcasts tend to go." As the list of episodes has grown, the atmosphere continues to be friendly and thoughtful enough to attract everyone from Bill Gates recounting his philanthropic work to Tom Cruise remembering his need for speed in the *Top Gun* days. Chris often travels to his guests to record the podcasts but also meets with them at the Nerdist Industries black box theater at Meltdown Comics in Hollywood. Hoping to keep his audience psyched even without guests, Chris introduced "Hostful" episodes that only feature him and comedian co-hosts Jonah Ray and Matt Mira discussing things like burger salads and bionic arms. These shows have the feel of a few friends catching up with each other and receive as many, if not more, downloads than many episodes with headlining names.

Build Your Platform Around Your Interests

So if you're Chris Hardwick and his Nerdist associates, how do you monetize a website and podcast that is getting all this love from fans? For starters, you don't rush to cash in. You put a pin in that question while you're building up your platform and community. Step 2 of the Influencer Economy is "Share," and we'll cover that later in the book. But Chris is a reminder that building trust is important when growing your platform. The entertainment you freely share with your audience, that big vision, builds a lot of good will by proving you prioritize giving away work over insisting to be paid for it. Don't worry. Your community won't forget this. They will buy your CDs and T-shirts when you make them available. They'll donate through crowdsourcing to ensure that you keep sharing cool content. In Chris's case, they showed up in droves to support his stand-up comedy and live podcast outings. More *Nerdist* downloads meant more folks going to shows at Meltdown Comics, or "Nerdmelt," as that performance space is known. The fans seeking out Chris and his co-hosts are people that he has said seem like friends because there is such a community vibe in the crowd.

Going from a few thousand listeners to the current *Nerdist* average of 400,000 per episode required Chris to become a multifaceted entrepreneur. The company's expansion has been a group effort, and yet its current 60-person Burbank headquarters wouldn't be up and running without the hustle of its founder. Nerdist has become a multichannel network of podcasts and a premium YouTube channel that features *Nerdist News*, *Chris Hardwick's All-Star Celebrity Bowling*, and a boatload of other geek, gamer, and comedy videos. There is an online publishing arm and a growing presence in cable television that includes AMC's *Talking Dead* and Comedy Central's *@midnight*, a game show where celebrities ponder hashtags and other weighty matters. Peter Levin, former CEO of Nerdist Industries, deserves some of the credit for diversifying the brand's channels, as he was Chris's early partner when Nerdist Industries really found its groove.

Dan Casey, host of *The Dan Cave*, does his pop culture "must-see" lists and commentary across various Nerdist channels. He's been in Chris Hardwick's circle since the company was only a blog and agreed that its growth has a lot to do with collaboration, as well as its reliably upbeat tone. Dan says, "Whether you love *Doctor Who*, or you love science, or anime, there's someone at Nerdist who geeks out about it as well. There's someone who gets you and understands you. There's so much negativity out there, and we really pride ourselves on trying to find, like, the positive in things. Because life is too short. You may as well enjoy the stuff you're passionate about."

When Chris launched his platform, he realized that the more interests you have, the better. If you're trying to create a point of view that the world has never seen before, make your podcast or video channel a fusion of a few favorite things. You'll be able to explain it to your audience because it will be your voice and your unique sensibility. *Nerdist* works because the show is essentially about three funny friends who enjoy geeking out with their guests and hanging out with each other. It's fun to listen to because it's fun for them to record. Should you wait for the next Super Bowl or for inspiration to otherwise strike you? Probably not. You already know what your passions are, and the idea that you alone were made to launch.

As you build your base, your fans become your top marketers, community builders, and partners. They will click that PayPal button or fund your Kickstarter to keep the work coming. The name you choose counts toward this principle. The right branded term defines the content that you make and is something to which your fans will be psyched to lay claim. "Nerdist" was an inspired choice, a nod to a community that Chris Hardwick considered active and creative. So how do you want your fans to think of *themselves*? That answer becomes more valuable when you remember that podcast audiences, for instance, are super-engaged and a draw for advertisers—especially on shows like *Nerdist* and its 400,000 average downloads per episode. Sure, millions more may tune in to a television show, but the Nerdist faithful and other podcast communities have proven that they're buying what their hosts are selling.[6]

To enable the creators on his network to focus on this passion-driven content with fewer distractions, Chris sold the company to Burbank-based Legendary Entertainment, a film production company looking for new leadership in its digital division. That went down in 2012 with guarantees from Legendary that Chris and his team would retain total creative control of their work. To this day, Chris thrives as the heart and soul of a digital media empire that all began with a modest, self-made podcast.

BONUS STORY

Launching the Influencer Platforms of Smart Girls and Felicia Day

Another measure of how far Chris Hardwick has come since that first Super Bowl Sunday *Nerdist* podcast is that he now doesn't need others for social proof. Instead, he shines a spotlight on his lesser-known guests and has even made Legendary Entertainment appealing to a lot of cool digital talent. Adam Rymer told me that he thinks having *Nerdist* on board helped make it possible to acquire *Amy Poehler's Smart Girls at the Party* and the Geek & Sundry network started by Felicia Day.

Smart Girls launched in 2008 when Poehler and her friends Meredith Walker and Amy Miles created an online community for young women with inspirational content, humor, and frequent dance parties. "Our goal is to model the behavior that we try to encourage in others," Meredith explained to me. "We want to be positive influences, and our concern for girls is that being snarky and commenting on things seems to outweigh normal participation in your own life. . . . We started with a small web series and what we wanted to do was celebrate the everyday, to show that just by being interested in something makes you interesting to yourself. That's how you feel like you have a fun, enriched life. We liked to focus on the girls who had actually found something that really held their interest and hadn't given it up just to fit in."

Both *Smart Girls* and Felicia Day's Geek & Sundry network joined Legendary in 2014, bringing their creators alongside Chris Hardwick's Nerdist empire. Felicia had already been coming on *The Nerdist Podcast* for years and attracts much the same audience with a mix of book club, gaming, live-action comedy, and other programming for geeks and the people who love them. A lifelong devotee of fantasy novels and video games, Felicia was a sporadically working actress in Hollywood when her obsession with playing *World of Warcraft* gave her an idea. In 2007 she filmed in locations like her garage, in which she began filming her own gaming-themed web series called *The Guild*.

Felicia's experiments with digital media and Chris Hardwick's career path both touch on an Influencer Economy step important to anyone shy about creating work: launch what you love. Unless you're Kanye West, no one is keeping track and judging you for what you find fulfilling. Felicia had landed roles on *Buffy the Vampire Slayer*, *Eureka,* and other TV shows and films, but mainstream platforms became less interesting to her than projects she was passionate about and could control on her own terms.

There can be an awesome upside to launching, as Felicia's experience shows. Episode 3 of *The Guild* was posted on the front page of YouTube and it took off like wildfire. People liked it and shared it, bringing more subscribers. When Felicia ran out of money, she put up a website with a PayPal button so she could ask her fans to help her produce more episodes. Microsoft eventually came aboard to sponsor the series, and millions of views plus multiple awards later, Felicia launched her Geek & Sundry premium YouTube channel and expanded it to over 30 shows, including *Felicia's Ark*, *Critical Role*, *Sword & Laser*, and the board game battles royale of *Tabletop*. "Finding success through embracing your individuality" is how Felicia sums up her career in a Google Talk regarding her memoir, *You're Never Weird on the Internet (Almost)*. She says she wrote her book "to inspire people to really pursue the things that make them an individual. Because I think that's where you find success and meaning in this world."[5]

It may be harder today, but it's not impossible for talented people to be the next Felicia Day or Chris Hardwick by making their marks on digital platforms. The trick is to establish who you are and what you represent to your fans. According to Adam Rymer, standing out online is definitely a function of being clear about your goals and identity. As he puts it, "Like if you just decided you're going to launch a new brand, a new channel focused on comic books, okay, well, why is somebody going to go to that channel? How in 10 seconds or less do you explain to somebody what that channel represents?" He thinks of *Nerdist* and Geek & Sundry as delivering that clarity. "This is a world of influencers where you can instantly assign aspects of what you expect from something that they're doing. It helps a lot. And there's a certain street cred that they bring, and an audience that they earned over time."

And to make that all happen, they launched.

Influencer School Lessons: What Chris Hardwick Can Teach You About Picking Your Platform

Lesson 1: Embrace Your Personality

Chris Hardwick launched his Nerdist.com media company off of one platform: a podcast. He picked his platform, consistently created regular episodes, and his mini empire grew over time into a 60+ person company. Nerdist the company took years to build, but it would have never existed if Chris had not hatched his podcast and grown a platform around his self-professed love of computer programming, chess, video games, and Dungeons & Dragons. He developed a platform edge around these "nerd powers."

What I love about Chris's story is how he researched the web to discover how people stand out from the crowd when launching a project on the Internet. He did the advance work and explored the creativity of bloggers like Perez Hilton, whose website PerezHilton.com was exploding at the time. Even though Perez's snarky brand was different from Chris's, Chris realized that personality was everything online.

In the modern digital age, we are inundated with a mind-boggling amount of information to process. All day we're clicking links, searching in Google, following friends on Snapchat. It's easy to get lost. Building the right platform for you and your idea makes you stand out from the herd, because it is the online manifestation of what I call big vision fulfillment. To fulfill your vision when building your platform, ask yourself two questions:

- ❖ What is the one thing in the world that I am prepared to do better than anyone else?
- ❖ What category can I lead and define on the Internet?

When answering these questions, always keep in mind that your personality is your competitive edge. Chris's personality was exemplified by curiosity about geek culture and a desire to express himself in a positive way. Chris valued treating others with respect, including his podcast guests, his listening audience, and even his Nerdist co-workers. Adam Rymer said that a lot of the Nerdist team "grew up in a culture of being bullied when they were younger for playing video games or reading fantasy books." Now, their employees are "lucky enough to be in a company that we support ourselves through, being those fans. And they feel pretty lucky about it. So there's no need for us to be negative about fan culture." They are themselves, and that's what makes their company great.

This welcoming atmosphere is bred into the Nerdist DNA. When you look at YouTube comments, Twitter chats on politics, or any type of online debate, you'll notice that social media has evolved into what digital marketing expert Aaron Dodez calls a modern-day Roman Colosseum. Conversations can turn ugly fast. For Nerdist, it was always about positivity and respect, which are defining and important traits of Chris's personality. Chris embracing his geek personality, being positive, and engaging in thoughtful conversations became a defining part of his Nerdist podcast and company.

Actions to Embrace Your Personality

1. Write down three traits of your personality that make you unique. Chris calls this "finding your voice," a term from the comedy world. These are three ideas that you can mash up into one thing that makes you unique. Remember that your personality is your competitive edge.

2. Then determine what the mash-up of those ideas looks like. Write a one-word description, a one-sentence

description, and a one-paragraph description of what your mashed idea encapsulates.

3. And finally write out why you're the right person to execute and build a platform on this idea.

How I Picked My Platform

Of the available platforms, why did I start my podcast? I knew that I was super passionate about what I called the Influencer Economy, the pivotal idea behind the podcast. But I also knew I needed an edge to make both my book and podcast unique.

I initially had the normal anxieties about leveraging a platform like a podcast: How do I book guests? Will I be interesting enough in the interviews? What if I fail and no one listens? But on a deeper level, I knew I had to address three questions:

1. What made me unique on this platform and what would make mine different from ALL the other podcasts?

2. Why would I be the best in the world at my podcast?

3. How did the podcast fulfill my big vision?

My confidence was spurred by three things:

1. I was writing a book on the Influencer Economy and the podcast could get my foot in the door with fascinating people I'd feature in it. The book was a bigger vision that people would hopefully be receptive to. I wasn't just another guy with a podcast—I had purpose.

2. I knew the world of YouTube marketing from my time as director of marketing at the pioneering YouTube video network Machinima.com. Our network served our community billions of YouTube videos a month, and I learned how to market online video from many experts. I also knew You-Tube creators and figured these YouTubers could be my

first podcast guests and that I could book other high-quality guests because of my contacts at Machinima.

3. I'm a former stand-up comedian and had enjoyed performing years ago. I kind of missed performing in front of audiences, and podcasting was a creative outlet for me. I can talk and improvise with people, and I think my personality translates well in conversations. And while working at Machinima.com, helping our YouTube creators thrive in growing their communities, it inspired me to want to emulate them in building a podcasting community.

When you pick your platform, determine what parts of your personality create your competitive edge. Think about why you ARE the best in the world to do what you're planning, because it's all based on YOU. You are actively pursuing this; it's not a passive experience! We're in the age where the individual creator has more opportunities to control his or her work than ever before. If you don't believe that you are the right person to launch your specific idea, then you won't succeed. When you find your edge, your confidence will grow and your big vision will start coming together. It's not easy, but it's very fulfilling when your ideas solidify and start to flourish.

Lesson 2: Pick the Platform That's Right for You

Your platform is the venue for you to create regular, consistent content in order to start introducing your big vision to a waiting world. Success comes with a commitment to produce. In chapter 1, the Vlogbrothers consistently created online videos over the course of 365 days. Chris Hardwick and *Nerdist* have over 600 podcast recordings. It may sound intimidating, so let's make it easy for you to pick your platform in order to start honing your craft.

What is a platform? A platform enables you to gain subscribers on a network or unique visitors to your website. Obviously then, you need your website operational to become your online hub. The content network is your channel that attracts people to your community and ultimately brings people to your website. Examples of platform content channels include:

❖ Video sites (Snapchat, YouTube, Vine)

❖ Podcasts

❖ E-mail newsletters

❖ Blogs

❖ Private groups (Slack, Facebook)

❖ Image communities (Instagram, Pinterest)

❖ Crowdfunding sites (Indiegogo, GoFundMe, Kickstarter)

This is important: you need to build a platform off of a content network, not merely a social media network. In fact, my advice to you is to ignore any social media marketers, gurus, or "thought leaders" who tell you that social media is as important as your content. They will give you strategies for increasing followers or likes, but they won't help your bottom line. Marketers are often full of BS. You need to focus on content, *not* on social media. Pick a channel like blogging, video, audio, or anything else that results in an actual piece of content. You want a system where people can easily subscribe to something you create on a regular basis. And then it's up to you to be creative and work hard to express your personality and point of view in a way that will capture people's attention.

I recommend producing mainly "evergreen" content, meaning you create stuff that can last over time. For example, my podcast is usually not topical around events like the Super Bowl or the presidential elections. I want people to listen to my episodes months and years from now and still get value. Ideally, you don't want your content to expire. Evergreen content is timeless in feel because the stories, lessons, and even jokes will never get old. That said, there *are* people who are skilled in creating evergreen content inspired by topical content. That works too. For example, you could create content around the Olympics and talk about the general pride countries feel about sports. Or make something around the 2016 election, but go into the evolution about how big money has become intertwined with politics through the years.

I also advise you to pick one platform to start. You may recall that Chris Hardwick started blogging for two years before he launched his first podcast episode. Even if your first platform isn't your last, we need to get you up and going. It will take time to grow your voice, find a community, and reach your larger goals. But you won't succeed if you don't launch. Remember the Kanye West rule: nobody cares if your early attempts are perfectly slick and shiny. People want authenticity and entertainment, not perfection.

Picking a platform is trial and error, and Chris talks about finding "holes or specific areas not being serviced in your field." This is important. Examine your platform options and find an online area that is less competitive. My podcast is business-focused around people's stories. When I researched business podcasts, I realized that most of the top shows were on subjects like "online marketing," "becoming a millionaire," or "steps to become an entrepreneur." My show was focused on stories of creative entrepreneurs who were reshaping business. My podcast wasn't yet another get-rich-quick show; instead, I saw and filled a big gap in the market.

The Joe Moore Rule: "It's called work for a reason"

My father-in-law, Joe Moore, is old school. He runs a company based in Raleigh, North Carolina, that repairs industrial boilers. It's called Joe Moore & Company. He knows the boiler business better than just about anyone else in the world. When I talk to him about work, in any field, he likes to say, "It's called work for a reason." What does he mean? He means it takes effort, sacrifice, and consistency to thrive. Joe told me that "you can't just follow your passions and dreams and expect to make money."

Joe has built a platform around repairing boilers. Even though he doesn't have a digital platform like a YouTube channel, podcast, or e-book, his platform reach is far and wide. He primarily markets his services via word-of-mouth referrals, or he and his team knock on doors for potential sales. And he is successful because he understands the boiler repair universe, and people look to him for answers. His platform isn't digital, but it's a platform nonetheless.

Joe has built a successful service-based business from his expertise. He is the go-to person for boiler repair in the Southeast. His knowledge is a big part of his platform.

Joe also gets hired because he makes people's lives easier. They can hire him and not have to worry about a subpar repair job. He solves a pain point for his customers.

Here's what we can learn from my father-in-law:

* Treat your platform like a job.

* Give people something special, something they don't get anywhere else in quite the same way.

* Develop knowledge or a skill that most people don't have, and then share it with them.

* Make people's lives better and easier. Solve pain points.

Actions to Pick Your Platform

1. Write down your goals for your platform. Ask yourself what your platform edge is, what you can do to grow your platform, and how it aligns with your big vision.

2. Research competitors within the platforms you are exploring. Identify the holes in the market that you can take advantage of. Create a matrix weighing the pros and

cons of each platform, listing how each may or may not work for you.

3. Write out your plan to produce content regularly and consistently. Whether it's daily, weekly, biweekly, or whatever, pick a program and stick to it. You need to think like an editor and publish your content with certainty.

Lesson 3: Find a Name and Create a Logo

Naming your idea can be an exhausting yet rewarding process. It's definitely not something that happens overnight. Naming your idea takes time and usually a few trial runs before you lock it down.

Naming is important but, again, don't get hung up on getting the details perfect. Know that many huge media companies have switched their names and even their business direction altogether. We call this a "pivot" in the tech world, where you change your business midstream and relaunch your idea. Did you know that Twitter was first called Odeo? The team behind Twitter launched an RSS-feed podcast tool back in 2005. After selling off that business, Evan Williams, Twitter's cofounder, pivoted his company to work on twttr, which eventually became Twitter. Even Instagram was originally a location-based app called Burbn, where users could "check in" to their locations via mobile devices. After that didn't get traction, they scrapped the idea and built a photo-sharing app called Instagram. So don't be hard on yourself if you have to rename your project; even large, successful technology companies like Instagram and Twitter had to rethink their names and businesses.

When naming your idea, follow what I call the "Naming Rule of Four." Your idea name should be four syllables or less. Almost all the brand names of the Influencer Economy stories profiled in this book are under four syllables. The Vlogbrothers, Nerdist, RocketJump, WTF, Boston Sports Guy, Rooster Teeth, *Red vs. Blue*, Sword & Laser,

Harto, VidCon, RocketJump, Nerdist—it's no coincidence that these names are short and sweet. Even our daily tech products like Facebook, Twitter, Google, Amazon, and Yahoo!—the brand names are concise and easy to remember. Keep it simple.

When naming an idea and moving on to the corollary task of creating a logo, I like to follow the "T-Shirt Rule," asking myself, "Would I wear a T-shirt with this logo on it?" If the answer is no, then the name and logo don't work. Not every logo needs to be worn by hipsters in Park Slope, Brooklyn, but still, think about designing a logo that will work well on T-shirts, stickers, and other merch. The logo should also be sharable online. In other words, it needs to look awesome posted on Pinterest and Instagram or look cool as a YouTube thumbnail. Your logo is a social object, something to be shared, worn, and passed around.

And again, *Google is your home page.* Without getting too technical, when thinking of a name, create something that you can own search results for. What's easy to remember? What will rise to the top of search results? When picking a website or branding an idea, create it, and become it.

Actions to Find Your Name and Create a Logo

1. Follow the "Naming Rule of Four" and come up with a list of brand names that are no more than four syllables. Run your list by friends for initial feedback.

2. Google your final choice of name and see if you can own the term. You don't want any competition in Google search results. Be creative when looking for competing names.

3. Create a simple logo using the "T-Shirt Rule." Think what would look cool on a T-shirt for your community. Your logo will become a social object, meaning it will be

passed around on the Internet. Make sure that your logo is something that you yourself would share online. Logos can be very difficult to make, and like your name you need to get it right, or as close to right, as possible. There are sites like Behance and 99Designs that connect designers with people hoping to make a reasonably priced and professional logo.

Lesson 4: Purchase Your Own Web Domain

I joke with friends that one of my favorite pastimes is pouring a big glass of wine, sitting down at my computer, and buying a bunch of domains for ideas that I have. Seriously, I love buying cool domains when I have new ideas! I'll let you in on a secret: when I started the Influencer Economy, it was with a glass of wine in hand.

Sometimes smaller steps like buying domains will help you accomplish larger goals. You need to take such smaller steps to make your idea more real. You have no idea how many people ask me for advice about how to launch a podcast, a book, or a mobile app. After we talk about the concrete steps they need to take to get going, they usually disappear. The number of people that don't ever start, or start and quit, is astounding.

When I talk about owning your domain, I mean it both in the literal online website domain sense and in the sense of the domain of expertise that you are acquiring. I don't equate gaining influence with gaining expertise, per se. But you need to believe that you are the best in the world at what you're doing. You need to justify to the people of the world why you are the right person to execute this idea. You will need to look inward and find the conviction to share your big vision to the world. Owning your domain is all about finding where you sit in the universe and making your idea happen.

Chris Hardwick took steps to make his idea a reality. He picked a solid name, he bought a domain, he started producing a blog, and he made sure that every step along the way he embraced his personality. You can do the same. So pick a name for your start-up idea and then go to a web hosting service like Dream-Host or Bluehost and see if the dot-com is available. If it is, buy it! It's that easy.

The action of buying a domain is empowering, and personally I'm a little bit paranoid that other people will swoop in and steal my domains if I don't grab them. Therefore I spend the $12 to sleep easier at night knowing that my bases are covered. Chris Hardwick bought Nerdist.com early in his platform-building process, and it still serves as the hub of his digital media universe.

Actions to Purchase Your Own Web Domain

1. Buy web domains for your big visions or idea. Specifically, buy a dot-com, because some people don't feel comfortable clicking on a dot-net, dot-ly, or anything with a hyphen (-) in it. Keep it simple and buy a domain based on what your mom would be likely to click on.

2. If you have the money and if you have more than one idea, buy multiple domain names just to be safe. Also, after you buy the .com, if you'd like to cover your bases, you can buy all the major top-level domains, which include .com, .net, and .org. Again, always keep your mom in mind.

3. If the dot-com is not available, think of other names for your idea. The dot-com is important enough that it's worth renaming your idea if it's not available. Or buy a derivative of your idea by including your city name or some self-identifier that allows you to get a dot-com. (i.e., www.Joespizzaatlanta.com)

Chapter 3

Book Your Own Gigs: The Jay Z Effect

"I'm not a businessman—I'm a business man."

—Jay Z

Chapter Playbook

Shawn Carter grew up in the Marcy Projects in Bedford-Stuyvesant, Brooklyn. He didn't advance beyond seventh grade, sold crack as a young kid, and has been shot multiple times. After surviving that rough neighborhood, Shawn—or, as he's known today, Jay Z—has evolved into a once-in-a-generation rapper.

At an early age, Jay Z learned how to book his own gigs and took on every job necessary to reach his goals and dreams. From freestyle battling against the best rappers in New York to working as a hype man for the rapper Big Daddy Kane to selling CDs out of his car after getting rejected for a traditional record deal, Jay Z did it all on his way to the top.

When launching your idea, you likely won't have the budget to hire a team or pay a staff, so you'll have to spend all your free moments doing it all. Your priorities will include programming, coding, project managing, marketing and PR, community building, graphic design, copywriting, and everything else involved with launching your idea. It is really hard work.

And you will get rejected a lot along the way to the top. When I performed stand-up comedy, I experienced rejection on a regular basis at open mic comedy nights. After getting back on stage again and again, I realized that anything in life is going to test you to see how bad you want it. And if you get rejected, it's up to you to not only book your own gigs but to find world-class teammates to help you launch your idea. Jay Z found the likes of Beyonce and Kanye to help him, and you need to find what we call your "launch team."

A student at the University of Pennsylvania kicked off his career writing in online forums about TV shows almost 25 years ago and booked his own gigs to self-publish a *New York Times* top 10 book.

Alan Sepinwall

Picture a world where there is no Facebook, Instagram, or any social media—in fact, the words *tweet* and *blog* don't yet exist. It's the fall of 1993, when people were just beginning to explore the early Internet, which was then a bit like the Wild West. Alan Sepinwall was a sophomore at the University of Pennsylvania and writing for the *Daily Pennsylvanian*, a student newspaper. He also made time each week to indulge his love for the hit TV series *NYPD Blue*.

While surfing the World Wide Web, Alan found a rec.arts.tv Usenet group—the Internet forum of its day—where other fans of *NYPD Blue* gathered online to discuss Detective Andy Sipowicz's drunken antics and the rest of life at New York's 15th Precinct. Late one night, when he saw a post from someone who had missed the latest episode of the show, Alan volunteered to write a recap. "A bunch of people said 'Hey, that's really good.' And so that became a thing I did," Alan told me. "At a certain point, the recap started to be combined with commentary. Eventually I set up my own website. It's still out there on the Penn servers. It looks really dated and primitive." But Alan was growing his platform, which enabled him to build his first community and give them information they appreciated about the show.

Because it was such a niche, Alan's writings became a powerful way for him to start attracting a following of *NYPD Blue* enthusiasts. He was writing every week about something he was passionate about, which is how you develop the consistent voice needed to keep your audience and even find new fans. Alan's goal was actually to become a print journalist, and his early mastery of a web format helped to make his writing samples stand out enough to land a job at the New Jersey *Star-Ledger.* The features editor at that newspaper knew online journalism was gaining traction and saw that Alan was already writing for an Internet audience. Then, when the paper's main TV critic couldn't attend a press tour in California, Alan got the chance to cover the event and quickly worked his way up to become a full-time critic. He had been out of college for all of a month.

For more than a dozen years, Alan covered television at the *Star-Ledger* and recapped shows on his popular blog, *What's Alan Watching?* He is now a well-respected and well-received online television critic who writes for the popular entertainment website HitFix.com. His fans include the people who watch TV as well as create it—many of whom go online after an hour of *Game of Thrones* or *Masters of Sex* to learn what Alan thinks about the episode. In other words, Alan watches *Breaking Bad* as intently as we do, and he creates an online article and thus a forum for us to discuss the show with him and others.

His articles and comments section are the modern-day version of workplace water cooler office chats. He has done as much as any critic to popularize the notion of the "golden age of TV" starting at the turn of the century. In addition to his successful HitFix column, he has hosted popular TV-themed podcasts. And if you read his Twitter mentions, he has the respect of fellow critics and TV fans alike. Alan's talent and influence extend far beyond the online world as well. He wrote the best-selling *The*

Revolution . . . Drama Forever, which was included in *New York Times* critic Michiko Kakutani's annual 10 Favorite Books list.

Given his influence, you'd think that the book publishing industry would have welcomed the opportunity to publish a book by Alan. Guess again.

Doing It Yourself

Many of us have cool insights about our industry or even a personal story—real or imagined—that might make a pretty good book. Whether fiction or nonfiction, a completed book is something tangible. In our professional lives, writing a book has become a valuable modern day business card and it can add to our credibility. In the Influencer Economy, self-publishing a book doesn't necessarily nix a book's integrity or sales potential. In fact, self-publishing is *more* empowering for writers, because it allows them to embrace their inner Jay Z to control the process from start to finish and gain more of the potential financial upside.

"People were skeptical that there would be an audience for this," Alan told me on my podcast about his book proposal that was circulating in 2011. "I got one pretty lowball offer. I sensed not a lot of enthusiasm from that publisher about it." The book idea that Alan and his literary agent were peddling became *The Revolution Was Televised.* Alan wanted to pay tribute to a dozen hour-long shows that altered our sense of what was possible on the small screen. The lure of creative freedom on HBO, AMC, and other cable channels meant that veteran TV writers could finally develop shows that dissed traditional network storytelling—most of which still clung to procedural and genre formats until the late 1990s. To hear Alan tell it, by greenlighting *Oz*, *The Sopranos*, *The Wire*, and *Deadwood*, HBO alone accounted for several millennium dramas that upped the game within their medium and even challenged the increasingly formulaic tent-pole plots in the movie business.

"The literary community doesn't necessarily know TV that well," Alan explained to me. "There was a similar book in the works at a publisher, and so nobody else necessarily wanted to touch mine." But this is what the publishing industry is still struggling to understand: there can be 10 books on the market that share DNA with a new book that comes along, but it won't significantly hurt sales if the author of the new book already has a committed following. Whether through social media or other forms of on- and offline presence, if you've done the Jay Z work of rallying your community, then a readership exists to check out your book.

There was another tool in place to convince Alan to bypass traditional publishers and go it alone. "Amazon had this print-on-demand program that I found really interesting," Alan said. "I owned a couple of books made by it, and they seemed indistinguishable from traditionally produced books. So I said, 'Sure, I've got this big social media following. Why not? I will do it myself. I won't have to give anybody else a cut, other than the collaborators I work with.' I tried that and it wound up working out spectacularly well."

Those collaborators he mentions are another key takeaway to all this, because they formed the nucleus of his launch team. Alan's editor was his friend Sarah Bunting, the founder of another popular TV criticism and recap blog, *Television Without Pity.* Another friend, Ken Levine, an Emmy Award–winning TV writer on *M*A*S*H* and other shows, gave Alan advice on the book's look and feel. A company called 52 Novels transferred the manuscript to its e-book format for less than a hundred dollars, allowing Alan to pony up for Jeroen Ten Berge, a freelance illustrator who designed the cover. Like a scrappy start-up company, *The*

Revolution Was Televised benefitted from various talent and resources to carry it across the finish line. It went on sale in November of 2012, only a few weeks after Alan had completed all the writing. That kind of turnaround would have been impossible with one of the big New York houses, which take months to bring out new titles, even after delivery and acceptance of a manuscript.

So here's Alan Sepinwall making all this sound pretty easy to me—on my podcast no less, which isn't a bad way to talk to a TV expert. I listened to him and felt inspired because I also had a book I wanted to write. And it even aimed to celebrate a kind of golden age of influence, with creators and builders who are also driving their own revolution through content channels like YouTube, blogs, and podcasts. But for me or anyone else to consider following in Alan's footsteps, we need to acknowledge that he's been building his community and team for several years. He could successfully be his own book distributor and sales rep because of his hard-won credibility with his fans. What's more important to mention here is that before he became a professional TV critic, Alan was writing for an online community that shared his interests. He was creating and giving away information to these folks for free, and even learning to refine his content per their feedback. More than once on my podcast, Alan referred to his success as a critic and author as a function of "luck," but if we really examine how he ended up on HitFix and a *New York Times* top 10 list, then we see how the Jay Z Effect principle comes into play.

Dealing with Rejection

Nir Eyal (who we'll talk about later in this chapter) is the author of *Hooked: How to Build Habit-Forming Products*, a fascinating look at strategies for creating behavior and habits that draw users back again and again.[1] Well, Alan did just that. His website prioritized the lure of community and great content before any thought of monetization (or selling a book) entered the mix. To this day, the habit for his fans stems from the pleasure of seeking out other fans—both of Alan's juicy recaps and of the shows themselves. Whether you visit his site after watching an episode in its normally scheduled hour or on your own time via DVR or On Demand, you are drawn to a conversation much like the engaging and multifaceted interaction that occurs on social media. The more specific the topic, the more impassioned the community.

"Some of my best and longest lasting friendships come from a Listserv I was on for the *Homicide* TV show on NBC," Alan said regarding folks he had befriended beyond his *NYPD Blue* community who also populated his blog and remained personally close. "People were at my wedding who were on that Listserv." It was by building this community that Alan nailed the confidence to self-produce his book and distribute it on his own without a mainstream publishing partner. He didn't need an old-school, offline company to give him credibility because he already had an eager and supportive group behind his success.

Tucker Max, author of the bestselling *I Hope They Serve Beer in Hell* and other "fratire" story collections, also spoke to me on the podcast about rallying your community versus relying on the publishing industry to put out a book. "I wasn't just rejected. I sent queries to all the mainstream publishers . . . and every magazine, newspaper, and whatever. I didn't just get zero interest. There were like five editors who took the time to write me about how terrible my writing was. How I was a horrible person and should never pick up a pen again. And I remember laughing at the time because I didn't define myself as a writer or think I was a writer at all." But because his friends and friends of friends had already passed his stories around the Internet by e-mail, Tucker had the confidence to build his own website where he could post his content. It was 2002, the era of Microsoft FrontPage, though Tucker ended up using a plain text HTML editor to upload those e-mails. "They were just funny things I wrote to my friends to make them laugh. This was back when people thought websites had to have dancing babies."

No question that Alan Sepinwall's television recaps and criticism aim for a different audience than Tucker Max's following, but both authors achieved major success by trusting their own communities. In Tucker's case, his website with its tales of womanizing and "absinthe donuts" was an early example of online self-publishing that went viral and led to an offline book deal. Yep, publishers finally came around to Tucker once they realized that his website tapped into a huge market of college-age readers. Alan also believed that his own community would justify writing a book that mainstream publishers didn't initially want. And by the time Alan began drafting his manuscript, the do-it-yourself model for authors often involved using the reach and resources of Amazon, which remains a powerful, if controversial, partner for writers in all genres.

Embracing the Jay Z Effect: Booking Your Own Gigs

Whether you're making a book, DVD, or some other kind of digital content, Amazon has a tool to help you self-publish and distribute your work to millions of people. Alan ultimately chose Amazon's self-publishing program because fans of *The Revolution Was Televised* seemed mostly interested in reading Alan Sepinwall regardless of how his book became available. Interestingly, he also told me that Amazon's print-on-demand option helped to prove that his community wanted whatever was best for him. "I would have people reach out to me and say, 'I'm debating whether I want to buy the Kindle version or the print version. Which would you make more money on?' That's awesome. There was a lot of good will I was getting at that time. It felt really nice."

The Amazon approach to book sales does have lots of critics, and a pricing standoff with the publishing conglomerate Hachette Book Group in 2014 was a public relations disaster for CEO Jeff Bezos.[2] Hachette books on Bezos's website couldn't be preordered, and suppressed inventories meant buyers had to wait weeks for new books by Stephen Colbert, Malcolm Gladwell, and other big-name authors. One of my guests on the podcast was Willie Geist, who co-wrote the best-selling Hachette book *Good Talk, Dad: The Birds and the Bees . . . and Other Conversations We Forgot to Have.*

Willie is a host on *The Today Show* and appears regularly on MSNBC's *Morning Joe.* He wrote the book with his father, Bill Geist, a long-time correspondent for *CBS: Sunday Morning.* The book chronicles funny stories—awkward father-son moments that the Geists forgot to talk about while Willie was growing up. Included is an anecdote from Willie and my Vanderbilt fraternity days when our friend Clay Neuman zip-lined down the frat house roof onto the basketball court to play the National Anthem during our fraternity's annual Big Sky Basketball Tournament. Neuman not only fired actual roman candles into the crowd of hundreds, but in an ode to *Animal House,* he shredded his guitar and smashed it into a thousand pieces on the court. Willie and Bill share these types of stories, riffing from chapter to chapter, and smartly released their book around Father's Day 2014 to tie in the holiday and move copies of their book.

Willie and Bill Geist released their book in the midst of Amazon's hardball negotiations with their publisher and still managed to reach number 17 on the *New York Times* best-seller list. "It's really hard nowadays to sell a book without Amazon," Willie told me. "[So] we called everybody we knew, called in every favor. Asked all our friends. We rallied people. We went on every radio show and TV show we could think of. We were all over social media, and so we felt we earned our spot on that list because it wasn't easy."

You could argue that the Geists and Alan Sepinwall have an advantage over lesser-known writers with or without publishing deals. Yes, Amazon plays a fascinating (some might say infuriating) role in launching a new book, regardless of whether it comes from a "Big Five" publisher or is a do-it-yourself publication.[3] But here's the real takeaway: When you finish your book, your work isn't done. You have to promote it. Even if you don't have the reach of people who have built up their audience over several years, you do have your own version of a community that you must tap. So you'll call everyone you know. You'll talk to your friends and ask them to buy your book, or help market it, or leave a nice online review. Maybe you can't snap your fingers and get on TV or radio—but you can try, and you can certainly use social media to raise awareness about your work. When it comes to sales on any platform, or just sharing the content that you create, you shouldn't expect results without asking people to look in your direction. And that's exactly what Alan did so that *The Revolution Was Televised* had the best possible chance for success.

He turned to his social media following and HitFix fans for support. Because he occasionally appeared on ESPN's influential *B.S. Report* podcast, Alan asked host Bill Simmons if he could come on again to discuss his book. That Bill Simmons "bump" certainly helped Alan's project. "I hear from people saying, 'I first heard of you on Simmons' podcast,'" Alan said to me. "It's absolutely the case that knowing him as tenuously as I know him has been very good for my career."

Nor was Alan shy when it came to asking critics to weigh in. "I had asked a friend at the *New York Times* if he knew how I would go about getting the book reviewed, but it seemed like the longest of long shots," he admitted. "Particularly after a few other newspaper people told me that their editors had a policy against reviewing self-published books. And my friend said he never heard back from the books editor. Then on Monday I got an e-mail from the *Times* photo editor asking for a headshot to accompany a review. I still don't entirely believe that that happened, under the circumstances."

The *New York Times* revered his book and that review ran on December 3, 2012. The critic, Michiko Kakutani, revealed herself to be both a fan of Alan's blog and his new book, which she acknowledged was self-published.[4] "He is probably most compelling in this volume explaining the magnetic pull of certain shows and their emotional power," she writes, "articulating just why we fell in love with the characters in *Friday Night Lights*, or why ordinary viewers can find stone-cold killers like Tony Soprano or Walt White so 'relatable.'"[5]

USA Today, The Huffington Post, Time, and the *New Yorker* also praised Alan's book, helping to drive sales and challenge the "policy" in some circles of not reviewing self-published work. Michiko Kakutani at the *Times* took this a step further when she named *The Revolution Was Televised* one of the year's best books, placing it on a list that included such top authors as Dave Eggers, Michael Chabon, and Oliver Sacks. The good press caught the attention of publishers, who wondered why they hadn't been given a chance to sign up Alan when he was shopping the book proposal. "Why didn't you bring this to us a year ago?" Alan recalled them saying. "And in certain cases I said, 'I did. You just didn't want it.' But I decided I had taken the self-published version of it as far as it could go. The traditional publishers were interested, and it would help get the book in many more places and physical bookstores. It would be available in more countries—lots of other things that I couldn't do with the apparatus I had set up."

To reach those additional goals, Alan signed with the Touchstone imprint of Simon & Schuster. But the *Times* review spelled out something that I think may be historic. A well-respected critic clearly accepted the self-publishing model and the importance of influence with an online community. As Michiko put it: "The Internet, in Mr. Sepinwall's opinion, wasn't a rival to TV, but a kind of partner. And for Mr. Sepinwall himself, the Internet has been the launching pad for an increasingly high-profile career—and now, a terrific book."[4]

Alan told me he had no idea that Michiko Kakutani was a fan of his blog. Rather than a hurdle, he also sensed that self-publishing in this case was a plus for her. "I think she was intrigued by the idea that I had done that," he said, making it sound like he had caught a break. But as I've noted, booking your own gigs, building out your launch team, and rallying your community is a lot more relevant here than luck—if that even applies to Alan Sepinwall.

Influencer School Lessons: What Alan Sepinwall Can Teach You About Booking Your Own Gigs

Lesson 1: Dealing with Rejection

Like many of us in the Influencer Economy, when we get rejected by the mainstream, we mobilize our resources and embrace a do-it-yourself mantra. In embracing the Jay Z Effect, you accept that you have to do every single job by yourself. But rather than being a drag, it's actually an inspiring time. There are a multitude of resources to help your ideas get seen. With the Internet, mobile devices, and social media, you can bounce back from rejection and create your own success and potentially reach a global audience in seconds. But it's also a very noisy time in that you need to make your voice heard amidst the clamor of the Internet, so when you launch you need to have your ducks in a row. It's all on you to get your work to the people.

When I performed stand-up comedy in the early 2000s I learned about the Jay Z Effect. I had to write my own jokes, book my own stage time at shows, network with other comedians to find new gigs, and perform at open mics to practice my material. When I finally performed at The Improv in Washington, DC, most of the hard work had been done. When I hit that stage, it was time to execute after the grind of just getting to that stage. But the hardest part of stand-up comedy is getting rejected by the audience. When no one laughs at your jokes, it's an awful feeling. When you tell a joke, you are putting yourself out there, almost naked, opening yourself up to judgment. And you get rejected. A lot.

After that experience, I now have the utmost respect for any creative entrepreneur who forges their own path and makes a living off of their ideas. It's hard getting visibility, and all creators will face rejection along the way. Building something from nothing is a daunting task that can seem impossible. When I heard Alan's story on the podcast, I couldn't help but think: even Alan Sepinwall was rejected by the mainstream. But what makes Alan's story so compelling is that he dealt with the rejection and went on to do it all himself.

Everyone gets rejected, even people at the top of their game. I know it's cliché, but it's really how you handle rejection that makes you succeed. And finding resourceful ways to get around gatekeepers helps you move on from rejection. The traditional book publishers were Alan's gatekeepers. His *What's Alan Watching?* blog is read by millions of people a month, but publishers failed to recognize that he had a large online audience that he could sell directly to. Of course, the irony of Alan's rejection was that after his self-published book gained traction, only *then* did publishers came knocking on his door.

Actions to Learn How to Deal with Rejection

1. Read stories about successful people who were rejected multiple times before they hit it big. Tucker Max, Alan Sepinwall, and even J. K. Rowling are well-known examples of authors. In fact, google "famous authors who were rejected" for an eye-opening look at the persistence and thick skin you'll need to endure in the Influencer Economy. I also created a page on my website, www.influencereconomy/rejections devoted to successful people's rejections. Hearing other people's stories with rejection can help you realize you're not alone.

2. Find out who are the decision makers in your industry. List out the investors, dealmakers, reviewers, and other traditional gatekeepers who may stand in your way. You'll always face people with more money, power, and experience that can stand in the way of your success. Figure out how much power your gatekeepers truly have (it may not be as much as you think), and then think of three creative ways to work around them.

3. Brainstorm ways to do it yourself and Jay Z your way to launching your idea. Determine whether avenues like crowdfunding or self-publishing are realistic ways for you to thrive by bypassing traditional gatekeepers. When you identify alternative paths to success, you will be more confident when dealing with gatekeepers and their rejection.

Getting My Book Rejected by Publishers

Stand-up comedy was not the only arena in which I faced rejection. When I was exploring a book deal for *The Influencer Economy*, 15 publishers rejected my proposal.

When I first set out to write the book, I didn't know if I would self-publish or go the traditional route. But I did write a proposal and shop it around to major and minor book publishers.

There are several pros to working with a traditional publisher. Publishers help authors with such services as editing, designing cover art, marketing, and distribution. They pay you money in advance while you finish the book. Getting paid to write is always awesome, and no one is going to turn down money. If getting into bookstores is your ultimate goal as a writer, major publishers have well-established relationships with the large bookstore chains to make that happen.

The cons of working with book publishers include the fact that it usually takes at least a year to get your book published after signing the deal. It's usually a slow process since you're working with larger corporations. Also, publishers are good at getting your book into bookstores, but how often do people really buy books in stores anymore when Amazon delivers titles right to your doorstep? The majority of book sales are digital these days. Traditional publishers also take a much larger cut of the profits from book sales but, to be fair, that's necessary to recoup their upfront costs to produce your book and bring it to market.

In general, self-publishing my book felt more in line with Influencer Economy principles, but I still needed to test the waters. I am a professional marketer and the book was years in the making. I felt pretty confident about my go-to-market launch plan. And I was building community via my podcast and e-mail list, so whether or not a book deal worked out, I felt good either way.

I signed on with an agent who did great work getting my proposal in front of 15 top-tier publishers. That was exciting. And then

I heard back from all 15 of them with one response: thanks, no thanks. They all passed. Every one of them. Some suggested that I didn't have a big enough platform. Others said I was potentially big in LA, but not national enough to get TV exposure. A few said they didn't like the "social media" themes of the book; they saw social media as too evolving to stay current. Some thought the book wouldn't stand out enough compared to similar titles. And still others didn't say much, except that it wasn't right for them.

These publishers were my gatekeepers. Like Alan, I was seeking a book deal and talking to agents. When Alan told me that he was rejected, and Tucker Max did as well, I felt even more encouraged that I could do it myself. I thought if a writer like Alan Sepinwall, who was well established as a TV critic, couldn't get a publishing deal to write a book about TV shows, then this model was broken. So I did what I had to do and went through Amazon to get self-published. And now you're reading my book, which is pretty awesome. If I had written this book in 2011, no one would have read it because I wouldn't have been able to book my own gigs and do all the work to self-publish.

Self-publishing is also more entrepreneurial. Even though I spent a lot of money and time up front working with editors and book designers, I knew that the high risk could pay off. With Amazon, I get a decent percentage of every book sold, whether the customer buys a physical or digital copy. But it's up to me to sell the books. It's high risk and high reward, and as an entrepreneur I thrive off those environments. And who knows? Perhaps a top-tier publisher is reading this book now and will offer me an attractive deal. Why? Because I booked my own gigs like Jay Z, saw my vision through to the end, and now have something to show for it.

Lesson 2: Build Your Launch Team (i.e., Find Your Kanye West and Beyoncé)

Alan realized his strength was in writing, but he had to identify all the other jobs that needed to get done in order to self-publish his book. He couldn't do it alone. Alan had to write the book—which was no small task, but as he said, "Someone was going to write this book—it may as well have been me." He was confident—Alan had been a writer his whole career, honing his craft for over a decade, and he knew the TV criticism universe as well as anyone. But to execute, he needed to find all-star teammates. He needed his Kanye and Beyoncé. He needed a launch team.

If you want to launch an idea, no matter what type of product it is, you too need to itemize the specific tasks that are needed and then mobilize your team to get it all done. Alan's jobs to launch his idea included the following:

1. Build a community of readers (which took years of work).

2. Write and publish consistent content to gain credibility in his field (which also took years to do).

3. Grow relationships with other writers and media personalities who would support him along the way (which you guessed it, took more years of work).

4. Write the book (the big job).

5. Hire an editor and work with her to polish the text.

6. Hire a designer to create a book cover.

7. Convert his manuscript into the Amazon self-publishing format.

8. Upload and submit his book to Amazon.

9. Book his media appearances on podcasts like Bill Simmons' *B.S. Report*.

10. Reach out to journalists at prominent newspapers like the *New York Times*.

11. Continue to engage regularly with his community on social media during the book release.

12. Reach out to his "friend list," i.e., his community of peers who were not only readers of his blog but also well connected in his industry. (More on this in the next lesson.)

That's a lot of work, which is why it's critical to create a team to help you launch your idea. A launch team helps you complete your final product more efficiently and effectively. And it helps you, the creator, stick to the task, because your teammates hold you accountable. By sharing your deadlines, you also get a kick in the pants from others who are depending on you.

I always advise creators and entrepreneurs to collaborate with others and never work in a vacuum. When you work alone in your office or garage, you often miss the structure and feedback that working with a team can give you. Don't isolate yourself.

Also, when you delegate tasks to members of your launch team, you feel more alive and accomplished. This is often an undervalued part of the Influencer Economy. It can light a fire under you. And it's more fun.

In the digital age you need to treat any idea, from a blog to a YouTube channel to a podcast, as a start-up. Entrepreneurship has allowed creative people to own their ideas. Alan Sepinwall formed his own start-up team and went deep into writing, editing, and packaging the book himself. It was a risk, but Alan knew he was practicing the Jay Z Effect—he was the author, distributor, marketer, PR agent, and everything else—and with the support of his team, he could create his own book and sell it direct to his readers.

Actions to Build Your Launch Team

1. Write down all the jobs you need to do to launch your idea. Simply write out the title, task, and order in which each job needs to be accomplished based on your launch timing and priorities.

2. Create a launch team "task matrix" to determine who will execute each of these jobs. There are three options: Do the job yourself, get help from a friend for free (including bartering with them), or hire someone to do the work. Each of these options comes with pros and cons that you need to list.

3. Determine who will hold you accountable. Who are the collaborators who will keep you on task? Think about who will keep you honest and focused on launching your idea. If you don't have a coworker to fill this role, find friends, colleagues, and teammates to help you along the way. And remember to have fun on the journey!

Click here for the Launch Team Task Matrix:

Influencereconomy.com/products

Lesson 3: Rally Your Friends

Right after you get your website up, I recommended that you create an e-mail group called a "friend list." These are the friends that you can really lean on to provide assistance, product feedback, and general support during your journey. Very few people can succeed while working in isolation, an operation that I call "building in a silo," hidden from the world. You need to find partners to help you fulfill your big vision. You need to get your product out the door, and these friends will help you accomplish that. Never build in a silo.

Your initial list should consist of people whom you can easily reach by e-mail. The list can be five people, or it can be 50 people or more. The number is not important. The priority is that you trust your friend list. These are your friends, relatives, former colleagues, college buddies, and anyone who will offer to pitch in when necessary. In turn, your responsibilities are simple: you ask them for help with small tasks; you never, ever spam them; and you reward them however you can along the way. You treat these friends like gold.

The people on your friend list are your alpha testers who will give you product feedback. They're the buddies who will share your idea on social media when you launch and eventually leave reviews on Amazon, iTunes, or wherever your product lives. You'll be surprised how happy these friends will be to support you, even if they are incredibly busy people. When you keep them in the loop with a somewhat regular e-mail, they'll feel engaged in your vision and invested in your progress. Even if you e-mail them general updates consisting of a few bullet points, it's enough. Creating can be a lonely job, and receiving an e-mail from a friend along the way saying "You're Awesome!" or "Congrats on the progress!" will make you feel good.

The Benihana Rule

Have you ever been to Benihana, the Japanese steakhouse where the chef cooks the meal in front of you and a small group of people? They were big in the '80s and '90s and remain so today. I frequented these restaurants as a kid, often celebrating my birthday with my family there.

What makes Benihana awesome isn't the food. (Actually, the food is not that great.) Benihana is all about the shared experience of watching a cook make your meal and then eating it with a group of people. Usually the chef performs tricks like flipping his knives around before chopping up the chicken or flipping shrimp from the grill onto your plate. Sometimes he hits the plate, sometimes he doesn't. It's fun. At Benihana, you typically are seated with a group of strangers, so it forces interaction. When my family and I went, we often laughed and made friends with the others at our table.

Building a friend list and letting your buddies into your launch process is like enjoying the meal experience at Benihana. I call it the "Benihana Rule," and it's important in the Influencer Economy. It creates a shared experience for many, including friends of yours who may not know each other. Moreover, once your idea launches, everyone experiences it together, just like eating your grilled chicken and fried rice at the Benihana dinner table. You are like the Japanese chef cooking a meal for a group of hungry eaters. You need to let your friends into the creative process for the good, bad, and sometimes the ugly. It will only help you along the way. Sharing your work with others, even when it's not completely polished, is a smart way to make your ideas stronger. It will also help you to galvanize a community for when you ultimately need them to help launch your idea.

Following the Benihana Rule, if you're a filmmaker, you can share storyboards. If you're a writer, you can share blog posts. If you're a technologist, you'll share an alpha version of your product. When I announced my podcast, the first group I e-mailed was my friend list. When I picked my book cover for *The Influencer Economy*, the first people I asked for feedback were in my friend group. I hope these friends will be with me over the long term of my creative career. And finally, the friend list will help grow your early adopter base that we'll talk more about in chapter 4, "Adopt New Technology Early and Often."

Actions to Rally Your Friends

1. Write out your friend list. Include a diverse group of younger, middle-aged, and older people, including your parents, current and former colleagues, high school friends, and anyone who may take an interest in supporting you. It doesn't matter if they are experts in your field; it just matters that they have your back.

2. When you think you're ready, send the entire friend list a group e-mail. Follow your gut on the timing, but it needs to be around when you have an announcement to make, like launching a new website. Welcome your friends into

the community that you are building, and tell them about your idea. Ask them if it's okay to include them in future correspondence about you building your idea. Express to them that you won't spam them, ever. And thank them. You can never thank these people enough.

3. Create a private Facebook Group (or Slack Group, if you are more technical) for your friend group. Invite these people into your creative processes as early as you can. By investing in them, they'll invest in you, and help you make a better product in the long run.

BONUS STORY

Nir Eyal and Building Proof of Concept for Your Idea

Do you know why you check Facebook when you're bored at work? Or why you look at Snapchat if you're feeling lonely? Maybe you just glanced at Instagram when reading this chapter. It's okay. We all have our little distractions. A 2013 study by the venture capital firm KPCB found that we check our smartphones about 150 times a day.[1] There's even an app called Checky that keeps track of how often we pull out our phones and is designed to help us understand our "phone habit." So yes, we've reached the point where an app can tell us how addicted we are to other apps—as well as to our e-mail accounts, text messages, and favorite websites.

But there is also a best-selling book that offers more insight. *Hooked: How to Build Habit-Forming Products* pulls back the curtain on what occurs in a user's mind during their love affair with a particular product or service. What's fascinating about the author, Nir Eyal, is that he never planned to write this widely-read book or amass a community of tech professionals and enthusiasts. His global audience discovered him and his passion for product design through his blog, *Nir and Far*. What began as a kind of journal or personal inquiry has led to a career as an influential speaker and lecturer, consultant, business writer, and angel investor (someone who invests very early in a company's development).

What helps to set Nir apart from other tech-focused authors is that he's also an entrepreneur. For much of his career, he worked in the video gaming and online advertising industries, cofounding two start-ups: Sunshine Business Development, which was acquired in 2007, and AdNectar, acquired in 2011. He understands the nuances of raising venture capital and launching a product, a fact that adds to his credibility with other aspiring and current tech founders.

After exiting AdNectar, Nir started consulting and also took time to research a question that had fascinated him for years. As a graduate student, he had been taught that the best products to develop are so-called "painkillers" because customers use them habitually. The students in his class were cautioned against launching companies that were merely "vitamins," offering value to a consumer's life without being indispensable. But here's the twist: on paper, some ideas appear to be vitamins, or start out that way, and then eventually become painkillers.

"A great example of that is Facebook," Nir told me. "I remember when I was at Stanford in the MBA program and Mark Zuckerberg was a guest speaker. It was 2007 and he had turned down the billion-dollar offer from Yahoo. Everybody in the class thought he was a big idiot. I mean, this twenty-something kid turned down a billion bucks. Well, he knew something, right? He knew that 50 percent of his users came back every day. These unbelievable engagement rates. His company is so valuable because for so many people it's a habit. It's something that people do with little or no conscious thought multiple times a day. Even though it started out as what many dismissed as a nice-to-have feature of somebody else's product. Something that's just like a toy."

Nir mentioned a grim hypothetical in which Zuckerberg one day decides that he's made enough money and shuts down Facebook. Given how important the product is to people, many would experience a form of withdrawal. If Facebook goes dark, that's a "big problem for a lot of folks." But how did Zuckerberg's company, or

Amazon, or Twitter, become so sticky for users in the first place? "I just started chiseling away at the psychology that unfortunately was kind of pent up in the ivory tower of academia," Nir said. "I read a lot of books, and I did a lot of interviews." The work of behaviorist B. F. Skinner factored into Nir's thinking as he began to formulate a four-part process that might help product development teams more fully understand consumer psychology, particularly what Nir calls "unprompted engagement." When talking with him about his book, you get the sense that he's an academic thinker trapped in the body of an entrepreneur.

A framework like *Hooked*, with its behavioral science origins and real-world applications, came along at the perfect moment to offer entrepreneurs a competitive edge. The best solutions don't necessarily win, right? If you use Google out of habit, then you may never find out if Bing is a decent search engine. A product that methodically follows the *Hooked* model has a better chance of outlasting brief viral popularity or a big advertising campaign and holding on to its market share. The growth is real and easier to defend against a similar product that just isn't as sticky.

The pressure to "get it right" can be intimidating for start-up founders or any builder inclined to join this generation's tech boom. Justin Jackson, host of the *Product People* and *Build and Launch* podcasts, told me that he reminds his listeners not to get hung up on building an epic idea or procrastinate over *Hooked* and other how-to blueprints. He advises to consider scaling down your initial launch: "This idea of actually just releasing [your product], sometimes even making it so small—you know, I think a lot of us have dreams about building really big things—but just making it so small that you could build it in a weekend."

Whatever the scope of a builder's new dot-com or app, there are powerful incentives for baking in concepts like the ones Nir Eyal began to post on his blog in 2012. As with most successful influencers, Nir had no initial thought of monetizing his content. But his desire to explore psychology in this context quickly caught on with an audience, which expanded with Nir's guest posts on other blogs and writing assignments for TechCrunch, *Forbes*, and

Psychology Today. These other trusted outlets helped to validate the ideas accumulating on *Nir and Far*, the blog that was serving as Nir's mother ship. So the combination of regular blog posts and e-mails to a growing list of *Nir and Far* subscribers helped to bring Nir's audience back to his website each week. The other blogs and publications requesting Nir's consumer psychology insights were only the start of his opportunities to expand his community.

"Lo and behold," Nir told me, "I was writing to answer my own questions, and then after about two and a half years, I had enough content that my readers were asking, 'Hey, where's the book? I want to give this to somebody. I want people to know what I read on your blog. How do I do that?' So that's when I decided we really have to make this book." If you think of *Hooked: How to Build Habit-Forming Products* as its own start-up, then all of the blog content on *Nir and Far* served as a minimum viable product that could be assessed and commented on by these readers. A form of collaboration occurred between Nir and his readers, one in which the work benefited by subscribers voicing their opinions and encouraging Nir to elaborate on or amend certain posts. By the time he decided that his blog could actually become a book, Nir had more specific ideas on how to give his readers value and, in a sense, pay them back for their fandom.

One of Nir's reader/fans was Ryan Hoover, an entrepreneur and blogger living in San Francisco. At the end of 2012, Ryan included Nir's name in a blog post, "13 People I Want to Meet in 2013." After Ryan put Nir's name into the universe as someone he'd love to chat with in person, Nir learned of the post, he agreed to meet Ryan, and the two grabbed lunch at a burger joint in Palo Alto. This quickly turned into an ongoing working relationship and a very interesting gig for Ryan, who came aboard as editor of *Hooked*. In the coming months, Ryan combed through the *Nir and Far* blog, assembling it into chapter form and ultimately a 256-page book that Nir self-published in late 2013. That collaboration was just the tip of the iceberg. Today, Ryan incorporates many of the *Hooked* theories into Product Hunt, a community he founded that's dedicated to curating the best new products every day, which also started its proof of concept as an e-mail newsletter to friends.

Instead of keeping his material guarded and gated, like a traditional publisher would expect, Nir broke those rules and used the Influencer Economy to reach an even bigger audience for *Hooked*. "*Backwards* is exactly the right word," said Nir when we talked about his path to publication. "Because when you think about the publishing industry a decade ago or less, an author would make and then sell a book proposal, then the book would come out in hardcover and paperback, and then maybe, eventually, some e-format when those became available. Well, I did that exactly backwards." First, Nir had his blog and, after that, an e-book. Then he self-published and ultimately got picked up by Portfolio, the business imprint of Penguin Group. *Hooked* became a best seller and is still available in bookstores worldwide. "That model worked really well for me because I could constantly revise and tweak [the book] and it never felt like a job, never felt like a career. It was just following my own curiosity. I mean, for an author, curiosity is rocket fuel."

The day that Nir and I spoke was something of a milestone for him and his book. "Just today I saw it for the first time in an airport bookstore. I said to myself a year ago, 'Oh man, if I ever get into an airport bookstore, that's it, that would be awesome.' And I just took a picture of it today. It's an amazing feeling." I managed not to ask him how many times he checked his mobile phone that day, but I wondered if there were any products he couldn't get enough of. "I find Twitter very habit-forming; I find my e-mail very habit-forming," Nir admitted. "And these products are great. I think they've enhanced my life, but I think we need a degree of caution about how we use them. I'm still trying to figure out where does technology belong and where does it not belong. How do I make sure that it's serving me and I'm not a slave to it? I still struggle with these technologies even though I know exactly what makes them habit-forming. I wrote the book on it."

Chapter 4

Adopt New Technology Early and Often

"The important thing is not to stop questioning. Curiosity has its own reason for existing."
—Albert Einstein

Chapter Playbook

There is one trait that nearly everyone who I have spoken to on my podcast exhibits: they are early adopters of technology. The Vlogbrothers from chapter 1 adopted YouTube very early when they created online videos for one another. Chapter 2's Chris Hardwick of Nerdist was an early podcaster adopter. And chapter 3's Alan Sepinwall was one of the earliest TV critics online, writing in Internet forums before *blog* was even a word.

It's no accident that these people are now thriving. Most of the people profiled in this book treat early adoption as a way of thinking, a mindset, and a philosophy for who they are as creators and entrepreneurs. Oftentimes curiosity about new technology mediums is all you need to figure out how to launch your idea.

Early adopters are people who start using technology products when they are first available. Without fail, they are people guided by a sense of learning something new and figuring out what's next in technology. That allows them to take control of their business or idea, and leverage online tools and resources to help them launch. Moving first on technology doesn't mean you need to be a social media expert or even a technologist; it means that you see technology as a tool and a process, and you aren't afraid to try new things. Technology can be intimidating, which is what holds people back. But in the Influencer Economy, people are self-empowered to be resourceful and to find their own solutions to problems. We are all bootstrapping our ideas with little budget, resources, and time. It pays to be curious about technology and find what works for you.

One USC film school graduate bypassed the traditional Hollywood business model for making films by adopting technology early, posting short videos on YouTube, and crowdfunding his films well ahead of the cultural curve.

Freddie Wong

A YouTube video posted in 2006 begins abruptly with a college-aged, bespectacled Chinese American rising from a dirt bike in his living room. Wearing a black leather jacket and linked chains, he grabs a microphone and says, "What's up, Internet? My name is Freddie." He tells us he's been "rocking faces" all day and is ready to rock ours. Freddie proceeds to play the video game *Guitar Hero II* on expert level, jamming out on his plastic guitar to the Rush song "YYZ." This was Freddie Wong's debut video on his newly launched FreddieW YouTube channel. To date, videos on this channel—including the groundbreaking *Video Game High School* web series—have earned over one billion views worldwide and enabled Freddie to totally rewrite the rules on crowdfunding in the age of the Internet.

Back when Freddie first rocked out in his living room, YouTube was mainly known as a source of pirated videos, such as Andy Samberg's "Lazy Sunday" *Saturday Night Live* digital short. NBCUniversal successfully pressured YouTube to remove the video, and Viacom had even filed suit against the company over

The Daily Show segments that fans had ripped straight from TV for upload. While these major corporations were fighting to remove content from YouTube, Freddie was posting his own new videos as quickly as he could. He also continued to rock. As a professional gamer, he leveled up and actually won the 2007 World Series of Video Games *Guitar Hero II* challenge. The prize was worth $2,635 and came with bragging rights that only helped to grow his online audience.

Pretending to play Rush songs was cool, but Freddie always saw himself as a filmmaker. In 2008, he graduated from the USC School of Cinematic Arts and, unlike most in his class, chose to continue building a community of online followers before launching any major film projects. To achieve this, he uploaded a video on his YouTube channel each week. While he had no way of knowing it at the time, such consistency is extremely important for building community, and Freddie created a habit for his audience by providing them with new work to view on a regular basis. Even when he wasn't getting paid for his videos with advertisements, he treated his schedule professionally and delivered content consistently.

Collaborate with Your Fellow Techies

It didn't hurt that the special effects Freddie began to include in his videos blew many people's minds. There was "Skydiving Out My Front Door" in which Freddie appears to leap out of his apartment building into a freefall, gaining speed and twisting in the air, before finally deploying his parachute. The fantastical "Real Life Mario Kart!" finds Freddie playing the video game *Mario Kart* at a go-kart track. In "Real Life Portal Gun," Freddie gets a video game gun that wreaks havoc by teleporting him throughout his apartment. Collaborating with his college friend Brandon Laatsch, Freddie's videos were often shorter than 90 seconds and usually starred him and his friends doing something funny or inspired by a video game. The special effects they learned at USC appealed to their audience of gamers, sci-fi fans, would-be filmmakers, and YouTube loyalists.

On my podcast, Freddie told me that to make this content he embraced his "inner nerd." That technique paid off. By being authentic, he created work that specifically landed with his subscribers. Even with his limited early budgets, he found his voice and stuck with it. His fans loved him for this and grew to regard him as a buddy and kindred spirit.

"The approach to greeting YouTube folks is much more like greeting a friend," Freddie says. "The experience of watching YouTube folks is more on the relatable level; it's more intimate—it's on your phone, computers, laptop." He calls himself "Internet famous," which means that he comes across as more accessible than some pop culture stars. In person, he's an easygoing, slightly built guy with the type of thin, graphite eyeglass frames you'd expect on a video gamer. Freddie was raised in Seattle, Washington, and can talk about John Woo movies until he turns blue. Much of his success is due to that sincere love for filmmaking and gaming displayed in his own work—frequently with fake blood and high body counts.

Content that is authentic to Freddie's personality and his relatable quality may have appealed to his core fans, but his collaborations with other YouTube creators were vital to expanding that audience.

A "collab," as it's called in the YouTube world, is another secret sauce ingredient in the Influencer Economy. In this case, it's when a YouTuber appears in another YouTuber's video. Each creator is able to share the other one's success, opening up new audiences for each other. It's a win/win way for YouTubers to help others and reach new communities. As far back as 2010, Freddie cast

YouTubers DeStorm Power, Shane Dawson, iJustine, and Philip DeFranco in his content. As of 2015, these four people collectively have over 12 million subscribers. They were "first movers" in 2010 and helped each other cross-promote their channels and attract new community members.

But what Freddie didn't have yet was a bigger canvas for his talents. Since graduating from USC, he had considered a web series to be the likely foundation of any films in his future—on or offline. He wanted a way to serialize his storytelling chops across an entire "season" of episodes. The FreddieW channel was now a YouTube partner, meaning he could advertise and make money on the site. But Freddie wasn't earning the kind of ad dollars he would need to launch a project on the scale he envisioned. There wasn't even comparable content at that time on YouTube, apart from Rooster Teeth's *Red vs. Blue* Machinima series. In 2010, the site wasn't yet the creative or branding machine that it is today. YouTube was starting to find its place in the world but much of the content still consisted of addictive "Charlie Bit My Finger" and "Keyboard Cat" novelties. Some videos went "viral," but their stars (including the cats) were usually one-hit wonders that weren't heard from again, at least online.

Move First on Technology

In 2011, Freddie increased his production capabilities by cofounding RocketJump Studios. Together with his partners, Freddie began to create original content in their own facility in Burbank, California. In an end-to-end model, they distributed that content directly to their audience and monetized it with ads. Freddie decided that the moment was right to launch his massive project, *Video Game High School* (*VGHS*), a web series featuring a bit of wish fulfillment. The action takes place in the near future when professional gaming is the most popular sport in the world. The main character, BrianD, is accepted into an elite high school that trains kids to become professional gamers. Despite the pro gaming backdrop and Michael Bay-level of special effects, the series is essentially a modern-day coming of age story. Freddie intended it to be aspirational and visually striking. The only catch was that he needed his audience to help him fund the project.

Around the time that the FreddieW channel gained a large following, crowdfunding emerged as a powerful resource for non-traditional film financing. Again, Freddie was an early adopter to a new technology medium. Crowdfunding at its most basic is the practice of funding a project or venture by raising small amounts of money from a large number of people. Websites such as Kickstarter and Indiegogo were allowing creators to put their ideas to the test. Would their networks of supporters actually come through with money? It was a gut check for many people posting projects, especially on Kickstarter, where the all-or-nothing policy meant you couldn't keep a single dollar if the entire fundraising goal wasn't met.

Freddie and his team hoped to raise $75,000 to finance the first season of *Video Game High School*. Once their campaign commenced, it took less than 24 hours for them to reach their goal, a record speed for the platform. By the end of their effort, they had raised $273,725 from 5,661 backers—almost $200,000 more than their announced budget. "It's been a crazy ride and we owe it all to you," Freddie told his community via Kickstarter. "We can't thank our fans enough. You are redefining how online content is made."[1]

By being an early adopter, Freddie helped shape and define the adoption of crowdfunding for more mainstream projects. RocketJump Studios scored significant media attention after the successful financing of *Video Game High School* and further established Internet crowdfunding as a legit solution for Spike

Lee, Zach Braff, the *Veronica Mars* movie creative team, and many other filmmakers and entrepreneurs. Freddie's transparency about the line items in the *VGHS* budget was one way he earned the trust of his backers. Fans who paid into the project understood where their money went.

Personalize the Technology

For *VGHS* season 2, Freddie also looked at the incentives offered to people who supported the series. In a crowdfunding campaign, a "perk" is a reward that gives back to the people who pledge money for your project, a way of saying "thank you" for their support. During our podcast chat, Freddie told me that thinking of perks to offer backers is part of the process. "It's all sitting around thinking of what would be fun and weird and kind of interesting," he said. For the next campaign, Freddie promised to fly anywhere in the world and deliver donuts to a financier's front door in exchange for $2,500. "Donuts or your cultural equivalent of fried dough," Freddie explained. He ended up at the home of a fan in New Jersey. For $5,000, backers received a perks package that included coproducer credit on the show and a trip to Disneyland with members of the *VGHS* cast and crew. The second season broke the record for film or video financing on Kickstarter with $808,341 from over 10,000 backers. Once again, RocketJump raised almost $200,000 more than their goal of $636,010.

The series itself went on to bring Freddie many new subscribers. He sometimes refers to it as "Harry Potter for video games." If you're a teenager or twenty-something gamer, you've no doubt heard of the *VGHS* trilogy and watched the videos. I asked some of its fans about the Harry Potter analogy, and many said that *VGHS* is more relatable to their lives. They know they'll never fly a broomstick like Harry, but they can totally see themselves video gaming for a living. The characters are also diverse in race and gender, and the idea of playing video games for a living is something many millennials find appealing.

To ensure the ongoing success of his web series and to further connect with his entire FreddieW channel audience, Freddie made himself available to his fans IRL (in real life). We'll cover this principle more in chapter 9, but the point here is that Freddie is accessible. This type of access and outreach is another important feature of the influencer model. Freddie remains a staple at most entertainment and gaming trade shows, where he is a "rock star" in the geek culture world. At Comic-Con and other fan-centric conferences, he meets and greets his fans, signing autographs for anyone and everyone. People wait in hundreds-deep lines to say hello and take a selfie with him.

Another way that Freddie personalizes the technology is that he has been able to educate and mentor his audience. A secondary YouTube channel called FreddieW2 features the behind-the-scenes process of making Freddie's videos. On his main channel viewers are simply entertained, but on the second they watch Brandon Laatsch and Freddie behind the scenes, showing how cars get blown up, and discussing the cameras they used or editing techniques for shooting lasers in a *Minecraft* video. When it launched in 2010, it was the closest thing to a DIY online film school. Since then Freddie launched RocketJump Film School to further mentor his audience.

Freddie's *VGHS* season 3 campaign in February of 2014 netted over $900,907, shattering the existing crowdfunding records for a web series on Indiegogo. That summer, Freddie and his *VGHS* codirector, Matt Arnold, were guests on Conan O'Brien's late night talk show. They debuted clips from the series and explained their filmmaking special effects. Conan said he hated Freddie and Matt because they were "too smart and successful for being so young," adding that their special effects were better than anything he'd ever done in his life. While filming a cameo with Conan for *VGHS*, Matt teased that Conan needed to do a second take, since his first one lacked emotion.

I wondered if the Conan O'Brien seal of approval (he has also appeared on Jimmy Kimmel's late night talk show) had changed Freddie's perception of his own fame, but he said he still regarded celebrities as a different breed. "There's a big marketing vehicle behind them . . . When you gain notoriety or recognition on YouTube, it's grassroots. It's one block at a time, one viewer at a time. You are known because you started from not being known at all, and you build yourself up. It's not a machine that is marketing itself to the masses. There's a fundamental difference, where the origins come from."

Create Your Own Technology-Based Do-It-Yourself Business

A new form of leadership is also flourishing in modern-day media companies that don't have experienced and dominant entertainment executives like Sumner Redstone, and Bob Iger at the helm. Redstone has been the executive chairman of both of the global companies, CBS and Viacom, while Iger has been the CEO and chairman at Disney. They are traditional entertainment executives running the companies behind the scenes. They aren't on-camera, filming, editing, or launching their creative ideas. They are old school executives. Freddie isn't just running a business, a man in a suit calling the shots from upstairs. He's creating the content, community, and brand, with his face out front. Modern-day media companies are built on the backs of creators. Their content and community are their priorities. Young creators like Freddie are visionaries because they own their content, build their brands with their audiences, and are entrepreneurial in defining their own careers. In other words, they aren't waiting for someone to discover them. They discover themselves.

Taryn Southern, YouTube actress and entrepreneur, was also a guest on the podcast. She pointed out, "In Hollywood, the norm is creating your idea and then you shop it around to studios and other people. You want them to pay you for your idea, so you can make it. In the era of YouTube and entrepreneurship, when you produce your videos, you take a risk . . . spending your own money, hoping to make money in the long run." It's a new technology-enabled mindset, embraced by entrepreneurs like Taryn and Freddie.

And she's right. If you look historically at the film industry or any major-media entertainment businesses from the past hundred years, Freddie Wong's early adopter thinking bucks the norms. Rather than shop his ideas around to someone else, he leveraged technology early to carve out his own success. "It's tough to make money on making videos these days," Freddie told me. "I think you have to stick to fundamentals. The videos I made back when I started wouldn't work now, because there's a lot more people doing it. But if what you make is fundamentally quality, good, and appealing, then that's where you start." Rather than focusing solely on the profit, Freddie recommended an alternate goal. "What you should really be thinking about is, are you attracting an audience . . . talking to people . . . engaging people?"

This is further evidence that the Internet, YouTube, and social media have redefined notions of celebrity and popular entertainment. Freddie's online audience has made him a new kind of star, one that first "rocked our faces" on desktops and mobile devices a decade ago. Freddie did have the advantage of arriving early on his chosen platforms. As he noted, there was less competition on YouTube back in the day, allowing him to rise quickly in the video ecosystem before reaching a mainstream audience. But he kept adopting new technologies, launching projects on Kickstarter, and even becoming one of the first partners to create on Snapchat. And he continues to evolve, reaching new audiences by placing content on Hulu and Netflix. This has made his micro-community into a mini-empire.

"We do know that having an audience that likes what you do is a powerful thing," Freddie told me. But it is still hard for him to fathom that today, seven million YouTube subscribers can follow his every move. His most watched video, "Future First Person Shooter," has over 26 million views. The entire *Video Game High School* series raised nearly two million dollars from its fans, and its view count is still climbing online. Like many in the Influencer Economy, when you think about how to leverage technology to super-charge your ideas, you can empower a large base of supporters, collaborators, and fellow influencers along the way.

Influencer School Lessons: What Freddie Wong Can Teach You About Adopting New Technology Early

Lesson 1: Move First on Technology

What's remarkable about Freddie Wong is not only that he was an early adopter creating videos and building an audience on YouTube, but he then was an early adopter on the crowdfunding site Kickstarter, running his own initial campaigns. And he continues to evolve as technology advances forward. In 2015, when Snapchat introduced original video series on their platform, Freddie was one of the first to partner with them. And when Hulu introduced original series from YouTube creators, *RocketJump: The Show* launched, which is a behind-the-scenes web series recorded at RocketJump Studios.

Freddie has thrived because he quickly learned how to tell stories on new and emergent platforms. He stays on the cutting edge of what's next in media. This mindset emerged after he graduated from the USC film school, where he went to learn how to make movies. Upon graduation he saw that technology was evolving. He envisioned a world where online videos were the future, so he adapted his film style to short, bite-sized web videos to be broadcast on YouTube. Now YouTube is the dominant video platform, and Freddie and his team are years ahead of other creators in terms of their number of YouTube subscribers. And he and RocketJump have gone on to gain a following off of additional platforms, leveraging the tech to build audience.

Early adopters of social media networks have an advantage because when networks first form and haven't yet caught on with the mainstream, there are fewer regular creators on the platforms. Thus there is less competition to gain visibility and early adopters get seen earlier and more often, building a community from the ground floor. Then, once the technology gets more popular, you already have your base of supporters. You earned it because you invested your time early.

Once you reach an influencer status on a network like YouTube, it's much easier to build community elsewhere. If someone's following you on YouTube, then they'll likely follow you on Instagram, Snapchat, or Periscope. When Freddie first wanted to crowdfund *VGHS*, he asked his YouTube community to support him on Kickstarter. He didn't have to reinvent himself, and he was able to accelerate his funding on Kickstarter because his YouTube community migrated over to the crowdfunding site.

Actions to Move First on Technology

1. Research new technologies in which you could become an early adopter. Think of ways you could leverage a new technology to grow a community.

2. If you are technophobic, learn how to embrace technology. Search for online courses and video tutorials on YouTube to teach you more about confusing technologies.

3. Register your social media networks. Sign up for a Twitter account and a Facebook page. Also, register a Pinterest page, YouTube Channel, Periscope account, and any site where large and emergent audiences live. You don't want to get into a branding situation where someone has taken your Instagram or Wordpress username, and your brand isn't consistent across all platforms. Do you need to start a LinkedIn group for your idea? Register everywhere. Think about the future and where you may need an account, and register it to be safe. You want to be discovered everywhere there are audiences online.

4. Write a blog post on your website or on Medium.com that explains your vision. (Medium is a free publishing platform for anyone with a blog idea.) Writing a blog is a great way to share your story with your friends and help you build new relationships, profiles, and web traffic.

Lesson 2: Collaborate with Your Fellow Techies

Collaboration is a theme that shows up continually in the Influencer Economy. We cover the concept in depth in step 2, "Share," but it is also an important part of the early adoption principle. Without collabing with other creators and entrepreneurs, you will make it difficult on yourself. As I've mentioned already, never build in a silo. You need friends, peers, supporters, customers, and fans to help you reach your goals. Back in 2010, Freddie found and collabed with fellow early adopters on YouTube like DeStorm

Power, Shane Dawson, iJustine, and Philip DeFranco as they were building their own followings on the platform. Today each of these creators has millions of subscribers, but back then Freddie and the group needed one another's support to find success.

On YouTube, when you collab and appear in someone else's video, you gain exposure to their subscribers. And it's a two-way street: when someone appears in your video, they are showcased to your followers. This applies across all other social media platforms, even when someone features you in their e-mail list. It's especially important to find the other early adopters and collaborate with them when the tech platforms are new and haven't reached the mainstream. Cross-promoting with other first movers is a great way to grow your community before everyone else jumps in. Even if you're not the first out of the gate, you need to focus on who the leaders and influencers are on your platform and work on building relationships with them.

James Altucher, author of the best-selling book *Choose Yourself*, told me on my podcast about a relevant and insightful concept called "finding your scene." He believes there are no "lone geniuses" and you need to find partners, friends, and collaborators in order to find your success. James highlights the stand-up comedy world as a great example of successful collaboration and finding your scene. He says, "If you watch interviews with comedians like Louis C.K., Jerry Seinfeld, Larry David, and Chris Rock, they all worked together in no-name clubs for years, each opening for the other over and over again, until they broke out one by one and pulled their talented friends along with them."[2]

DeStorm Power, iJustine, Phil DeFranco, Shane Dawson, and other YouTube early adopters who collabed with Freddie Wong back in 2010 today lead dominant YouTube channels and companies. Similar to the comedians that James mentions, all these early YouTubers found their scene and helped "pull their talented friends" to reach success. Collaborating with fellow early adopters allows all of you to find success together.

Actions to Start Collaborating with Your Fellow Techies

1. List the people who are your heroes on different platforms. Think about influencers who you want to collaborate with in the long run. Determine what makes collabing with them a unique opportunity. Write out a longer-term roadmap for how you can reach these creators. Put this into the universe on a blog post, video, or somewhere that people can see it.

2. Determine who you can collaborate with while you're just starting out. Realize that you need to start realistically and if you're looking to collaborate with influencers like Freddie Wong, it may be hard to reach them. But you can look for others to help create "your scene." List friends and colleagues in your field who are potential techies to collaborate with. Focus on those who are at your level in skill and experience.

3. Write a blog post that gives knowledge or helps people in your field. Publish it on your blog or at Medium.com. Research bigger websites and blogs with more web traffic that may publish your post. Present yourself as a "guest poster" and see if any bite. This type of collaboration can help build your profile.

MY INFLUENCER ECONOMY STORY

Early Adopting My Podcast

Launching my podcast in early 2014 was an exhilarating experience. I recorded my first interview with Burnie Burns in December 2013 and when I booked most of my early guests, including

Freddie Wong, podcasting was mostly a niche activity. I was just enough of an early adopter that when I asked someone like Freddie to come on my show, it was a novel enough experience that they said yes. If I were to have started my podcast in 2016, I think I would have been lost in the clutter. It would have been more competitive to book A+ guests, and there is no way the show would have gotten as much traction and grown into what it is today. But because I adopted tech early, I had an advantage.

My podcast was rewarding on many fronts. I love talking to new and interesting people, and the podcast afforded me a chance to speak with my heroes and peers. I am a former stand-up comedian, and the podcast got me back into the performance space. And, of course, it helped to fuel the research for this book.

During the first year of my show I booked fun and fascinating guests like Freddie Wong, Alan Sepinwall, Willie Geist, and Tucker Max. But then the technology transformed drastically. Podcasts like *Serial* came along and really made people rethink the value of the medium. Additionally, Bluetooth devices and Internet-connected cars broadened everyone's access to podcasts. Over time podcasts will become even more mainstream, but I was fortunate to be an early adopter back when fewer people were creating and consuming podcasts and it was more of a niche industry.

Lesson 3: Personalize the Technology

On tech platforms, you and your community are co-builders, co-creators, and partners. You have an understood agreement with your audience once you connect online. Freddie deeply connected with his community by giving them perks on crowdfunding sites like Kickstarter and Indiegogo. A perk is similar to when you get a free coffee at your local coffee shop, or the bartender at your neighborhood pub buys you a beer—it's something personal that makes you feel valued. And it endears you to the giver.

Crowdfunding is not just a platform to raise money—it's a new way of thinking and a vehicle to connect with and reward your fans. Andy Baio was the founding CTO of Kickstarter who helped on-board some of the largest projects on the platform. He told me on the podcast, "Kickstarter is not a store. You're not browsing Amazon and deciding on something that it ships to you. It's a patronage, and you're supporting someone's project, while they are obligated to keep you in the process, to keep you in the know for what's happening. It's an alternative to the traditional publishing structure, where fans can fund a project and become part of the story and process."

Technology empowers you to connect directly with your community, audience, or customer base. Just as you can go directly to the consumer in delivering a product, you can go direct to the consumer to communicate with them. People talk about "lifetime customers" a lot in the marketing world. Customers who are with you for the long haul are extremely valuable to your business. They help you to keep the lights on and power your operation.

The "patronage" that Andy Baio speaks about can be transferred to any project, even if you're not crowdfunding. People who back and support you need to be kept in the loop, whether it's your launch team, your friend list, your potential investors, customers, or any other group. Keep an updated list of whom you need to keep informed about your idea. People get busy, and you need to keep them all updated on your progress.

And give your community perks, all the time. People love free stuff. If you're in the business sector, publish free online courses, give away free e-books, teach people via a free YouTube series. Mentorship is something empowering about our modern age. Freddie created an entire YouTube channel, FreddieW2, to post behind-the-scenes videos of tutorials and walkthroughs. By teaching his community through RocketJump's film school, he is empowering his community to become filmmakers like him. He took the technology and used it to teach others. You, too, can mentor and help others via your content and ideas.

Actions to Personalize the Technology

1. Pick five perks that you want to give to your community. Think like your community and ask yourself what they would want from you. Determine how you will give these perks to your community.

2. Determine something of value that you can give to people online for free. It can be as simple as a blog post or online video discussing something that can be helpful to others. Write out five ways you can teach people something of value to help them out. Make it personal and relevant to your audience.

3. Brainstorm ways you can share your ideas to mentor others. Determine if you can record a video tutorial, teach an online lesson or take people behind the scenes of your creative process. When creative people share their truths around both successes and failures, we can all learn so much more. Write out five ways you can mentor your community.

Lesson 4: Embrace Technology and Data

Technology is not your enemy. You have to figure out how to upload your podcast, download a video file, or hack code your blog if you want to bootstrap your way to the top of your industry. If you can't figure it out, ask someone to help you. You can't let fear of technology get in the way of your success. Grasping the technology can be a really big hurdle for some people to start creating anything on the Internet, but in the Influencer Economy, technology is your friend.

You can start by optimizing your website and other online properties so they come up in search results, called search engine optimization (SEO). Search engines like Google crawl the web and decide which sites will show up on their front page during search results. When choosing the name and branding for your idea, you want all of you efforts and content to show up on the first page of Google. You want to create consistent content and own all the search results for your idea, ideally for all the major search engines (Yahoo, Bing, etc.) but especially for Google. When someone searches for "influencer economy," my goal is for the first pages of Google to contain 100 percent results with my website or properties. Your goal is for people to easily discover your work, and that your branding is consistent and dominant in Google search results.

I've done pretty well on this front. When I first started *The Influencer Economy* podcast in 2014, the majority of search results on Google were my YouTube videos, website, Twitter and Pinterest accounts, and other social networks where I had posted. Even though my book had yet to launch, the SEO results were all based on my work.

Just because you know how to use social media as a consumer doesn't mean you know how to use social media for business. There's a big difference between uploading your favorite wedding photo to Facebook and running a major media campaign on FB. To understand the business of social media, you need to understand the business of social media companies. Companies like Facebook, Twitter, and LinkedIn all sell media services that connect you with collaborators, potential partners, and your audience. It's helpful to strategically and intelligently understand how these networks monetize their websites and communities. You don't need to necessarily spend a lot of money on media-buying on these sites. I'd leave that to professionals. But testing and experimenting with buying media can help teach you more about how the sites actually work.

Actions to Embrace Tech and Data

1. Google your idea and find out if you own the search terms. If not, start syndicating your content on your social media channels ASAP. Get the word out there about what you're building and ask your friend list to share your content as well. You want to control Google, and oftentimes an active blog or social media channel will help you own more search terms.

2. Study social networks and start using them. Set up $5 media buys to promote your content on Facebook, Twitter, Pinterest, or anywhere you think your audience lives. Learning a little about media buying will help you understand the economics of social media, which gives you more knowledge and control in the long run. Log into the advertising dashboards of your targeted sites and spend a couple ad dollars.

3. Install Google Analytics on your website, or google "how to install Google Analytics" if you're unsure how the installation works. If you can't teach yourself, ask someone to help, or pay someone for help. You need to understand your web traffic and data. Once you get up and running with Google Analytics, monitor where your traffic is coming from.

4. Google Analytics is critical to understanding your website's traffic. Once you install GA on your site, challenge yourself to learn from the tools it offers. Determine what your top five traffic drivers are, your top five states where people find your website, and your top

five web pages that people visit on your site. Even if you get a little bit of traffic, it's important to finding out more about how your website works. Start early and get into the habit of checking this data out.

Lesson 5: Start Collecting E-mails Now!

Don't ignore your e-mail list—start collecting e-mail addresses now. I cannot repeat that enough. When people ask me for advice about building their community or customer base, my immediate recommendation is to build their e-mail list ASAP. And my second recommendation is to leverage technology to acquire e-mails on their website.

E-mails are the lifeblood to help you keep a healthy and direct line of communication to your community. Social media marketers will tell you that you need Facebook likes or Twitter followers or other BS in order to sell you their products and services. I'm calling all those people out right now. They're wrong. E-mail is gold. It's never too early to start gathering e-mails. Learn to use e-mail tech on your website to your advantage. Start by adding an e-mail acquisition feature or function to your website.

E-mail is not going away. In fact, I check e-mail before I go to bed and after I wake up. Do you check it in bed like I do? We are addicted to e-mail. Social media networks are essential to grow a community, but e-mail is how you'll sell your product. People call it "growing your list" in the writing industry. You need to start growing your list now. Start collecting e-mails now.

John Corcoran is a former White House speechwriter who hosts the *Smart Business Revolution* podcast and has written several books on helping entrepreneurs. He is an expert in how to build an e-mail list. He told me, "Some people will say, 'E-mail is dead, man, isn't it? Don't you need a YouTube channel, Twitter, all that kind of stuff?' But across the board, if you look at the statistics, the engagement and response rate of e-mail far outranks any social media platform. The bottom line is people still read their e-mail. The statistics say that people spend on average over 11 hours per week in their in-box." In other words, your e-mail in-box isn't going anywhere, and it's where a large percentage of your potential audience members live.

Another key element to growing your e-mail list is to give away a FREE product or service in exchange for someone's e-mail. Whether it's a FREE online course, educational resource, video content, or e-book, people love FREE stuff. And if you keep giving them something of value for FREE, they will stay with you for potentially years as e-mail subscribers. Eventually when you have a larger item to charge people for like a book, movie, song, or product, you will have built up enough loyalty that people will support you without any hesitation. When you give great value for FREE people will be more interested in receiving your e-mails. And treat your list like gold, never spam them.

Actions to Begin Collecting E-mails

1. Add an e-mail sign-up button to your website.

2. Use a service like SumoMe or LeadPages to optimize your website to gather e-mails.

3. Connect a technology like MailChimp or AWeber to create a database of e-mails. Ask people for their first name and e-mail when they sign up.

4. Create an e-mail acquisition pop-up to appear on your website. Most of us don't have ads on our websites, so a pop-up is not considered spammy. It's survival. You need to grab people's e-mails in a non-intrusive way, so be clear in your e-mail pop-up messaging that you will never spam them, ever. And also create pop-ups that do

not appear to repeat customers on your website. Respect people's wishes if they don't want to subscribe, for the pop-up to not show up again.

5. Create a way to give away a free perk when people provide their e-mail. I gave away a "how to start a podcast" tip sheet when people first signed up for my e-mail list. The perk should be in a digital format and of reasonable size for quick downloading. Make it easy.

BONUS STORY

Minecraft—Building Your Product with Your Early Adopters

As mentioned, I worked at the Los Angeles–based start-up Machinima.com, a pioneering video network on YouTube. In 2014, we were getting upwards of four billion YouTube video views a month. Yes, that's what you read—four billion. And we were valued at over $200 million by our investors and we were in the middle of the online video revolution on YouTube. Even Google (who owns YouTube) invested in our company. We were on the cutting edge.

Our YouTube videos often featured people playing popular video games like *Call of Duty* and *World of Warcraft*. These gamers would play video games, tell funny stories, or narrate their gameplay and then upload their videos to YouTube. It's amazing to think that most of the players were under the age of 25, some still living at home or working day jobs they hated. Machinima also produced videos around events like E3 and Comic-Con and created stuff like live-action zombie series and animations, but gameplay was an area where we thrived.

In the summer of 2010, one game was becoming an Internet obsession: *Minecraft*. A PC-based "sandbox" game, *Minecraft* was bubbling up within the gaming community and on the cusp of becoming a global phenomenon. If you're not familiar with it, think of *Minecraft* as digital Legos, where you play in an online world where everything appears as 3-D building blocks. Gamers have activities where they explore, gather resources, and craft their way through different worlds. In the game, a player runs around as a block character interacting on different maps and worlds.

The developer of *Minecraft*, Markus Persson (a.k.a. Notch), lived in another realm, building the game at his house in Sweden. His company, Mojang, published the alpha version in 2009. By 2010, the game started to explode in usage. By 2013, 70 million people played *Minecraft*, and its revenue was at a staggering $200 million. In 2014, Microsoft bought *Minecraft* for $2.5 billion.

At Machinima, we played *Minecraft* in our office with Notch back in February 2011, just as it was catching on like wildfire. We caught him and his girlfriend on their way back to Sweden after they had traveled to Mexico. *Minecraft* had originally debuted as a downloadable game, playable on your PC, and had zero dollars for its marketing budget. It had only five worlds to explore and was a single-player game. *Minecraft* was still in its alpha phase, a work in progress, playable to the community but buggy and not completely finished.

Minecraft became a gaming giant because Notch built the game with his community. As he recalled, "It's a weird way of making a game. You just put it out and keep working on it as you're making it . . . I tried to make sure it's clear 'This is not the game [that the buyers will see].' I'm just working on it, and you can play it while I'm making it." But still, he had found his early adopters and they made the game better. They reported bugs and, more importantly, created "mods," which were new worlds, characters, and items for gamers to play with inside *Minecraft*.

One of Notch's best moves, even if he didn't realize it at the time, was releasing the game to the "right" early adopters within the gaming industry. Early influencer YouTubers with massive video subscriber followings found the game and were captivated by it. In that sense *Minecraft* struck gold—it reached influencers that any indie video game or film creator would give anything to reach. These were gamers who could not have been hired in a media buy or reached through a PR firm. It was all organic. It was a secret, a cult game with a rabid following.

The early *Minecraft* gameplay creators were named SeaNanners, iHasCupquake, and Yogscast, and they are the equivalent of rock stars in the gaming industry. The majority of the mainstream entertainment world hasn't heard of any of these influencers, but if you're wired into the gaming and YouTube ecosystem, then you've heard of them. And if you're a sixth grader and love *Call of Duty*, *Minecraft*, or any other trending video game, you definitely know of them by their gamer tags.

Minecraft was like a tech start-up in its initial launch phase, as its early community provided the initial growth and adoption. When you're a start-up with minimal budget and resources, word of mouth is the primary driver of usage. Whereas Facebook's early users were college kids and Instagram's were San Francisco Bay–area techies, *Minecraft*'s early ambassadors were YouTubers who were hyper-famous in the gaming industry. Without these early adopters collaborating to make the game better, we may have never heard of *Minecraft*, and the industry would have passed it by. Instead, the Influencer Economy launched the game to the world, and revolutionized how games and entertainment properties will launch in the future.

Step 2: Share

Once you "launch" and get through the first four principles of the Influencer Economy, then your next step is to share your idea and build community. It is the most important step you can take to help you thrive in the digital age. And it's not easy growing a community. It's actually very difficult to grow a following of any sort. In the digital age, your project backers, online subscribers, and digital network are what defines you. Without great people surrounding and supporting you, you will struggle to find success with your idea. I advise people to "never build in a silo," meaning you never should create an idea by yourself and alone. You constantly need feedback, assistance, and for people to have your back. When you have a loyal community coalescing around your idea, you can do amazing things.

Everyone I have spoken to on my podcast has been a world-class community builder, so I've been lucky to learn from some of the best. Taking a page from their playbook, I always recommend one thing when students ask me about launching their idea: start building community now. It's never too early to share your idea, even if it's well ahead of your launch. When I wrote my book, it took more than two years to finish and then publish it. The community I built along the way is one of the most awesome things to come from that journey. I am most grateful for the people who subscribed to my podcast well ahead of the book launch.

I'll say this one more time: it's never too early to think about building community. Share your idea. Start to collect feedback on your idea, listen to other people's feedback to make your idea better and allow a community to build alongside you. Over time your community will become your biggest advocates, supporters, and customers. Consider how you can share your idea before you launch your idea.

Chapter 5

Strive for Authenticity

"To find yourself, think for yourself."

—Socrates

Chapter Playbook

Authenticity is a word that gets thrown around a lot in the digital media world. I have a love/hate relationship with the word because although it has become a little hackneyed, it's still a vital concept for building community.

Authenticity means finding your voice, identifying your true self, and embracing your vulnerabilities that make you *you*. Authentic people stand up for their ideas and don't back down in the face of outside pressure or when others disagree with them. I still like to use the word because when you find your own authentic self, amazing things can happen.

In the Influencer Economy, the majority of successful people have found their authentic voice, and they didn't do so by passively sitting back and hoping others would recognize it in them. You have to take risks and open up yourself to potential criticism if you want to find authenticity.

When I was growing up, my mom encouraged me to "be myself" and to make my own choices by not following the crowd. When you're a kid, it's not always cool to follow your mom's advice, but in the digital age, everyone should follow what Mom Williams told me. What makes you uniquely you and what makes you different from everyone else *is* your authentic voice. In the Influencer Economy, personality is king and individual people rather than large companies have the power. We are all our own personality-driven media networks.

The bottom line is you can't buy authenticity. An authentic person with a strong community can challenge the largest media companies in the world for respect. When you're authentic, you can gain control of the decisions you make because you have earned that right.

One podcaster in a northeast-side Los Angeles garage found his authentic voice sharing stories of his past alcohol and drug abuse. He connected with his podcast guests—major comedians, actors, and artists—enabling them to open up and equally be authentic.

Marc Maron

It's not every day that you come home from vacation to find a sniper perched on your garage, 40 or so United States Secret Service personnel on your property, and uniformed cops from the Los Angeles Police Department guarding the perimeter of your house. We're talking a modest two-bedroom home in the LA suburb of Highland Park—not the sort of address one associates with a presidential security detail and a highly choreographed visit from the leader of the free world. But Barack Obama was indeed flying by helicopter to Rose Bowl Stadium in nearby Pasadena and traveling by motorcade to this private residence, which is home to the host of the hugely popular podcast *WTF with Marc Maron.* As an additional security precaution, Maron's driveway had been tented for the occasion. And that garage with the sniper on top? That's where the majority of *WTF* podcasts are recorded, and Marc's interview with the president was on schedule to become the podcast's episode number 613—just as soon as Marc locked his two cats in the bedroom and allowed bomb-sniffing dogs to finish their sweep of the garage and surrounding area.

Apart from the podcast, Marc stars in a half-hour sitcom on IFC about a twice-divorced stand-up comedian who hosts a podcast in his Highland Park garage and is a cat lover. Like the off-screen Maron, his television character keeps a soul patch and favors western-style shirts. It's not a total hall of mirrors, but the show, *Maron*, also gets the details right about his 16 years of sobriety and admitted tendency to agonize about matters great and small.

Marc's vacation in Kauai prior to President Obama's visit in June of 2015 didn't exactly relieve his angst about the podcast interview. His long-time business partner and podcast producer, Brendan McDonald, assisted the Secret Service and other agencies while Marc stayed away from home to clear his head. Brendan told me on my podcast, "Having the White House reach out to us is the reason that [the interview] happened. We wouldn't have been so bold as to go the other way. I think that was just a huge win for podcasting in general. [Obama] has his pick of media outlets, a lot of options at the disposal of the president if he wants to communicate to the country and the world. So it's very validating to know that podcasting had achieved a level of acceptance in the media landscape."

The significance of the opportunity wasn't lost on Marc, though he'd had trouble believing that President Obama would follow through on his promise to schlep all the way out to a garage in northeast LA. Marc and Brendan had first heard from the White House via e-mail in 2014 without any specific mention of the president appearing on the podcast. But staffers in Obama's circle who are fans of the show knew it would be a venue that allowed the president to speak about more than just the press pool news of the day. Obama had talked sports with Bill Simmons on ESPN's *B.S. Report* podcast and popped up on the web talk show parody *Between Two Ferns with Zach Galifianakis*, so he was open to booking himself on different platforms if it meant exposure to new audiences. When it was clear that he hoped to be the first politician to appear on *WTF*, a podcast that surpassed 100 million downloads by the beginning of 2014, Marc assumed that they would tape the interview in the Oval Office or somewhere else convenient for Obama. No, the president wanted to come to Maron.[1]

Find the Truth by Being Yourself

So what exactly was the draw? If *WTF with Marc Maron* was strictly a comedy podcast, then perhaps the White House might never have planned its trip to Highland Park. But since launching the show in 2009, Marc has developed a conversational style that manages to probe his guests in a thoughtful way, rather than chase easy laughs with them. His own edgy sense of humor is just as often directed at himself, especially during the unscripted monologues at the start of each episode that have addressed his failed marriages, career frustrations, past substance abuse, and other painfully honest revelations.

As *WTF*'s producer, Brendan has heard plenty of these recollections, and he edits each podcast with a unique understanding of the stories Marc shares with his audience. Some things do remain behind the scenes, or start out that way, such as the text message Marc sent Brendan on the night before Obama and his entourage were due to arrive for the interview. "He was getting himself a little psyched out that, you know, something bad was going to happen to him," Brendan said. "When I was trying to talk him down from it, he mentioned that he kind of does that on purpose to ground himself. A little freak out might keep his nerves calmer than if he were to try to ignore it. I think that's a good representation of how we work together. He has a very amped personality, and mine, as you can tell from talking to me, is pretty low key."

Marc and Brendan had actually been working together as far back as Maron's multiple hosting gigs at Air America, the liberal talk radio network that employed him on *Morning Sedition* and *Breakroom Live with Maron & Seder*. After his relationship with Air America fell apart and his various shows were dropped, Marc couldn't exactly fall back on his stand-up career, though he had appeared regularly on *The Late Show with David Letterman* and *Late Night with Conan O'Brien*. Podcasting as a medium was still finding its feet when Marc and Brendan began experimenting with *WTF*, the new platform that he hoped would somehow earn him a living. He and Brendan recorded the first several episodes by sneaking back into the Air America studios in New York City—both guys had been laid off but used their two-month notice to return for these after-hours sessions. The first guest was comedian Jeffrey Ross, a friend of Maron's who helped set the tone for what Marc still calls "a show born out of desperation."[2]

Obviously much has changed with respect to podcasting since then, partly because of the success of Marc and Brendan's teamwork. Marc's 2010 interview with comedian Louis C.K. ranked #1 on *Slate's* list of the "25 Best Podcast Episodes Ever," and *WTF with Marc Maron* earned "Best Comedy Podcast" at the 2012 Comedy Central Comedy Awards. And a day after the Obama *WTF* episode posted, almost a million people had downloaded it. Listeners discovered that Marc, for all his insecurities, had pulled his shit together and conducted another of his typically disarming interviews.

"Our temperaments are very different, even though our minds are kind of the same," Brendan told me regarding their successful partnership. "A lot of things that I think about are things that Marc thinks about on a daily basis. We have the same philosophical questions about life, the same fears and anxieties, and we just go about our business dealing with them in different ways."

Marc is based in LA and Brendan is in New York. While the team around them has grown since they started, it's Marc who knows how to draw out the guests during his interviews, and Brendan who edits these conversations so that they are as clear and compelling as possible. After that first upload, it's basically been two guys with complementary skills who have worked together to build a significant media property. "That kind of yin and yang makes the relationship work—not just as professional colleagues," Brendan says. "We've been friends for 11 years now."

So you can bet that Brendan had flown to Los Angeles to personally assist the Secret Service and otherwise guarantee that the president's hour of *WTF* ran smoothly. He sat outside the garage with members of Obama's staff, all of them wearing headphones and noting any highlights or potential problems during the interview.

It wasn't easy for Marc and his *WTF* team to fathom just who was visiting "the Cat Ranch," the nickname of his feline-friendly home. "You're like a big cheese now," the president stated when he first met Marc and had a look at the garage. Regarding a photo of two cats having sex, Obama noted, "You've got drawings and pictures that we can't really discuss." A *Gimme Shelter* poster also hangs on the wall, along with photos of the guitarist Muddy Waters and other musicians. Marc himself plays a little guitar, and he has said that strumming a few songs before the president arrived had helped him to relax.

His preparation for the interview actually began that spring when Marc read President Obama's memoir, *Dreams from My Father: A Story of Race and Inheritance*. The book includes candid details of young "Barry" Obama's identity crisis and use of drugs while at Occidental College in neighboring Eagle Rock, California. One of Marc's questions early in the interview is characteristic of his direct approach with guests.

"How far away are you from that guy? Are there still struggles?"

"Stuff that was bugging you," the president told Marc, "by the time you're 53, either you've worked it out or you've just forgiven yourself. And you've said, 'That's who I am.'" Obama continued to bring it full circle. "Listen, I'm a big fan," he said of *WTF*. "And I love conversations like this because if I thought to myself when I was in college that I'd be in a garage a couple miles away doing an interview as president with a comedian—I think that's a pretty hard scenario. It's not possible to imagine."

The fact that Marc's marriages didn't work, and that he is so honest with his audience and guests about his troubled relationships or other problems, may be the most significant element of his success. The importance of creating authentic content that is relevant to your community is one of the core Influencer Economy principles. Many fans of *WTF* who are facing their own challenges have been impressed by Marc's willingness to publicly bare his soul. In fact, the show launched during what might be called his midlife crisis. "The first hundred episodes are me asking celebrities for help," Marc admitted.[3] But his rawness and transparency became staples of the show, encouraging his audience to root for him once he left New York behind to start his new life in LA.

Fans heard all about his good days in Highland Park as well as the bad. Marc wrote on the *WTF* blog in October of 2013 that he had decided to break things off with his former fiancée, Jessica Sanchez: "On the show this week, I'll fill you in a bit on what has been a couple of the most difficult weeks of my life. It's weird to have the relationship with you that I do. I can't keep things hidden because I would feel like I was being disingenuous or dishonest. I don't think most entertainers have the same problem."[4] Even the disappearance of one of Marc's cats generated an outpouring of

sympathy from his audience and led to the "Boomer lives!" rallying cry for his show.

Authenticity: How Marc Maron Nailed
the Biggest Interview of His Career

One of the main reasons the president went to Marc's LA garage
to chat on the *WTF* podcast was because Marc is a fantastic
interviewer. And this episode of *WTF* fell in line with all the other
episodes, as Marc asked the right questions to get the president
to open up. Obama was honest and up front about his past, as
much as any other guest before him had been. Marc delivered an
intimate and personal conversation with the most powerful man in
America.

On the podcast, Marc talks earnestly and openly about his
past marriages and divorces, so you can bet when the president
came on *WTF* that the topic of marriage would come up. And it did,
turning into an ordinary and normal conversation about wives. "If
Michelle says, 'Would you stop that, please?' What is she talking
about?" This was how Marc burrowed into the president's personal
life. "Being late," Obama replied. "When we first started dating . . .
I used to say, 'Why are you stressing me not to be late? Fifteen minutes late, 10 minutes late, what's the big deal?' And then, I don't
remember how long we were in the relationship, she described how
her dad had to wake up an hour earlier than everyone else 'cause
he had multiple sclerosis. Just to put on his shirt and button his
own shirt was a big task." For the future president to arrive early
or at least on time for events with Michelle's family was a sign of
respect. "It wasn't just about being late," Obama explained. "That's
one of the beauties of marriage. If it works, it's because you start
figuring out that the fights you have are never about the thing you're
fighting about. It's always about something else. It's about a story;
it's about respect; it's about recognition. Something deep."

Marc had read *Dreams from My Father* to research the president's early life, and it influenced their conversation in equally

candid ways. On *WTF*, Obama mentioned that the movie *Shaft* made a strong impression on him as a young man who took up smoking in college and tried to seem cool to other students. Some of his memories from those partying days are "through a haze," he admitted. Marc could sympathize, though his hard living lasted well into his adult life.

"You just made his life," Marc said when he learned that the president considered Louis C.K. one of his favorite comedians. Richard Pryor and Dick Gregory also made the list. Fine, so Maron isn't one of Obama's faves. But you can hear the host bite back his jealousy. Louis?! Did our nation's commander in chief really just give a shout-out to Louis C.K.? That moment is good news for fans of the show. No matter how much of a star or how wealthy Marc Maron becomes, one suspects that he will always find a way to take aim at the world or himself. Even the Obama interview had the same format and line of connection that Marc has with any of his past guests. He will always fall back on his authentic voice, even when he's nailing the biggest interview of his career.

Develop a Relationship with Your Audience

I spoke to Dan Pashman, who hosts the popular podcast, *The Sporkful* and is another of Marc's former producers at Air America. Dan knows a good deal about authenticity, he has authored the best-selling book *Eat More Better: How to Make Every Bite More Delicious*. Dan's creative culinary exploration comes with both humor and his passion for eating, as you quickly understand when hearing *The Sporkful's* tagline: "It's for eaters, not foodies." Dan thinks that the eater community is underserved online and he literally delivers the goods for that food-seeking audience. Dan gets the finer points of building audience relationships.

Dan believes that Marc has become a better podcast host than stand-up comedian. In describing Marc's approach to authenticity, Pashman told me, "Maron isn't the kind of guy to 'machine gun' you with punch lines. His approach is more about developing a relationship with an audience, and he has an extraordinary ability to develop relationships with people very quickly, and to read them and to read a crowd. And he's also become a really good interviewer, which he honed at Air America. His mind works extremely quickly; he can react and adjust his tone and style in a matter of split seconds."

Some of the most effective moments in Marc's interviews aren't even derived from questions. Instead, he delivers to a guest his occasionally rambling perceptions of them or their career and then waits for them to respond. Likely not the technique taught in journalism school, but the honesty of his observations tends to prompt similarly candid statements—as if Marc's breach of interview protocol gives people on his show permission to say things that are deeper than the canned answers they normally serve to the press. On the Louis C.K. episode of *WTF*, when the conversation shifted to Louis's memories of becoming a father, even weeping as he recalled the circumstances of his first daughter's birth, admitting that he had never publicly told the story or divulged his feelings. Other *WTF* interviews found Robin Williams humbly addressing accusations of joke theft and describing a night in a hotel when he contemplated suicide. The comedian Todd Glass chose to come out of the closet on Marc's show. Not every episode is confessional or gets the waterworks flowing from guests, but many are surprisingly poignant.

Divorce Yourself from Agenda

Marc also travels to do his show, as he did for the Robin Williams episode and another very popular visit with Zach Galifianakis. Even on the road, Marc's conversations with his high-profile friends from the comedy world can achieve a certain keep-it-real intimacy. During the show's first year, these household names helped to validate the new series and give it the social proof that's so valuable in the Influencer Economy. Judd Apatow, Ben Stiller, and others helped to pull the podcast into the limelight just by showing up and talking into a microphone. And *WTF* has found a way to pay these folks back without losing its hype-free zone sensibility.

"In the episodes we've done, we won't do promotional interviews for the full episode," Brendan McDonald explained. "Marc will graciously have his friends over sometimes and do 10 minutes at the beginning of an episode to help somebody that has a book out or a movie out, or something like that. His feeling about that is it's kind of like an 'everybody can help everybody out' situation. It's not that we go requesting promotional stuff. It's that people were gracious enough to appear on our show, which helped raise our tide quite a bit, so of course we're going to pay the favor back." But even the fellow comedians who arrive for the Maron treatment know better than to overdo bits from their acts or to simply try out new material. This all earns a form of street cred that the show's audience seems to appreciate. Nor do *WTF* fans mind branded terms of endearment such as "What the Fuckers" and "What the Fuck Buddies," which is how Marc salutes his community of listeners at the start of each podcast. The brief W-T-F of the show's name itself is the kind of short and sweet handle that catches on with an audience and allows Maron to give his community ownership of his brand and provides a firm sense that both the host and the community are spirits in the same universe.

Build Community First, Monetization Later

"No one really knew how to make money with podcasting," Marc told *Bostonia*, the alumni magazine of Boston University, his alma mater. "It's really just becoming clearer now for some people. Our first hurdle was getting people to listen. We knew we had to use new media, so we had to learn all that. We used Facebook, Twitter, and iTunes, of course, and we partnered with our server on an app."[5] Marc still relies on social media to grow, and also hits up the listeners he has amassed to donate "shekels," as he likes to call money. He and Brendan were eventually able to land a variety of sponsors, ranging from Stamps.com and Audible.com to programming on Comedy Central and HBO looking to reach the *WTF* crowd. "Pow! I just crapped my pants" is the tagline Marc made up for his very first sponsor, Just Coffee Cooperative. The java company gives Marc 10 percent of every sale made with the *WTF* code on justcoffee.coop. This arrangement has proven so lucrative for both parties that there is now a WTF Roast blend with tasting notes that include "complex, spicy, and chocolatey." Once upon a time, Brendan had been in charge of dealing with these sponsorships but now they have such a vast audience that an agency handles their advertising.

Jeff Ullrich is the founder of Earwolf, a popular podcast network, and Midroll, a podcast advertising network. He told me that consistency is vital to building any content mechanism, and *WTF* certainly embraces that notion by offering new shows every Monday and Thursday without fail. "I would say that another thing is to stay true to your voice," Jeff added when giving advice to would-be podcasters. "At the end of the day, authentic people who have their own perspective and point of view—and they're willing to share it and stand behind it—are the people who create the most compelling content."

Marc Maron's show is squarely in that camp. Marc is a performer, and his ongoing work as a stand-up comic with very personal material plays perfectly to the strengths of podcasting's distinctive impact on audiences. In this medium, hosts like Marc speak directly into their listeners' earbuds or go along for the ride on car speakers. It's an intimate bond that is only helped by the on-demand nature of the format. Podcasting audio is easy to binge on as is Netflix and Amazon video programming. With more and more Internet-connected cars on the road and a rising global smartphone adoption rate, traditional radio is likely to be eclipsed. Eventually your car will even auto-download your favorite shows, and your home will be Bluetooth-wired so you can listen to podcasts in any room.

Will the hosts of this medium become the new kings and queens of audio? If so, Marc Maron may be first in line to the throne. *WTF* can be considered an essential oral history of American comedy and pop culture. The initial 100 episodes were catalogued at the Library of Congress, making *WTF* the first podcast archived at that institution. Off-platform success for Marc has also opened new doors for him. WNYC, New York's public radio station, began carrying abridged versions of the series in 2011. His TV show has been renewed for a fourth season. In the years prior to his podcast, Marc had released comedy albums with titles such as *Not Sold Out* and *Tickets Still Available*. But his Maronation stand-up tour in the spring of 2015 was frequently standing room only and a great example of an IRL opportunity to meet with fans. In that same vein, Marc and Brendan have experimented with doing the podcast live in front of an audience. What the Fuckers who want to curl up with a good book can read Marc's *Attempting Normal*, published by Spiegel & Grau. There are DVDs available (*Thinky Pain*) and more TV specials in the works. None of it would have been possible if Marc hadn't spent years delivering his unique brand of authentic content and building a loyal audience who ate it up.

Even after getting sober, there were many years of personal and career setbacks before *WTF* punched Maron's ticket. And all of that failure and frustration made for great, cringe-worthy comedy. But now that Marc is doing so well and seemingly on a path to even greater success, will his good fortune make it impossible to use his trademarked envy and brutal honesty as shtick? Does authenticity change when you make money? I don't know. Marc's closest modern-day comparison would be Howard Stern, who has cultivated a rabid following and A+ guest list, and he seems to have kept his authenticity along the way. And Stern has made hundreds of millions of dollars from his SiriusXM partnership. So, perhaps the best is yet to come with *WTF*, as Marc's community grows and he's able to reach more people. And, hundreds of podcasts later, can could say that he is still just as authentic as he was on his very first one.

Influencer School Lessons: What Marc Maron Can Teach You About Striving for Authenticity

Lesson 1: Find Your Authentic Self

It is hard to describe authenticity. It looks different on different types of people. As Justice Potter Stewart once said when describing pornography in the Supreme Court case *Jacobellis v. Ohio*, "I know it when I see it." Authenticity can be described the same way: you know it when you see it. And you can't fake it.

There is no formula for accessing your own authenticity. Finding your voice can take time. And "being yourself" like Mom Williams advised me isn't as easy as you think. We are all programmed to act certain ways that are not always authentic. With creators like Marc Maron, their success comes from letting people deep into their world. Marc literally lets people into his inner monologue. For better or worse you know what he thinks, loves, and hates about his life. When you give people a chance to understand the real you, amazing things can happen.

In the Influencer Economy, the most successful people are the ones who are naturally authentic. Yes, you have to find your authentic voice, but it's not something you can simply develop or create; it happens organically, from a variety of circumstances. True authenticity comes from a wide array of defining angles that come together to help people see your complete picture.

How did *WTF* become such a successful show? For starters, Marc interviewed well-known comedians and entertainers from the beginning. You can't overlook the fact that he had years of relationships in the comedy world and could book A+ list guests on the podcast. He had paid his dues for decades on the comedy circuit, appearing over 40 times on Conan's old NBC *Late Night* show alone. If you have a large network in advance of building your community, it will accelerate your community growth.

But that's not the reason why *WTF* took off like it did. Just getting celebrities on your podcast won't make you a winner. It worked because Marc related to his community on an intimate level. The *WTF* community feels like he is their friend and buddy. I would imagine some people in Marc's audience know more about him than they even do about some of their close friends.

It's worth listing some key authentic ingredients of Maron's universe:

❖ **Marc records his podcast in a garage.** He doesn't have a formal office and doesn't even record in a studio. It feels more intimate when you're a guest in someone's house, let alone their garage. It almost sounds unprofessional that he works in his garage, but that's the appeal. His environment is less buttoned-up. It's hard to fathom that Marc would host a hugely popular show from his garage, let alone that the President of the United States would stop by to record an interview. But the garage only adds to the mythology of the show and makes Marc more accessible.

❖ *Marc admits his own faults and imperfections.*
Marc shares his personal details, warts and all. After battling alcohol and drugs for years, he got sober in 1999. On
the show he speaks candidly about his former drug bend-
ers, struggles with alcohol, and his lifestyle of cutting lines
of cocaine for comedians like Sam Kinison. Marc opens
up to his audience, sharing his inner demons, even talking
about his two marriages that ended in divorce. He exter-
nalizes his insecurities, neurosis, and pain, and it's real.

❖ *Marc lives in a house nicknamed "the Cat Ranch."*
Marc lives with a bunch of cats. He has his own cats, and
also takes care of and feeds local stray cats. When his
feline Boomer disappeared, fans made "Boomer Lives"
T-shirts, and Marc often calls out "Boomer lives" at the
end of his podcast.

❖ *Marc gets his guests to open up and be vulnerable.*
As mentioned, Marc says his first 100 episodes were interviewing famous people to talk about *his* problems. He is
vulnerable talking about his own issues, and in return the
guests feel comfortable sharing their own personal stories.
He raises the stakes by opening up himself, and then gets
candid interviews from his guests. Marc also isn't afraid to
get uncomfortable. James Franco and Larry King are just
two of the guests who Marc obviously did not get along
with due to his interviewing style.

❖ *Marc gives his community an online home.* Marc
affectionately calls his community What the Fuckers and
What The Fuckaneers, among other derivatives of WTF.
He forms an authentic bond with his listeners by giving
them a tongue-in-cheek name. It's not only funny when he
calls his community the What the Fuck Buddies, but it

also makes people feel a part of something bigger than themselves.

Actions to Find Your Authentic Self

1. Think about your "big picture" self. Consider what you stand for and how you can stand behind what you think and say. Authenticity comes from several defining angles that come together to paint a true picture of who you are. Look inward to discover the unique elements of your life that are worth sharing with an online community.

2. Write out what you are passionate about that relates to your platform. Think about how you can convey these passions to your community. It can be funny things like sharing with people that you own a bunch of cats, or hobbies like telling people you're a video gamer, or it can be something earnest like how much you love your family. These traits are small elements that let people inside and get to know you.

3. Determine if you can take a risk to connect with others by being honest and vulnerable. Remember, in the digital age you are a personality-driven media network. When people google you and your ideas, they will instantly find out what you stand for. Make those results count. It's important to take risks to express vulnerabilities. Are there parts of your personality that might be accessible and relatable to others? Also determine whether it's worth taking this risk to connect. For example, if you need to keep your day job and maintain a certain professional profile, it may not be the right time to reveal a lot of personal traits to the wider world.

Authenticity with Stand-Up Comedy

Have you ever tried stand-up comedy? If so, you realize there's a big difference between sharing funny stories with your friends and telling jokes at a comedy club to people you have never met. In stand-up, it can take years to find your authentic voice. I have performed stand-up comedy more than 50 times at open-mic nights and paid gigs around the DC/Baltimore area. When I started performing, I learned quickly that comedians take years to hone their craft because it's hard to tell jokes to strangers who don't give a damn about you and your feelings. Oftentimes comedy fans go to a show after a long, stressful day of work, hoping to unwind with friends, a plate of buffalo chicken wings, and a few drinks. They want to laugh—the question is whether it will be with you or at you. The first time I had the guts to go on stage in a stand-up comedy show was in 2003. I had written jokes in a journal, videotaped myself doing material in my one-bedroom studio, and attended a few open-mic nights as a spectator to get a feel for the experience. In my own mind I was as ready as ever to cut my teeth performing jokes in front of strangers.

I had heard of an open-mic night at a now closed spot called Winchesters in Baltimore. It was above a bar in downtown Baltimore by the inner harbor. The crowd was diverse and raw. I showed up early and put my name on the list to perform at 8:10 p.m. I brought a small piece of paper, disguised as a cocktail napkin, which was really my set list. I had eight jokes lined up. The host said, "Next on stage is Ryan Williams; give it up for him!" I walked up and told a joke, barely making my way through it, and crap, I had a brain fart. Without knowing what my second joke was, I went to the cocktail napkin with my set list. This crowd was not the most compassionate and understanding group and they started heckling me for not knowing my material. Within seconds, I had lost the crowd and it was over. I fought through the nervous feelings and finished my set, but literally no one laughed for five minutes. Ouch.

After I performed at the DC Improv, which was my peak performance, I packed it in. My then girlfriend, who is now my wife, helped me to see that I was a much better marketer of comedy than comedy performer anyway. I'm glad I did it, though. That stand-up experience has really helped my career. Now when I host a podcast and things go awry, I can think on my feet quickly. Or when I'm giving a keynote lecture or presenting a PowerPoint in an executive meeting, I know I can get through a difficult stretch. When you perform stand-up, you know what it's like when no one laughs, and it hurts. When I give a talk or speak in a meeting these days, at the very least I know I won't get heckled like at Winchesters!

When finding your authentic voice, it's like performing stand-up comedy. You may fail at first, get heckled along the way, and even lose your set list. But in the end, by putting yourself out there, you find rewards.

What I love about creating in the digital age is that you get do-overs. You get a chance to remake the content, again and again. If a YouTube video only gets a few views, you can reshoot it. If your e-book fails to reach an audience, you can write another version. And if you screw up your product launch, you can rebuild your software and publish a new version. You get a lot of chances to fashion your idea and find your authentic stride.

Lesson 2: Divorce Yourself from an Agenda

Brendan McDonald revealed to me that one of the main reasons why the *WTF* podcast thrives is because it is agenda-free, meaning that the conversations are about people and their stories, not about hawking movies or selling products. Marc Maron's lack of an agenda creates a forum and opportunity for him to do what he does: focusing on recording great interviews. And McDonald can focus on his expertise: producing an awesome show.

When Maron and McDonald were let go by Air America, they turned to podcasting as a last resort, and building community was the main priority. They never wanted to sell out and do promotional episodes where guests came on to talk about their upcoming movie or TV show. During traditional press junkets, comedians, actors, and performers go on media tours, appearing on *Ellen* and *The Tonight Show* to talk about the projects they are promoting. We've all seen these segments where some writer or actor sits on a couch for five minutes, launching into a quick story that helps promote their new project. It can feel very contrived. However revealing these segments can sometimes be, in the end they are promos, and they lack the depth that a conversation on *WTF* does.

Brendan told me, "We won't do promotional interviews for the full episode." As mentioned, sometimes Marc will do a friend a favor by talking about an upcoming book, TV special, or product, but even those shows typically lack any heavy self-promotion. Instead, people as diverse as Terry Gross, Robin Williams, and President Obama appear on Marc's show to have real, long-form conversations. The guests get deep. They talk about their upbringings and get into serious life issues that are both complimentary and often not very flattering. The guests bare themselves in an honest way and go into the garage knowing that they too need to be authentic.

Marc sets the tone on his show by being completely honest with his guests. And as a by-product, his guests open up. They know it's a space for them to be 100 percent real. And the audience loves it because this agenda-free environment helps create trust with them as well. They keep coming back knowing they'll hear compelling interviews rather than have to endure mindless promotion or product hard sell.

If you divorce yourself from agenda, then you too will be able to build trust with your community. Always have the motives of your community in mind. Do not sell them out for a quick buck, and think about the long-term relationship you are looking to build and grow. Take the long view with your community.

Actions to Divorce Yourself from an Agenda

1. Determine five goals that you want to achieve with your community. Think about where you'd like to be with your community in six months, one year, and five years. Take the long view.

2. Brainstorm ways to build and sustain a community without monetizing your idea. Think about ways you can build your community without burning bridges to make a quick dollar.

3. Determine how you will make money while building community. Define whether you need to sell ads, products, or services to survive while building your audience. Consider if the pressure to monetize will negatively influence what you are creating.

Lesson 3: Find the Truth in What You Do

Marc Maron is a great podcast host because he bonds with his community by expressing the truth about himself. He is a former stand-up comedian, so he's used to revealing his insecurities and neuroses to others in a public forum. Not all of us have that training. Many comedians start their careers by taking improvisation classes and performing with improv troupes to hone their craft. Marc didn't take the improvisation route, but many of his comedian podcast guests have. Improv is basically "a form of live theatre in which the plot, characters, and dialogue of a game, scene, or story are made up in the moment." Improv performances are usually constructed around an audience suggestion or other randomly determined starting topic."[6]

I took improv classes when I was performing stand-up comedy, and it provided a great training ground for experimenting with my ideas. Early on in my improv days, someone recommended a book on improvisation called *Truth in Comedy* by Charna Halpern, Del Close, and Kim "Howard" Johnson. Del Close was a pioneer in the improv community and a famed teacher at Second City in Chicago. He created a defining improv storytelling structure called "The Harold."

The book is a training guide to help improvisers get better at their craft. It provides powerful yet easy-to-learn lessons for performing scenes with other improvisers. The book's focus is to help people find truth in their performance of comedy, training improvisers to "be honest and in the moment because the truth is funny. Honest discovery, observation, and reaction is better than contrived invention." The book also describes the importance of a comfortable, open relationship between performer and audience: "when we're relaxing, we don't have to entertain each other with jokes."

These theories are not only true for comedians but for anyone looking to grow an authentic community in the digital age. When you're interacting with others online, you need to find the truth in yourself. You need to relax, open up, and be honest. Observations and reactions that are honest are authentic ways to connect with others whom you don't know. Finding the truth in what you do is as important as anything else in the Influencer Economy.

Actions to Find the Truth in What You Do

1. Identify the truth in what you do. Write down five reasons you want to launch your idea. Explain your motivations to your community and ask for feedback.

2. Ask your community how you can help them. Send out a poll asking what challenges they face, what they hope to

accomplish, or what they would like to see from you. See if there's something out there that can improve your relationship with your audience. Take their ideas in feedback to help make your idea better.

Lesson 4: Build Community First, Monetize Later

Finding your authentic voice, growing your community, and launching your idea can take years. There is no silver bullet. When you start, you'll be working on your own time and your own dime. In other words, like Marc Maron, you may start out fired from your job, looking for work, and drawing out ideas from a place of desperation. Other people may work on their ideas as side projects, while still others may raise outside investment from investors and stay afloat with other people's money.

At first, while your community is still growing, it's hard to make any money. You have to be real about that. But over time, if you grow your community and find your truth, you can build and sell not only your primary idea but other ideas from your platform.

In 2009, Marc Maron started his podcasting career interviewing well-known comedians, first in the Air America studio and then in his garage. Podcasting wasn't even a business back then; it was a hobby for the majority of participants. There were no direct paths to monetization.

But as Marc got more popular, his podcast became his platform for larger monetization opportunities. He promoted his TV shows, comedy tours, and books via his podcast, talking authentically about them and piquing audience interest. He invited his listeners to live comedy shows, talked at length about making his *Maron* TV show, and even shared updates on his book release ahead of its launch.

It took years for Marc to build his platform and grow a community large enough to support his many projects. In 2009, when *WTF* kicked off, Marc and Brendan posted only 34 episodes that year. In 2013 you can start to see how Marc's efforts to grow his community began to pay off. He launched bigger products and more ideas than at any time during his career. In 2013, Marc published a national best-selling book, *Attempting Normal,* and kicked off his IFC TV show *Maron,* which he executive-produces, stars in, and writes. Not falling too far from the tree, the show is about a comedian who records podcasts in his garage. He also released a Netflix stand-up comedy special called *Thinky Pain.* Two years later, he was playing to capacity crowds during his Maronation stand-up tour. He's a great example of a creator whose community supports him on multiple platforms because of the trust he has built with them over time.

When launching your idea and wondering if it can help you make a living, you too must think about the long run, not the short term. Students often ask: "Should I quit my day job to pursue my idea?" There is no easy answer, but I usually advise "No!" I advise people to stay employed as long as possible. I know that some people need to be 100 percent focused on their idea to get it done, while others need to maintain a full-time job in order to save money to pursue their idea in the long run. Marc and Brendan bootstrapped their show for years before making any substantial money. Marc had comedy to keep paying his bills, and Brendan produced radio programs to pay his. Many of us have spouses and children (or both) to provide for or student debt to pay off, and for us it's not realistic to jump full-force into launching an idea. But if you can bootstrap like the *WTF* team, making it up as you go along, you can eke out an acceptable living while devoting your remaining time and energy to your idea.

I tend to follow the advice of podcast guest Chris Yeh, who wrote the business book *The Alliance: Managing Talent in the Networked Age* along with LinkedIn cofounder Reid Hoffman and author Ben Casnocha. Chris told me that when working on an idea as a side project, you should not quit your day job to pursue it. In order to create a large runway for success, you need time to find your "product market fit." In other words, when you start fleshing out your idea it may change drastically from when you start, and it takes time to refine your product for the market. That development is based on the feedback that you get from your early community members who serve as alpha testers. Chris says "you're probably thinking about your side project at least four hours a day at your job, so you are practically robbing them blind while working there." In other words, don't quit your day job.

It can take years to grow community around your idea, and consequently, making money around your idea can also take years. Marc launched his podcast in 2009, but it wasn't until 2013 that his influence grew enough to sell a lot of different products to his community. Making money from your idea isn't easy, and you should never take your community for granted. As John Green of the Vlogbrothers, who I focus on in chapter 1, "Craft Your Big Vision," has said, "What's good for your community is good for your business. And what's bad for your community is bad for your business." Take the long view with all of your ideas and think about how to pay the bills in other ways while you build your audience.

Actions to Build Community First, Monetize Later

1. Determine whether you can bootstrap your idea or if you need to raise outside capital. In other words, answer the question, "Can I support myself while building a community and product over time?" Determine how

much money you need to support yourself while you build your idea.

2. If you need outside investment, whether through small business loans or venture capital investments, define how much you realistically need to raise in order to launch your idea. Pick a date when you want to start making money from your idea. Determine how much time per week you need to budget for working on your idea, then double that number. Ideas always take double the amount of time to monetize than you plan for. Then factor in how a day job fits into your weekly schedule in addition to pursuing your idea. Determine your monetization timetable from this exercise.

Chapter 6

Collaborate

"Luck is the residue of design."

—Branch Rickey

Chapter Playbook

In the Influencer Economy, you want your idea to get seen and heard above the noise. To achieve that, I've learned firsthand from my podcast guests that you need to build a movement around your idea. A movement results from teaming up, or collaborating, with both your community and other influencers.

Community collaboration is a bread and butter ingredient of the Influencer Economy. We've touched upon this principle already—it results from teaming up, or collaborating, with both your community and other influencers, brick by brick. You work in tandem with your community and you grow one e-mail, one follower, and one fan at a time. And by sheer force of will and hard work, you build your community by consistently putting out great work and material. You need to play the long game and realize this won't happen overnight. Oftentimes, community collaboration can lead to bigger job opportunities, which can open new doors to grow your audience.

When you build a website it's imperative to start collecting e-mails and dedicate yourself to working together with your community. I collaborate weekly with my e-mail list, and send personal notes and writing to help people learn about how to launch their ideas. E-mail is my prioritized channel for communication and the place where I most collaborate. Not only do I focus on sending thoughtful and value-adding e-mails, but I often receive even more thoughtful and inspiring responses back from my community. It's a win/win and it only makes my final product better.

Influencer collaboration is a secret sauce ingredient in the Influencer Economy. It is when you collaborate with an influencer in your field to make a product together or when someone with pull or influence supports you and your idea. Think of it as an endorsement, and that that person's involvement gives you "street cred" in your industry. When you collab, the influencer opens up you and your work to a new audience. In essence, they are sharing their larger, more established community with you. It's a powerful thing, and when I collaborated with podcast guests like Alan Sepinwall, Freddie Wong, and Burnie Burns early in my podcast career, they helped me to gain more credibility as a podcaster. Not only did these collaborations help open the door to new podcast listeners, but I gained more street cred as a podcaster and was able to book better guests on the show. When you get influencers to enter your world, it can help define and become a catalyst to further define the movement around your idea.

One column writer who originated his career in a local sports market built a nationwide collaborative community as the ultimate voice of the fan. He then acquired great influence to launch well-listened to podcast and popular podcasts where he could pass his influence onto others.

Bill Simmons

Fans of Boston's sports teams have had much to celebrate over the years. The Celtics have 17 NBA banners hanging on the roof of the Boston Garden, the Patriots own their share of Tom Brady–led Super Bowl rings (four), and the Bruins are a classic hockey franchise, one of the original six NHL teams.

Then there's the Red Sox. As a storied Major League Baseball franchise, for 86 years their home stadium, Fenway Park, hadn't hosted a new World Series championship team. During that epic drought, at the end of each season, Sox fans used their team's failure as character-building lessons for their children and tried to live with chronic frustration. But in 2004, all of that changed.

By that time, Bill Simmons had launched his career by covering the Boston sports scene and was a leading national sports columnist and writer at ESPN.com. At the time when the Sox won the World Series, Bill said, "ESPN.com was really starting to take off, and the Red Sox in 2004, that's when they had their little run."[1] Even though he was fired from ESPN in 2015, Bill had spent 14 years working for the company, and back in 2004 this was a big moment for his team and employer. On their way to winning the '04 series, the Red Sox came back from a three games to zero deficit against the rival New York Yankees in the American League playoffs. Simmons called the start of that rally one of the greatest experiences he's ever had in sports.

Bill had been waiting his whole life for that moment—and not just because the Red Sox were on a path to redemption. He had a hit column on the well-trafficked "Page 2" section of ESPN.com. It was his dream job. Years later, Bill built upon his career at ESPN with the incredibly popular *B.S. Report* podcast, where he spoke with everyone from legendary Boston sports figures like Larry Bird to comedians like Louis C.K. and even with friends from his youth like Joe House (now with his own website and brand, House from DC). He also oversaw a website called Grantland. com, which was launched in conjunction with ESPN. At Grantland, Bill managed his own staff of talented sports and pop culture writers. On top of that, he partnered with ESPN Films to executive produce the Emmy Award–winning *30 for 30* sports documentary series, a collaborative effort with filmmakers such as Barry Levinson, who directed *The Band That Wouldn't Die*, a story about the famed Baltimore Colts marching band, and Ice Cube's *Straight Outta L.A.*, which chronicled the city of Los Angeles's relationship with the Los Angeles Raiders.

Bill Simmons clearly knew how to use his voice as a sports fan and writer to notch successes in many aspects of digital media. The way he developed his vision is a bootstrap story that pulls together a lot of principles in building community through collaboration.

Community Collaboration—Embrace Your Outsider Standing

"I was going to try to freelance. And it was going to go great," Bill said on the *B.S. Report*, describing his misplaced optimism several years before he joined the ESPN.com team. He had quit a dead-end job at the copy desk of the *Boston Herald* and was using his master's degree in print journalism from Boston University to write for New England newspapers and hopefully score his own column. "Three months pass and I don't get a single freelance job other than, I think, I got one feature for the *Worcester Phoenix*. So at this point, I'm 26 years old and my writing career has just gone down in flames. And I got no idea what I'm going to do."[2] Bill thought he was a little too old to ask his mom for money, so he found a bartending gig to pay the rent on his Charlestown apartment.

But he also began to badger the editor of the Boston edition of AOL's *Digital City*, a sort of group blog that offered local content for many America Online markets back in 1997. Bill noticed that the site had someone known as "Boston Movie Guy" to write film reviews, so he pitched himself as "Boston Sports Guy" because he loved that arena and thought he knew how to create authentic and relevant content for a growing audience. "My idea at the time was if I'm going to go down in flames, I'm going down in flames like *me*. I'm not going to try to write like a traditional newspaper columnist. I'm going to write from a fan's perspective. I'm going to write about the stuff my buddies and I talk about."[3]

In the Influencer Economy, it's always valuable to embrace an outsider perspective when fighting against a traditional industrial media machine, which in the case of Simmons involved unapologetically rooting for the Patriots, Celtics, and Red Sox—a total departure from the way sportswriters were covering the beat in those days. And if you're going to pioneer a new online journalistic voice, you may as well do it from your living room couch. Bill had no access to the Boston sports teams' locker rooms or press boxes. And he didn't need it. He was a proud outsider, writing for a young audience who related to his barroom fan perspective. Also, his column began to catch on because readers liked the way his writing extended to sports data and statistics, along with movies and other pop culture references that weren't normally in the sports journalism playbook.

In a "Boston Sports Guy" column from September 2000, Bill talks up his qualifications to appear on an ESPN game show called *Two Minute Drill*: "You need to know one thing about me: as far as sports trivia goes, I'm Pedro [Martínez]. It's that simple. I throw in the mid nineties; I have four pitches and I throw all of them for strikes. I was born for this type of game show. It's like that scene in *Jaws* when Richard Dreyfuss is describing the great white shark to the Amity mayor and says, 'This is a killing machine. All this animal does is swim and eat. That's it. It's a miracle of evolution.'" He continues: "For whatever reason, my brain possesses the startling capacity to remember dumb, trivial things. And it's not just limited to games/players/events from the sports world; it extends to television and movies as well. I couldn't name six senators in the United States right now, yet I could tell you who played Arnold's buddy on *Diff'rent Strokes* (Shavar Ross) and what the Celtics' record was at the Garden during the '86 season (47-1; they also won two games in Hartford) . . . I'm the King of Knowing Dumb Things."[4]

Community Collaboration—Honing Your Craft While Building Community

A growing community of readers ate this stuff up. Simmons was a leader in collaborating with his audience. He and his community were partners in crime. Bill also got his readers more invested in his column by publishing a mailbag correspondence where he answered their questions and generally riffed off of reader feedback. He borrowed this idea and some of the sarcastic tone from talk show host David Letterman, who Bill had long admired. Another unique format choice within his column was the "running diary" he occasionally kept while watching games and other media. It was like the live blog or live Twitter session that we see today, and it gave Bill a chance to time-stamp plenty of jokes and one-liners. These running diaries made readers relate to him more as a funny friend rather than a buttoned-up journalist.

Bill continually honed this fresh perspective, and his columns started to take off. His material felt more like having a conversation with him rather than reading a traditional sportswriter talking at you, or even down to you. It was like he was cracking the jokes that you and your friends did too.

Although the "Boston Sports Guy" was turning into a fairly innovative column, he wasn't getting rich—for some of his years at *Digital City*, AOL paid Bill $50 a week. But he kept at it, writing online, hoping to build an audience and launch a career because assignments in print journalism were so scarce. He didn't get hung up wondering if this was the right direction for him. If it meant control over his own column, Bill was willing to go down in flames, as he's fond of saying. So what if he wasn't writing for the *Boston Globe*? Borrowing a term from sports training, he was getting what he called his "reps" as a writer by turning in three to four columns a week, and that regular schedule of publication helped build his community and reputation. By 2000, Bill estimated that he had 10,000 loyal readers. The *Globe* had actually run a story on Boston Sports Guy, acknowledging that this columnist was on the Internet, taking shots at a local sports radio station (WEEI), and otherwise filing stories from his couch.[5]

Community Collaboration—Fighting Through the Dip

That *Globe* story gave Simmons some credibility in the Boston market, and it helped him to renegotiate his deal with AOL and finally quit his bartending job. And old-media freelance opportunities became a little easier to line up, which gave him more chances to shine and grow his writing portfolio.

What's interesting is that Bill wasn't encouraged by his progress. On the *B.S. Report* podcast, he recalled turning 30 and being filled with doubt about his status as a journalist. FOX Sports had come after him regarding a job but then cooled off. There didn't seem to be any other prospects with such high visibility. "Maybe late summer 2000, I remember going to dinner with my girlfriend at the time, who is now my wife, and my mom and my stepdad, who is in commercial real estate, and seriously thinking it might be time to give this up. I'm making $32,000 a year, $35,000. I have friends who are making three to four times as much money as me. I don't know what to do. Is it time to just say this didn't work out? Everybody convinced me: you've got to give it one more year."[6]

Bill was fighting through the Dip, a term coined by entrepreneur and marketer Seth Godin, who also wrote a book of the same name. It's a favorite book of mine and when I spoke with

Seth on the podcast, he told me "the only way to become the best at one thing is to quit something else. And the thesis of the book is that we live in a culture where supposedly quitting is a bad thing. But people quit stuff all the time." Yet in his book, Seth also advises people to "never quit something with great long-term potential just because you can't deal with the stress of the moment."[7] When at a crossroads like Bill was, Seth told me that "you need to figure out if you quit or stick," but you also need to know that the Dip is "a temporary setback that can be overcome with persistence."[8]

Bill got through the Dip and stuck with it. His family helped him to realize it was worth pushing through rather than quitting, and his 14 years at ESPN show that he made the right call.

But all of that was still to come. Less than a year after his crisis of conscience, Bill would write the column that put him on the road to real success. ESPN airs its own version of the Oscars or Emmy Awards known as the ESPYs, which stands for Excellence in Sports Performance Yearly Awards. The annual show is hosted by a celebrity of some kind and tries not to take itself too seriously, though its scripted efforts at humor can be painful. Bill decided to publish one of his running diary columns for the ESPYs in February of 2000. America Online no longer has an archive of "Boston Sports Guy" columns, but here's a taste of a different Bill's notorious ESPY diary republished by *Deadspin*:[9]

> 8:03 — The show kicks off with a mock opera opening, featuring Dick Vitale as the showstopper. I'm not making this up.
>
> 8:04 — Just slammed my head against the coffee table for 30 seconds.

> 8:22 — Steve Largent reads the ESPY rules . . . allegedly a
> comedy segment. I've watched funerals for slain
> policeman that were packed with more comedy.
>
> 8:32 — Is this hell?

He goes on in this vein all evening, entitling the piece, "The 1999 ESPY Awards: Greatest Night In Sports . . . Or TV Holocaust?" Bill had a friend who worked for ESPN but hadn't been able to get any traction with the editors there, even on a freelance basis. His early columns spread mainly via word of mouth—many of Bill's readers liked to e-mail his columns to their friends, which was how his audience grew during his *Digital City* years. But when Bill wrote a second ESPY diary, he learned that his columns were starting to make the rounds at ESPN headquarters in Bristol, Connecticut. In fact, executive editor John Walsh had binged on several weeks' worth of columns and thought his voice was right for the new "Page 2" section of the company's website. They asked if they could try him out on a few assignments, which led to an article on Red Sox shortstop Nomar Garciaparra, and another on former Sox pitcher Roger Clemens that Bill entitled "Is Clemens the Antichrist?"[10] With these new ESPN writing assignments, Bill had gotten a break that would change the trajectory of his career.

Community Collaboration—New Jobs Can Help Grow Your Community

Getting a break in business can help you grow your community, especially when a larger company wants to hire you for your work, and that's exactly how it unfolded with Bill. When readers of ESPN.com took notice of this new writer and looked for more of his work at bostonsportsguy.com, Bill's old employers at the

Boston Herald were also noticing his rising profile and decided to make their former copy desk intern an offer. Why not bring his whole website into the *Herald* and write for them? He'd be a star player in their digital media effort and have a steady, respectable job at the number two newspaper in his hometown. Bill was engaged to his girlfriend by then and was very tempted by this opportunity, especially because he knew he had taken his work with AOL and *Digital City* as far as it could go.

But after he told his editors at ESPN.com that he was about to sign with the *Herald*, John Walsh himself summoned Bill to his executive suite. In his 27 years with the company, Walsh had widely been thought of as the godfather of ESPN and is credited with successfully beefing up both its newsroom and online presence.[11] Bill had been warned about him: "I was told that Walsh is someone who waits you out, who stares you down. He'll use silence as his weapon."[12] The bloated ESPY Awards were also Walsh's baby, and he remained a strong defender of the show when others in Bristol considered it an unnecessary expense. Meanwhile, Bill had compared the annual pageant of the ESPY to the Holocaust. You might not think that would be a great calling card, but Walsh considered it an asset to have a young and irreverent voice on ESPN.com. He offered Bill a permanent column on "Page 2" and a chance to become simply the "Sports Guy," shedding "Boston" from the name in favor of a large national audience. Bill took the offer.

At first he battled with editors at ESPN with his outsider perspective as they edited out some of his more provocative jokes and observations. But when they discovered that his column significantly increased traffic to their site, they eventually allowed him more rope and indulged his honesty with his fans.

It was a win/win for both Simmons and the company. While Bill's candor and passion in his writing helped fuel his community's loyal support, ESPN reaped the rewards of providing a stage for such an unconventional and popular sportswriter. Staying true to himself at all costs helped cement Bill's legacy, and his community supports him to this day on multiple platforms.

At ESPN, there were 14 years in which Bill amassed tremendous influence by experimenting with his flagship column and branching out into other formats. His pop culture references helped him to write for readers nationwide who wouldn't understand the local Boston color in his pieces prior to ESPN. He was the first at that company to write about fantasy leagues, which was still regarded as a nerds-only hobby back in the early 2000s. He even championed for the Talented Mr. Roto, Matthew Berry, to get hired at ESPN as their first fantasy football analyst. And Bill wouldn't be Bill if he didn't occasionally piss off portions of his audience. He got death threats a year after joining "Page 2" for "Growing Queasy in the Big Easy," a story he filed from New Orleans during Super Bowl week in which he wrote, "The natives speak in some sort of Creole gibberish that's nearly impossible to understand. Remember Adam Sandler's old 'Cajun Man' skit on *SNL*? He wasn't kidding."[13]

If some folks were alienated by Bill's sense of humor, others hoped to borrow it from ESPN. In 2002, the comedian Jimmy Kimmel offered him a job writing for his late-night talk show on ABC, *Jimmy Kimmel Live!* The position required him to move to Los Angeles and scale back the three columns a week he wrote as the Sports Guy. Disney, the parent company of both ESPN and ABC, gave Bill its blessing to try writing for their broadcast network.

After writing for Kimmel's inaugural year, Bill missed sports and wanted that emphasis back, saying he had "unfinished business" with his ESPN career. He resumed his column full-time and looked for ways to do more than write for the company website, turning that astonishing 2004 Red Sox World Series victory into a best-selling sports anthology entitled *Now I Can Die in Peace: How ESPN's Sports Guy Found Salvation With a Little Help from Nomar, Pedro, Shawshank, and the 2004 Red Sox.* But that year at *JKL* was another career-defining experience for Bill. It opened doors into the entertainment world, which helped him launch what would become the super-popular *B.S. Report* on an up-and-coming medium: podcasting.

Influencer Collaboration—Expanding Your Vision with Outside Help

In the Influencer Economy, creators sometimes accelerate their success and community building by collaborating with influential people in their field. With Bill, this approach helped pivot his career toward fresh opportunities and new ideas. Podcasting was very new in May of 2007 when he launched an interview format show that he first called *Eye of the Sports Guy* and later renamed *The B.S. Report.* On these weekly hour-long podcasts, Bill talked to sports people and media personalities, or he would talk with old friends about sports. A group of his former colleagues from *Jimmy Kimmel Live!*—including Kimmel himself and comedian Adam Carolla—were early guests. Kimmel's "Cousin Sal," Salvatore Iacono, became a *B.S. Report* regular who discussed the Vegas gambling picks on National Football League games. The NFL is opposed to legalized sports betting and has a broadcast deal with ESPN, yet Simmons' podcast wasted no time ignoring the will of his employer's powerful corporate partner.

But listeners loved the picks episodes, as well as Bill's heated arguments with "JackO," an old college buddy of his who was a New York Yankees fan. Just like his online column, *The B.S. Report* thrived by being amusingly candid and a showcase for Bill's pop culture interests. The Pulitzer Prize–winning journalist Wesley

Morris talked movies with him, and the influential television critic Alan Sepinwall (the subject of chapter 3, "Book Your Own Gigs: The Jay Z Effect") was also a guest. Even Barack Obama agreed to chat with Bill at the White House. In its eight-year run, over 30 million annual downloads of these episodes meant that Simmons headed up a lucrative pioneering media property at ESPN.

The popularity of *The B.S. Report* generated something I call "the Simmons Bump." It's a phenomenon where guests on the show might suddenly see increased web traffic, sales, subscriptions, and so on—especially if they had their own online platform. Alan Sepinwall told me that in addition to discussing television shows on *The B.S. Report*, Bill gave Alan the chance to talk about his self-published book, *The Revolution Was Televised: The Cops, Crooks, Slingers, and Slayers Who Changed TV Drama Forever.* "There has absolutely been a Bill Simmons bump," Alan says. "I interviewed him around the time *30 for 30* was debuting, and he knew who I was, and he said, 'Hey, you should come on the podcast.' If you look at the bump in my Twitter followers every time I would appear on *B.S. Report* after that, and the number of times I hear from people saying I first heard of you on Simmons' podcast, it's absolutely the case that knowing him as tenuously as I know him has been very good for my career." Bill not only benefitted from influencers coming on his show at its launch, but his podcast guests got their own influencer bump as Bill's profile continued to grow.

Influencer Collaboration—Passing Along Your Influence to Help Others

Once Bill reached a certain level of notoriety and, more importantly, had established a larger community, he was able to lend his influence to give credibility to others' work. When you become the influencer, you can help others draft off your success. You can help empower them to launch their own projects, gain new jobs, and pursue new opportunities. It can be a transcendent experience when you help others to thrive in the Influencer Economy.

The *30 for 30* that Alan Sepinwall referred to is a sports documentary series at ESPN that Bill began to develop with a team of producers and creative people he knew. As an executive producer, Bill worked with filmmakers who he trusted to tell 30, hour-long sports stories to celebrate ESPN's 30-year anniversary. These stories had once made headlines but weren't necessarily familiar to today's audiences. Peter Berg helmed the first hour that aired in October 2009, a film about the sudden popularity of hockey in Southern California after the 1988 trade of Wayne Gretzky to the Los Angeles Kings. Subsequent *30 for 30* films dealt with an obsessive fan's efforts to purchase the original rules of basketball, a profile of "big wave" surfer Eddie Aikau, and the tragic overdose of University of Maryland's Len Bias only two days after the Boston Celtics had drafted him.

When I asked screenwriter and former Grantland contributor Brian Koppelman how he got involved in the *30 for 30* series, he told me, "I was on a plane one day, and Simmons and I were e-mailing, and he said you guys should direct a *30 for 30*." Brian was flying with his creative partner, David Levien, and the two men immediately knew who they wanted to make a film about. "I wrote back, 'Jimmy Connors' and Simmons said, 'Done.'" I learned from Brian that this exchange was typical of the confidence Bill had in the people with whom he collaborated. He was a hands-off producer, enabling filmmakers to bring their own visions to the series and benefit collectively when it earned a Peabody Award and an Emmy for *30 for 30 Shorts*, the short-format version that he also created. His award-winning film series lifted the boats of the extended creative team of producers, filmmakers, and even ESPN.

When Brian Koppelman's *30 for 30* film came out, Simmons had him on *The B.S. Report* to discuss it. Koppelman, who is known as the co- writer of *Ocean's 13* and the poker movie, *Rounders*. Koppelman first heard from Simmons back in 2006 when Simmons would email questions to sports or media personalities and then publish their correspondence in his *Page 2* column as "The Curious Guy." Their friendship and collaboration grew out of Simmons' interest in *Rounders* and did progress across ESPN Films, Koppelman's many written contributions to Grantland, and launching the *The Moment* podcast, a show in which Koppelman interviews creators about pivotal moments of inspiration.

Bill also helped to grow community for writers that he hired to work on Grantland.com, an ESPN-affiliated sports and pop culture website that became the new home of Simmons' "Sports Guy" column and *The B.S. Report*, along with multiple new columnists and podcast hosts that he handpicked. Bill was a fan of a *New York Times* best seller called *The Extra 2%: How Wall Street Strategies Took a Major League Baseball Team from Worst to First*. The author, Jonah Keri, delved into baseball statistics and wrote a book about how sports data enabled the small-market Tampa Bay Rays to compete with wealthy baseball teams like the Boston Red Sox and New York Yankees. "I think that the reason I got hired at Grantland was largely the book, largely *The Extra 2%*," Jonah told me regarding his former dual role as a columnist and podcaster in the Grantland network. "People really liked [the book]. Simmons in particular really liked it, and also my body of work at that point. I've written for *Baseball Prospectus*, ESPN.com, and I had a different approach because I had this business background. And also, I'm big into stats. I do the analytical thing."

That "thing" that Keri does, as well as Brian Koppelman's creativity, as well as the talents of each contributor to Grantland, were a fit with Bill's sensibilities and not part of a corporate hiring strategy. Bill made personal connections with creative people and he could staff his website based on what his gut told him would make cool content and grow a community based on their collective interests. His "no assholes" rule was the only quasi human resources guideline for expanding the team.

Jonah Keri called his chance to join Grantland "fun and a great coincidence that Simmons ended up being my boss." Like many other aspiring sportswriters, he had read Bill's stuff for years and wanted a career that resembled the Sports Guy's. He said that he covered Wall Street and the business beat for so long because, well, it's hard to become the next Bill Simmons. "I didn't actually sign my first real Grantland contract until I was 37 years old. I was 14 years out of college by the time I joined Grantland. That's a long, long slog. I was writing for a living, but I wanted to be a sportswriter." Jonah said that he was third oldest person at Grantland, which employed many people in their twenties. "Simmons and the other editors of the site had a really good eye and said we want to give these people a bigger platform and a chance to do well. So I think [25-year-olds] should be reassured that if they're listening to this and want to do 'X', but they don't feel that they're going to get there, somebody *is* paying attention to them somewhere—if not now, then by next year, or next week, or next month. Just keep creating and doing stuff."

To bring influencer collaboration full circle, when I reached out to both Keri and Koppelman to appear on my podcast, I had hosted my show for less than a year and had roughly 25 episodes under my belt. Yet they both agreed to come on and chat with me—Jonah, in fact, agreed to come on the show after a single encounter I had with him at a sports blog conference years ago. It reflects a mentality in the majority of my podcast guests where they are willing to help and collaborate with others after they've reached a degree of success, and this held true for both Jonah Keri and Brian Koppelman. They were extremely generous with their time.

Influencer Collaboration—Maintaining Your Outsider Perspective

The Bill Simmons hyphenated title while he was at ESPN would have to include columnist, author, podcaster, television talking head, and film executive producer, to name a few hats he wore. Grantland.com alone had about three million unique monthly readers at its peak. But in the fall of 2014, the fact that Bill was essentially paid to be opinionated couldn't save him from a three-week suspension for criticizing National Football League commissioner Roger Goodell. Earlier that year, Goodell had reviewed a video showing Ray Rice, a Baltimore Ravens running back, dragging his fiancée out of an Atlantic City hotel elevator. Goodell gave Rice a light punishment at first, but later suspended him for the entire season when the celebrity gossip website TMZ located a second video in which Rice is seen brutally hitting his future wife. Why had Goodell claimed that he hadn't watched both videos? How could the NFL be so indifferent to a graphic incident of domestic violence within their ranks? Bill had an answer on his podcast: "Goodell, if he didn't know what was on that tape, he's a liar. I'm just saying it. He is lying . . . For all these people to pretend they didn't know is such fucking bullshit. It really is—it's such fucking bullshit. And for him to go in that press conference and pretend otherwise, I was so insulted. I really was."

ESPN made the mistake of taking down that episode in which Bill went on to announce, "I really hope somebody calls me or e-mails me and says I'm in trouble for anything I say about Roger Goodell . . . The commissioner's a liar and I get to talk about that on my podcast. Please, call me and say I'm in trouble. I dare you." When ESPN withdrew the episode, it only drew more attention to it. Sports blogs such as *Deadspin* and *The Big Lead* sniffed it out and embedded the story on their sites. The hashtag #FreeSimmons quickly became a global Twitter trend after Bill was suspended.[14] Plenty of fans and journalists shared his view that ESPN couldn't be totally objective when the NFL was making that network so much money. If his comments were a tad incautious, maybe job security wasn't a priority, and he was ready to take on a new challenge. Despite popular support and a killer record of achievement at ESPN, the company's president, John Skipper, chose not to renew the Sports Guy's contract in 2015.

Bill Simmons didn't remain a free agent for long. He has a TV deal with HBO to host a weekly sportscast with other topical content, and he'll be creating programming for HBO's digital platforms while consulting with HBO Sports. Not a bad gig. Fans of the old podcast can still find archives on Grantland, but the new *Bill Simmons Podcast* launched in October 2015, with Cousin Sal doing his Guess the Lines duties, Joe House talking about the NBA, and other Grantland friends like Andy Greenwald, Chris Ryan, and Juliet Litman. He has also launched his own podcast network, media company, and website.

So far Bill has proved able to reunite his audience. And this time it really is *his* podcast, website, and company—not something that he made for ESPN and never owned. He has jumped full-tilt into entrepreneurship.

It's hard to succeed as an independent voice and creator these days. Without sponsors or companies that bankroll your ideas, building out your own platform can seem impossible. Not all of us are early adopters of YouTube and social media, and not all of us can bootstrap our way to success. But Bill applied community collaboration, working brick by brick to grow his audience, and then found outside collaboration, partnering with a bigger company, ESPN, to expand his community even more. He leveraged his position at ESPN to make connections that raised his own profile, allowing him to collaborate with influencers in the big-time sports and entertainment worlds and launch his singular career as an entertainment business icon.

And yet today, he's still Bill Simmons, whether speaking his mind on his new podcast, appearing on a premium cable show, or sitting at a Boston bar and watching the Red Sox. Twenty years ago, he was mixing drinks to pay his bills, busting his butt to be a writer. Today he is one of the pioneers and true leaders of the Influencer Economy.

Influencer School Lessons: What Bill Simmons Can Teach You About Collaboration

Lesson 1: Embrace Your Outsider Standing

Bill Simmons found his authentic voice early as a writer. He began his writing career in the late 1990s, when he wrote about Boston sports from his couch and didn't hide his allegiances to Boston sports teams. He wrote how normal sports fans talk about sports. He wasn't a traditional journalist. When reading his column, it was like you were at the bar with him, chatting about the Celtics while drinking a bottle of Budweiser. Bill had a distinct voice that stood out from the crowd. He was real.

When building your community, pay attention to something I call "community-building efficiency." This refers to your ability to be more efficient than others you are competing with. Bill's CBE was off the charts because he was able to write content that was fresh and original, publish it immediately online, and distribute these early "Boston Sports Guy" columns via his early community of friends and fans. He was incredibly efficient. Meanwhile his competition—traditional writers in the Boston sports market—were typing up their articles and submitting them to editors to run in the newspaper the next day. Theirs was a stodgy insider's game; Bill was on to the new rules before these guys even realized the game had changed.

Bill embraced his outsider standing because he had no access. He had to find his edge and unique voice because, as he put it, if he was going to go down in flames, he wanted to do it as himself rather then conforming to the norm. But it didn't turn out that way—his grassroots beginnings served him well in distributing his columns to new readers. In his efficient DIY model, his buddies in Boston served as his early community builders and marketing team, passing the columns in e-mails from friend to friend. Without embracing the Internet, other Boston sports journalists were incredibly inefficient, and their readership was limited to their paper's print edition circulation figures. Although traditional journalists were making a lot more money than Bill at the time, they had no control over their work or community. Bill was much more efficient in not only writing on AOL's website, which was a big player back then, but also in marketing his work via a growing community in Boston.

To thrive in the Influencer Economy, you have to bypass the barriers in your industry and go around them. Bill wasn't in the good old boys network of journalists. He thrived because his columns were read on the web. That was where he grew his community brick by brick, building his audience one member at a time. This is what made him efficient. In those days, these tactics were not ordinary for writers, even though it's now the norm. He was an underdog, and the early audience that found him and championed his work was his underground partner.

None of this happened overnight; it took him years to build out his community. But all that long effort helped him land his big opportunity to work at ESPN. If you follow the playbook like Bill, you will wake up months, even years later and suddenly find you have a community.

Building community is hard. But when you have nothing to lose, you have everything to gain. Bill Simmons' outsider status helped him build a following as he pioneered a new journalistic voice. And through it all, he had fun infiltrating and ultimately disrupting a big, older, and more established industry.

Actions to Embrace Your Outsider Standing

1. Determine how you are more efficient than more established players in your industry. Determine how you work better, harder, and smarter than them.

2. Define how you are an outsider in your field and how you can use that underdog status to your advantage. Consider what makes you authentic, as well as how your perspective is different than the establishment.

3. Determine how you can collaborate with your community. For Simmons, answering mailbag questions was one tactic. Another was writing like he was just another fan, or a friend at the corner bar. List ways you can help make your community part of your work.

Lesson 2: Hone Your Craft While Building Community

Here are the steps Bill Simmons took to hone his craft while simultaneously building his community:

❖ *He embraced his personality.* In 1997, Bill was bartending in Boston, writing sports columns on the web while getting his online "Boston Sports Guy" column off the ground. Whether writing his running diaries about the ESPYs or answering mailbag questions from his readers or talking about taboo subjects like sports gambling, he instinctively clicked with his natural audience—sports fans just like him.

- **He had no access, which became his unique vantage point.** Bill managed to maintain his voice as an independent sports fan, watching the games from his living room, without any access to athletes or, for that matter, any access to companies and brands like ESPN or the NFL.

- **He made less money to pursue his vision.** He was making only $30,000 a year from writing while many of his other friends were making six figures. Although he questioned it at times, this deliberate sacrifice enabled him to stick with his path and slowly build community as he slowly built his independent writing career.

- **He collab'ed with his friends.** Bill's buds spread his Internet columns around to their buds via e-mail. It was old-school word-of-mouth marketing.

- **He got his reps writing online earlier than most sports journalists.** Bill was writing on the web before it was cool and back when sports journalists had to wait for someone to die in order to get promoted. He was years ahead of other Internet sportswriters.

- **He got a job at ESPN to grow his profile.** When you get a job at a big company like ESPN, it can be an incredible opportunity to get national exposure and grow your profile. When Bill was an underdog writer as the Boston Sports Guy, he made fun of ESPN. Then they hired him because he had such an impactful community and strong perspective.

❖ ***He jumped over to work on the Jimmy Kimmel show as a comedy writer.*** Bill moved to LA to pursue his writing career, and this job opened doors to a bigger entertainment career. He picked up a new craft, writing comedy for a late-night talk show.

❖ ***He collabed with influencers when he launched his podcast.*** Many of Bill's first guests were friends from *Jimmy Kimmel Live!,* including Adam Corolla and Cousin Sal. He also collab'ed with filmmakers on the *30 for 30* documentaries and writers/podcasters on Grantland in the influencer role himself. He helped to grow the profile of many creative people via these projects.

❖ ***He was fired by ESPN but he still could start his new podcast and website with his preexisting community.*** Bill had over a decade of community building and audience development under his belt. When he was fired by ESPN, he was able to launch his own podcast network, media network, and HBO show in less than a year after leaving ESPN. His community was loyal and followed him, because he continually honed his craft while continually building a community.

Actions to Hone Your Craft While Building Community

1. Write down five ways you can hone your craft while building community. Think about ways you can create a community simultaneously while woodshedding your idea.

2. Determine and refine your goals for how you can continue growing community ahead of your project launch. Establish your launch date and work backwards to figure out the number of community members you

think you'll need to launch your idea. Pick a number and go with it, realizing it will change over time.

3. Determine if you need a company or partner to give you a larger platform to succeed. Sometimes community collaboration can accelerate when you get a better job with a higher profile. Do you need a better/bigger job to grow your idea? If yes, it's okay—not everyone needs to go the completely independent route.

Lesson 3: Get Your Reps Before You're Famous (When No One Is Watching)

When you're famous everyone is watching you. They know when you succeed, but they also know when you fail. That comes with the territory of success. As such, it's important to perfect your craft early on in your journey. Bill calls it getting your "reps," because when you are training to be the champ, you have to get your practice in the gym when no one is watching. Preparation and practice make successful creative entrepreneurs.

At ESPN in 2008, Bill wrote about reps when describing how LeBron James and other athletes get better in their performance: "Reps are easy to understand: The more you do something, the better you will be."[15]

In regards to podcasting, Bill told Peter Kafka of the website Re/Code how he honed his craft on such a new platform: "I got all these reps the first two years, when a lot of people didn't even have iTunes yet, and people were listening on ESPN.com files. Podcasts didn't really take off as a medium, I don't think, until the fall of 2009, maybe even a little into 2010. But those first two years for me were a real advantage on ESPN.com, because they would promote them. . . . Now there are so many of them. It's really hard to stand out. I'm lucky enough to stand out just because I was there so early."[16]

Actions to Get Your Reps Before You're Famous

1. Determine how you can get your reps in early in your process. Find time to practice when no one is looking. Think about how you can work on your particular Influencer Economy craft in your spare time, when you are just starting out. If it's podcasting, start recording interviews. If it's graphic design, start designing logos for friends and family. If it's writing, schedule sessions to write out your ideas and thoughts. Get in your reps early and often.

2. Establish how many hours a week you can dedicate to practicing. If you have a day job, commit to a number of hours and make it happen. If you are pursuing your idea full-time, commit to working as much as necessary without burning out.

Lesson 4: Grow Your Profile and Community with New Jobs

Landing a better job, especially one that is "right" for you, can often be part of your strategy for success. Partnering or collaborating with a larger website or company can accelerate your growth and open new doors for your idea. Bill was the beneficiary of a better job when he got his first big break writing full-time for "Page 2" at ESPN. For a writer like Simmons, getting a job at a big company like ESPN was an incredible opportunity to get national exposure. And it was the right job because he could still be himself, only now on a bigger stage. He even updated his writing name to go national, switching from the local Boston Sports Guy to the more broad Sports Guy. His ability to add to his growing community piggybacked off of ESPN's widespread popularity.

When considering your career options, you have to think about how new jobs can expand your network and grow your community. For example, if you have an opening with a company that will pay for you to attend large conferences and other networking events to grow their business, that may be a great career move if it aligns with your goals. Or if you're a start-up founder building a mobile app and Google wants to hire you or, better yet, acquire your company, that sounds like the right career path. If you are trying to grow your profile as an online commentator, partnering with a larger media website like Bill did will help accelerate your community building.

Taking advantage of the right job opportunity is often overlooked when people are deep in the world of community collaboration. However glamorous it is to do it yourself and build out your own ideas, often the most efficient path may be to ride the wave of another company's resources and success.

Actions to Grow Your Profile and Community with New Jobs

1. Determine if your goals to grow your idea and community align with a bigger job opportunity. Research five companies that may be interested in partnering with you or acquiring what you're working on. Even if you aren't thinking about this now, you should at least consider how a bigger website or business partnership could conceivably grow your profile.

2. Determine how you can meet with the five companies you identified in your research. Whether it's via a cold e-mail, warm intro, or networking at a conference, write out a road map to reach these companies. You don't need to be in a hurry to meet them, but you need to consider how realistic it is for you to forge these types of business partnerships. Ask yourself how you can best put yourself in position to succeed.

Lesson 5: Grow Your Profile and Community with Influencer Collaboration

When Bill Simmons was launching his podcast, he earned credibility early on by booking high-profile guests. Well-known comedians and TV hosts like Adam Corolla and Jimmy Kimmel were early guests, as were respected sports personalities like Marv Albert and Michael Wilbon. Even David Stern, the commissioner of the NBA, made an early appearance on his podcast. He set his bar for guest bookings very high—his guests were influencers in both entertainment and sports. It's a great example of influencer collaboration.

Influencer collaboration is important for the launch of your idea. It gives you street cred in your field or industry. People often think influencers have to be global celebrities like Leonardo DiCaprio or Lady Gaga, but celebrities are not necessarily influencers in the digital world. You are looking for influential people in a specific category on the Internet. And often the more segmented the interests of the influencer, the more influential they are among the types of followers you're trying to attract.

For example, when I worked at Machinima, a lot of our video gaming personalities, the guys and gals who played *Minecraft* and uploaded their gameplay to YouTube, had hundreds of thousands of Twitter followers. They weren't household names like Beyoncé, but they had a global and rabid following nonetheless. Often their Twitter interaction rates were 10 to 15 percent of their total audience, a phenomenal return. These gamers were building big businesses off their digital work and, as with most influencers, their community was incredibly loyal.

The right influencers can move the needle when you launch your idea, so determine the ideal personalities to collaborate with. Think about the bigger and broader influencers in your category, but also go very specific. At Machinima, we differentiated between gamers who played *Minecraft* and gamers who played *Call of Duty* for certain initiatives. Segment your influencer group as much as possible when thinking about your collaborations.

Important: *Do not* reach out to influencers as soon as you start creating your project. Wait until you have your reps and practice and are very good at your craft before reaching out. Think strategically about when the outreach makes sense. For my podcast, I didn't book Jonah Keri and Brian Koppelman on day one; I waited until I had 25 well-done, high-quality episodes in the can ahead of time. With other well-known guests, I waited until I had even more top-notch people on the podcast in order to show these bigger names that I was taking my work seriously. Don't rush to reach an influencer when your ducks aren't in a row. Otherwise, you won't be showcasing your best work, and you may only get one chance to impress someone.

And finally, when you've reached a certain level of success, don't neglect to collab with others on their way up. When Bill hired Jonah and Brian for Grantland and *30 for 30*, he gave each of them a great gig and work opportunity. They got hired for cool and interesting projects that gave them a bigger platform and opportunity to grow their own communities and visions.

Actions to Grow Your Profile and Community with Influencer Collabing

1. Make a list of 10 influencers you'd like to collaborate with. Think about both the bigger and broader influencers in your category and the very specific. In other words, if you're reaching out to tech influencers, consider those in both the broader tech community and in your specific tech category. Segment your influencer group as much as possible.

2. Create a timeline for when you need to reach out to these influencers. Consider how many reps you have in and how experienced you are before you make your move. Also, determine if you even need credibility from other influencers before you reach out. Be strategic as you carefully build your influencer launch plan for your idea.

Lesson 6: Commit to Your Idea for the Long Haul

It's normal during the community-building phase in the Influencer Economy for people to want to quit. It can take years to successfully build a loyal community, and it takes dedication to do it right. But in his book *The Dip*, Seth Godin writes that you "never quit something with great long-term potential just because you can't deal with the stress of the moment." You need to stay on course.

Bill Simmons went through the Dip during his career and he didn't quit his goal to make it as a columnist. He stuck with it. He pushed through the Dip. I agree with Godin in that "there is a long slog between starting and mastery,"[17] but, like Bill, you need to commit to becoming the best in the world at what you are doing. Know, too, that when others in your field give up, it creates opportunities and openings for you.

But there's a flip side to all this. If you find you just aren't passionate about your idea, your work, or your product, it's okay to quit. You want to be the best in the world at what you do, but if you don't have that passion, it's not worth it to keep trying. Find something else to be the best in the world at doing. By quitting, you will free up your own mind space to focus on what you want to master.

Actions to Commit to Your Idea for the Long Haul

1. Determine if you're in this for the long haul. Look inward to find out if you want to be the best in the world at what you do. Decide if you're going to stick with what you're doing. If not, it's okay to quit. Only you can decide if it's something you want to persevere through.

2. When you reach a tough spot when launching your idea, analyze if you're in the Dip and just going through a rough patch. Consider that everyone has a rocky path to success, and it's not easy to build a community. It's okay to quit your idea if you want to be the best in the world at something else. Brainstorm a list of other ideas you might want to pursue if your first one doesn't work out. Don't get too detailed about this; just sketch out ideas that interest you or otherwise might be a good fit for your talents.

BONUS STORY

The Pivot with Troy Carter

When you walk into Troy Carter's Atom Factory office space in the Culver City neighborhood of Los Angeles, you immediately sense a cool mash-up of culture. The library, where we chatted, features a sleek and modern fully stocked bar toward the back. The walls and shelves are blanketed with awards, posters, and artwork, including a framed photo of Neil Armstrong walking on the moon, and numerous moon man statues Troy won from the MTV Music Awards. There is a smooth leather couch emblazoned with an American flag imprint, and after a couple of glances I noticed his silver coffee table spelled out L-O-V-E.

Many in the Los Angeles entertainment industry know Troy from his work in music management, successfully helping navigate the careers of Eve, Lady Gaga, and John Legend. Others in the

Silicon Valley technology industry know of his tech investments in companies like Warby Parker, Uber, and Dropbox. He's seamlessly intersected the worlds of entertainment and technology like few in the business world today, and the key to his success has been his ability to pivot—meaning his willingness to evolve his career throughout his life, sometimes re-calibrating his career into a bold new direction.

Born in 1972, Troy grew up in West Philadelphia in a poorer part of the city and dropped out of high school as a teenager. Growing up, he said if "I want[ed] sneakers, I can't go, 'Hey Mom, I want Air Jordans' or anything like that because we didn't have the money to be able to afford those." Troy's parents divorced when he was two years old and when Troy was seven, his father shot and killed his new wife's brother after an argument. After twelve years in prison, Troy's father rebuilt his life, and now Troy calls him his hero.[18]

Yet while Troy's dad was in prison Troy learned quickly how to make money on his own. Whether cutting grass in the summer or shoveling snow in the winter, this entrepreneurial "hustle" as he calls it eventually brought him a middle-school side gig promoting house parties in his neighborhood. "My friends had a speakeasy in the basement of their house [that] their father built," Troy told me, "and he was a doctor by day and at night he had this after-hours illegal spot. But we promoted parties there from about nine until midnight." This promotional skill would serve him well later in life.

Around this time, the Fresh Prince (Will Smith) and DJ Jazzy Jeff were one of Philly's prized hip-hop duos. Inspired, Troy and his friends formed a hip-hop group called 2 Too Many. "If we ever meet Jazzy Jeff and the Fresh Prince, they are going to give us a record deal," Troy told me his crew naively thought. Eventually 2 Too Many met their idols, and Smith and Jazzy Jeff took the group under their wing. Troy said that's when reality hit him: "We found out really quickly that we weren't that talented, [but I] wanted to just really be around music and learn about the business." With his sense of self-awareness, this was his career first pivot.

When I asked Troy about the advice he'd give new artists wanting to become the next Lady Gaga or new entrepreneurs hoping to build the next Warby Parker, he recommended that people should not be afraid to pivot. "You need to develop that personal internal gauge that tells you when it's time to pivot," he told me. "I was really passionate about being an artist and wanting to do it, but I really understood when it was time that this thing [wasn't] quite for me." Troy understood that his passion to perform drove him to a certain spot in his career, but ultimately he channeled his passion into other business-related work around music. Troy's internal gauge helped him to see the road ahead: "I still want to be in this [music] space and I still love music. I still want to be a part of it, but I think it's time for me to switch gears."

Years later in Philly, Troy honed his chops by promoting rap shows for heavy-hitter hip-hop artists like Wu-Tang Clan, Jay Z, Foxy Brown, and Biggie Smalls (who later became Notorious B.I.G.). He always had a strong ability to size people up. "I think that's just part of coming from where I come from," he told me. "You better be good at sizing people up, that's just part of it. You come from tough neighborhoods, you've got to be able to read a room . . . [and] be able to sense bad situations."

Troy's promotion business booked shows in local nightclubs and banquet halls, and one night he had a show on the UPenn campus with Biggie Smalls, who at the time was being managed by Sean "Puff" Combs. But much to Troy's frustration, Biggie was a no-show for the gig. However frustrating this was, Troy thought that Biggie and Puff showed character with the refund and he told Puff, "I want to come work for you." Troy ultimately went to work for Puff's Bad Boy Records and was mentored by Kirk Burrowes, the president of the company at the time.

Troy has survived to live many lives in music. After working for James Lassiter's Overbrook Entertainment Company, James fired Troy. And after working with the rapper Eve for eight years, she fired him. And after years of success with Lady GaGa, he and she split up. Like many in the Influencer Economy, he has dealt with rejection and moved onto bigger opportunities.

Maybe that's why Troy wasn't content just working in music. He was curious about tech and Silicon Valley, so he embarked on the next major pivot of his career. He was introduced to some of the most successful investors and entrepreneurs in that region and went on to learn more about tech culture. As he put it, "I think a lot of people up there up in the valley, there [are] a lot of music lovers, and I think they were curious about our world and what we do. So it's kind of like us landing on Mars and us finding life on Mars."

Pivoting is also about seizing new opportunities and taking risks with new endeavors, which is how Troy moved over to tech so seamlessly. In 2015, Troy and his Atom Factory team launched Smashd Labs, a start-up accelerator at the intersection of tech and media, in addition to founding Cross Culture Ventures, a venture capital group that invests in start-ups at the early stage of their careers. With some of the entrepreneurs he works with, he notices that when they pivot, "it's like their company might be going one way and all of a sudden [one] day they make a switch and then all of a sudden they're on fire." The same can be true for most artists and creative people in the Influencer Economy. They have to have a vision, but they also have to remain flexible and open to new opportunities.

Chapter 7

Capture Lightning in a Bottle

"Some are born great, some achieve greatness, and some have greatness thrust upon them."

—William Shakespeare

Chapter Playbook

The final element of the "Share" step of the Influencer Economy is how to capture lightning in a bottle. Capturing lightning in a bottle is when you experience a burst of attention and popularity and use that moment to accelerate your audience growth to new levels. It's when you start to come into your own as a leader in your field. When it occurs, your platform, products, and website need to be ready in order to take full advantage of the opportunity.

Capturing your lightning moment stems from both community and influencer collaborations. With the latter, it involves leveraging your new status to collaborate with bigger fish in your pond. With the former, it goes back to the one principle that's threaded through the Influencer Economy ecosystem perhaps more than any other—finding and nurturing your core community.

Once your idea starts gaining an audience, a group will emerge that I call your micro-community. We have talked about how you need to rally your friends and fellow early adopters, and from that group your micro-community will form. This group will become your most loyal supporters, backers, and subscribers, the heart and soul of your effort. Pay attention to what they want and reward them for their support, as this is the group who will have your back for the long haul. This is an active step. You need to lean into your micro-community and listen to this core audience. Ask them questions to reveal who they are, plan in-person meet-ups, and even give them free stuff when you can. Your micro-community already knows a lot about you, and these gestures will help you get to know them.

A German DJ caught his lightning in a bottle and worked his tail off afterward to serve his micro-community with creative community and influencer collaboration.

Flula Borg

Many aspiring actors, musicians, and artists from around the world chase success in America by trying to start new lives in Hollywood. But because they're off the bus from much farther away than Nebraska, problematic visas occasionally force these talented folks to return home sooner than they might wish. Flula Borg, a native of Erlangen, Germany, found himself in a predicament in 2007 when he was deported back to his home country due to a work visa situation. Known simply as Flula, or DJ Flula, he shies away from discussing the details that led to his leaving Los Angeles while pursuing a music and possible on-camera career nearly a decade ago. "Long story, yah. This is two beers—five beers. We need *five* beers for this story."

But what happened next is pure Flula and another instance of how the Influencer Economy creates surprising, if not life-changing opportunities. To cheer himself up after his deportation setback, Flula used his mobile phone to make a techno music video in which he stars, rocking a black turtleneck and dancing with his grandfather ("Opa"), two fluffy poodles, a kebob sandwich, and other partners in his Bavarian hometown. The video, "Flula in Germany,"

received about 2,000 views when it first appeared on the DJ Flula
YouTube channel. Those aren't numbers to yodel about. But four
years later it was posted on Reddit, which bills itself as the "front
page of the Internet," and quickly amassed 400,000 views. By then,
Flula had been able to return to Los Angeles, though he hadn't yet
figured out how making music videos and pursuing his other DJ
endeavors might steadily attract a large following.

"Like *boom*, look at this" was how Flula described the sudden
effect of Reddit on his YouTube views. *Boom!* is a favorite word of
Flula's, the one he uses to start many videos—just as "everybody
dance!" is a frequent sign-off, as if he hopes his audience will keep
the party going on its own. "I was realizing this is the path. I think
for me you can try other things, but YouTube you have control. You
can make things how you like it. That was my start, and I realized,
great, every week I shall now make a video. Minimum one video.
I'm Flula, so Tuesday is 'Fluesday,' and so Fluesday, new video."

Define Your Micro-Community

A micro-community is the initial community that develops after
you start to thrive in the digital economy. This group forms after
your earliest adopters have come on board, and you have to work
hard to serve and meet its needs. When Flula caught lightning in a
bottle with his burst of viral popularity, he was motivated as a creator to make more videos and start to deliver more to his growing
community. You've got your lightning in a bottle. Now what? Some
creators on these digital platforms catch a short wave of success
before losing their focus, but influencers such as Flula understand
that uploading regular work is vital to growing your audience. Flula
now has around one million YouTube subscribers and roughly 100
million total views, along with high-profile interview and hosting
gigs, television roles, and a movie career thanks to performances in
Pitch Perfect 2, Killing Hasselhoff, and more.

Consistency about posting content for his fans was just the start. Flula was also quick to give them rewards: T-shirts to the people who watched him initially on Reddit, and now an eclectic line of merchandise for sale. In the market for sunglasses attached to a bandana with a binder clip? Try Flula's "Shadeanas" for $12.99. There's also his "Flalendar: the Flula Kalendar" featuring photos of Flula and a dozen different dogs for each month of the year. "I am loving pooches so very hard," he says.

Where Flula's lilting Bavarian accent and eyebrow-raising English is concerned, he is very much in on the joke, particularly as it plays with an American audience. As for Flula, it helps to think of him as a devotee of '80s and '90s American pop culture and hip-hop. He was a German kid who beatboxed growing up, loving Michael Jackson and LL Cool J, then producing his own songs while working as a DJ at the local beer halls. His first trip to America was as a foreign exchange student, where he spent a semester at the University of North Carolina at Chapel Hill. He was even the mascot of the UNC men's basketball team, the Tar Heels, donning the ram costume of "Rameses" for eight games.

Today, when asked to describe what he does for a living, Flula has the same trouble as other influencers who wear many hats. "I would say musician is really my only thing, but the world is different now. You have all these mediums. You have video, you have live things, and so I just use everything. People also will say, 'Oh, you're a comedian!' I don't know what I'm doing; I'm just making things. If people are liking it for a reason that's funny, or weird, or who knows what? Great." This is the Jay Z Effect in action, where Flula appears on YouTube in videos that he writes or improvises, films, and edits himself, then uploads—along with performing live and on other platforms.

But it's hard to say where Flula would be now if the Reddit community hadn't responded so positively to his old deportation/

homecoming video. He might still have found an audience eventually, but Reddit's contribution to his sudden popularity, as well as other people that the website has "discovered," is itself a fascinating phenomenon. The site has a reach of over a billion unique visitors a month and may be best known for its "Ask Me Anything" (AMA) content, essentially a crowdsourced forum for users to ask famous or noteworthy people whatever they want. Everyone from President Obama to the porn actress Nina Hartley has subjected themselves to questions from the site's registered members. "Ask Me Anything" is one of many "subreddits" that cover a range of topics and rely on "redditors," the site's users, to post links from elsewhere on the web related to current events, television shows, or anything that might appeal to these individual Reddit communities. People can also vote posts up or down, which means that sometimes a video or other content is plucked from obscurity and quickly becomes Internet front-page news.

Creatively Brand Your Ideas

But if your goal is to make sharable content that can build out your platform, or even attract an audience that may one day support you financially, the path of Flula Borg is again worth considering. He wasn't precious about the videos he made and posted each "Fluesday" because he played down his 2011 exposure on Reddit. In regard to putting out weekly content, warts and all, Flula said, "You're not Garth Brooks. You're Johnny Schnoop Schnoop. I just learn to make a video. Just make it. And then people shall tell you if it is terrible or not because many times I do not know." Also, the truth is that people are watching far less live content these days. They're binge-watching videos on their own schedules, which means that it's important to give them as much of your work as possible to catch up on. "On-demand is where the viewership is," said Shira Lazar, host of YouTube's *What's*

Trending. "It's about building up your archive." It doesn't matter if your audience is watching your content months or years after you've made it. If you're not willing to just start creating work, and consistently add more, no one can watch your progress or cheer you on as you grow.

Making a new music video each week was kind of a stretch for Flula, so he also began to post vlogs, or "flogs," as he calls his video blogs. Many of these are musings on English words and phrases that Flula pretends to find bizarre. "Jennifer Is a Party Pooper," "Daddy Long Legs," and other improvised monologues have clocked millions of views from people, including English teachers and their students, who enjoy watching Flula act confused about American idioms. It was another happy accident. If Flula hadn't honored his promise to give his fans weekly content, he wouldn't have cooked up this other extremely popular comedy playlist.

Meanwhile, Flula is actually branding his own terms with those "Fluesdays," "flogs," and similar Flula-speak. Not that he thinks of himself as a brand. "I'm just Flula. Which sounds like a kind of species," he suggested. But just as Hannah Hart has her "Hartosexuals," and "Tease it!" is big within the Rooster Teeth lexicon, the many Flula phrases on his YouTube channel and beyond help to give his community ownership of all things Flula. That's a win for any creator who wants an audience to feel like they have a special connection to the identity underlying the content. Whether it's the perks in the form of those T-shirts, calendars, and other Flula Borg merchandise, or his personalized catchphrases, Flula has built himself a world that offers his community many ways to feel included. You'd be right if you guessed there's also a financial incentive to creating a cool bond with your audience, especially your core supporters.

Embracing Kevin Kelly's 1,000 True Fans Principle

Kevin Kelly, the founding executive editor of *Wired*, writes about the value of finding the "true fans" who can sustain your efforts. "Assume conservatively that your True Fans will each spend one day's wages per year in support of what you do. That 'one-day-wage' is an average, because of course your truest fans will spend a lot more than that. Let's peg that *per diem* each True Fan spends at $100 per year. If you have 1,000 fans, that sums up to $100,000 per year, which minus some modest expenses, is a living for most folks. One thousand is a feasible number. You could count to 1,000. If you added one fan a day, it would take only three years. True Fanship is doable."[1]

Kelly thinks that pleasing a true fan encourages the creator to remain consistent and disciplined, to focus on the unique aspects of their work and the qualities that true fans appreciate. But Flula Borg tries to strike a balance between giving his hard-core fans more of what they expect from him and not becoming a caricature of himself. His idea of making something that's a departure from previous work has its own logic. "You have to not be so different that you lose everyone. I will still be Flula. I will still be German. I will still love techno. I cannot all of the sudden be a Bolivian hillbilly who speaks Afrikaans."

Stepping Up Your Collaboration Game

Flula's love of techno music is definitely not a pose, and it created a useful opportunity to introduce himself to a mainstream audience. When the cast of *Anchorman 2* appeared at a press junket to promote their movie, Flula got five minutes with Will Ferrell and the rest of the ensemble—but as his own flavor of entertainment. Instead of doing a traditional interview to post on his YouTube channel, Flula orchestrated a "techno banger" in which the cast supplied the sounds he later mixed into another viral video hit. The actress Christina Applegate looks a bit startled when Flula begins their session by shouting his customary "Bang!" "That's your thing,"[2] she quickly realizes.

When watching the video, you get the sense that these movie stars may not be familiar with the Flula phenomenon—a case of Hollywood looking to get more comfortable with the whole You-Tube thing, especially if it helps to introduce a new film to the hard-to-reach millennial crowd. *Star Wars: The Force Awakens*, *The Hunger Games* franchise, and many other tent-pole releases are working with YouTube channels on content marketing strategies, even opening up movie sets and making actual costumes and props available to creators for videos. It's not at all surprising that Flula would be in the mix for these opportunities, and while they also expose him to new audiences, his YouTube collabs with other digital content influencers have been the most direct route to gaining more subscribers for his own channel.

"You need some milk, you need some flour, and you need some eggs," Flula told Hannah Hart when he appeared on her *My Drunk Kitchen* YouTube show. Together they make spätzle, "Like tiny tiny dumplings."[3] They also drink a lot of German beer. It's hard to overstate the importance of the collab when trying to grow your audience, and YouTube navigation encourages viewers to click over to related channels so that creators on the platform can easily benefit each other. Hannah Hart, Grace Helbig, Chester See, and other YouTubers with more subscribers than Flula have all worked with him, extending their coattails and getting some love in exchange from Flula's fans. His *Auto Tunes* series on his own channel finds Flula in a car doing song covers with the above YouTube stars and everyone else, from Sir Mix-A-Lot ("Baby Got Back") to Flula's basketball hero, Dirk Nowitzki

(Rolling Stones' "Satisfaction" accompanied by two Dallas Maverick cheerleaders).

Ever since redditors up-voted Flula to Internet acclaim, he seems like he is doing just fine. *Pitch Perfect 2*, the comedy in which Flula plays the evil lead singer of Das Sound Machine, a German a cappella group, earned almost $300 million in worldwide box office the summer of its release. He has more movie and television roles coming his way even as he continues to make YouTube videos. Talk about free speech, in one of his *Auto Tunes* bits, Flula drives to a supermarket and mixes his own version of "The Fox (What Does the Fox Say?)" by Ylvis, singing at the top of his lungs as incredulous shoppers stare at him in the parking lot. The video inches him closer to the late, great Andy Kaufman's sensibility, if Andy sounded like Brüno Gehard and wore a fanny pack and headphones. "For me," Flula says, "I like to try things that do not work. I cannot really sing so great. I cannot be Brad Pitt. But I would love to do that. I fit every place because I fit no place."

Flula caught lightning in a bottle and engineered a way to harness that energy and build a sustained micro-community that he still serves every Fluesday.

Influencer Economy Lessons: What Flula Borg Can Teach You About Capturing Lightning in a Bottle

Lesson 1: Define Your Micro-Community

When you start growing and scaling up your idea, your micro-community will emerge. These loyal backers, supporters, and subscribers are the group that you need to create stuff for.
It took me well over a year to pinpoint my micro-community as I was hosting the podcast and writing this book. It formed around start-up entrepreneurs in areas like tech, e-commerce, and small

businesses. Think of your micro-community as the archetypes of your audience, the main types of people who love what you do. I had to actively meet, chat with, and collaborate with my audience to discover who this group was. Eventually, I found a micro-community of three types of people:

- ❖ Those who wanted to leave their traditional corporate day job to launch a start-up.
- ❖ Those who worked for a start-up and wanted to eventually build their own company.
- ❖ Those who worked in a stable profession that they liked, but wanted to launch a side project.

After identifying this core group, I started building my work around their needs, and soon I realized these people were just like me. I created *The Influencer Economy* as a playbook for them, one I wish I had when I started. I wanted to synthesize the stories of successful creators and entrepreneurs, with actionable lessons, that could be understood by everyone with a big idea. Because the micro-community is the subsection of your audience who your idea is made for, they will often teach you more about your idea than any other group in your community. They help define your efforts.

Unlike Flula, most of us will never land on the front page of Reddit. But like Flula, we all have our Reddit-like opportunities where we can get a burst of new eyeballs on our idea. When you capture your Flula moment, you have to do everything in your power and work your butt off to sustain it. There's no guarantee it will hit, but if and when it does, be ready. You need to have the technology, ideas, and support behind you to succeed.

Most of us work hard to collaborate with our communities to achieve growth "brick by brick," as you've heard me say often. But when your product launches, you need to ask yourself:

❖ "Am I ready for success?"

❖ "Do I have a back-end strategy for my website to make money?"

❖ "Can I make the time to work longer hours to make my idea work?"

❖ "Am I willing to dedicate the amount of effort it takes to be the best in the world in my field?"

Flula became the creator that he wanted to be due to a viral moment, but as you start building community, you'll soon discover how hard it is to find even a couple of fans for anything you create. And when considering Kevin Kelly's philosophy of finding a thousand "true fans," it becomes an even steeper challenge. But when you do find your micro-community, consider them your lifeline to sustaining a business around your idea. They are your community leaders, top customers, and people who will support you at all times.

For this final principle of the building-community step of the Influencer Economy, I want you to think realistically about your business. Start thinking more and more about products and revenue streams. It's hard to make a living just from your core supporters' enthusiasm for your creativity. Turning these people into paying customers is a delicate balance, but it can transform your business and life when executed properly. You don't want to spam people. As Mom Williams used to tell me, "Treat others how you want to be treated." No one likes spam.

Also, don't set yourself up for failure by miscalculating how many true fans you can reach. Don't think your business is suddenly thriving just because you have a big community. Having 10,000 community members doesn't mean that a thousand of them will buy a product from you. When you build a community, assume that less than 10 percent of that group will convert to paying customers. Don't overestimate your influence.

Actions to Define Your Micro-Community

1. Discover who your micro-community is by engaging with and getting to know your community better. Do something that allows you a chance to talk to members of the group. You could organize a community meet-up for getting to know people IRL (in real life, the subject of chapter 9). Or you can host a giveaway—people like free stuff—and ask them questions along the way. Your micro-community already knows you, so invest in getting to know them. Provide something of value for them that allows you to deepen the connection and gives you a better understanding of their interests and expectations.

2. Determine if your website is able to handle a massive spike in traffic. Don't let your website crash when things really start to take off. If you start scaling up your big idea, be prepared for when it hits. Success is awesome, but you need your tech to be 100 percent ready.

3. Ask your community to take a survey about how you can help better serve them. Write to your e-mail list, make a call to action in your videos, or otherwise reach out to your community through your preferred channel. Survey, in a nice way, if they'd want to buy a book from you, or if they're interested in an event to meet with you and other members of the community, or if they would want some type of private coaching (if you're in the business field). Don't worry about it seeming pushy or moneygrubbing; just make it authentic and ask what they'd like you to do to help them. Then, sit back and listen.

Lesson 2: Creatively Brand Your Ideas

When trying to make your mark in the Influencer Economy, you want to create stuff that people want to share to their networks. Creatively branding your ideas into shareable content can help you grow your audience. You want people to tell their friends about your stuff via digital platforms like text messages, Facebook posts, or e-mails. You want people to share your idea to their own communities.

Flula did a fantastic job cleverly branding himself. Every Tuesday he posted a video, calling that day "Fluesday." And he added a personal touch to his vlog videos, calling them "flogs." This creative Flula-speak also contributed to his Flalendar, which is his hilarious calendar, and his *Auto Tunes* segments, which are him singing in his car with other YouTubers or people of note. He made his YouTube videos stand out with fun and interesting naming choices. And he also mailed out free T-shirts and schwag to fans as a thank-you for their support.

Sharable content works in two ways:

- ❖ *It makes the recipient feel smarter.* Often this entails handy information delivered in a new or funny way. You share it with your friends to help make them smarter too.

- ❖ *It makes the recipient feel good.* You laugh, smile, or enjoy it. You share it with your friends to give them the same feelings.

Flula's videos are the latter. He makes you feel good and makes you laugh. He also did a great job creating merch—the calendar, T-shirts, and other schwag with personalized catchphrases like *Boom!*. He made his merch memorable and catchy, which helped form a personal connection with his community and spread his message. While his community loves to go along with him on the ride of all his fun ideas, Flula gladly keeps them as wingman while they are part of the journey.

Having a clever idea goes a long way in the Influencer Economy. You don't need to be incredibly witty, just clever enough that it sticks in people's minds.

Actions to Creatively Brand Your Ideas

1. Determine how you can creatively brand your ideas. Think about what type of content you will create for your community. (At this point, you should already be giving stuff to them regularly.) Define if you're making people feel good, making them feel smarter, or both. If you can communicate a combination of the two, you will be better in the long run.

2. Come up with your own versions of Fluesdays, Flalendars, and flogs. Create your own language or nomenclature that gives your followers something to remember. Think about something simple enough that can be hashtagged in social media.

3. Decide if you want to make and sell merch. If so, make stickers, T-shirts, hats, or any other branded merchandise to give away or eventually sell to your fans. Remember the T-Shirt Rule from chapter 2—every logo you create needs to look cool on a T-shirt.

BONUS STORY

Franchesca Ramsey Captures Her Moment

In 2012, Franchesca Ramsey's life went viral. Literally. Her video "Shit White Girls Say to Black Girls" took off like wildfire across the Internet. She had a lightning in a bottle moment as the video gained a million views in one day and six million views in a week.

It landed on the front page of major heavy-hitter media websites like MSNBC, the BBC, and MTV. Even Anderson Cooper's talk show booked her as a featured guest to discuss why the video resonated with audiences and why it also made people upset. She told me that her success was "ridiculous, and there was no way to prepare for it."

Franchesca had been making and posting videos for six years as a fun hobby to pay her cell phone bill and buy some nice clothes from her "YouTube money," but this sudden notoriety was a game changer. After the amazing popularity of her video, a multitude of career opportunities were suddenly knocking at her door. Franchesca soon quit her nine-to-five day job as a graphic designer, got an agent, worked on a TV pilot, went on a college speaking tour, had a potential book deal, and considered some big new career opportunities.

When I asked Franchesca how she describes herself when she meets people at parties, she said she calls herself an actress, comedian, activist, and YouTube creator. Her YouTube videos often take important subjects that are difficult to talk about and find creative ways to address them through humor.

"Shit White Girls Say to Black Girls" is emblematic of her disarmingly edgy approach. It features Franchesca in a blonde wig, speaking directly to the camera, saying one-liners in a series of quick-cutting scenes. Her character makes a series of fast, flippant comments like:

- ❖ "That's so ghetto."
- ❖ "Not to be racist, but . . ."
- ❖ "Can I touch your hair?"
- ❖ "Well, how come you can say the N word but if I say it, it's racist?"

The video is a blend of pop culture commentary and comedy, to make people both laugh and think. The reaction? In the digital age, as my friend Aaron Dodez says, "Online comments are like the modern-day Roman Colosseum," and in this case, the comments were either laughing hysterically at her comedy or calling it racist—there was virtually no middle ground. But being the only black person in her community growing up in Florida, and dealing with some of these insensitive questions that are oftentimes very unintentionally hurtful, she made the video because it was real life to her.

Looking back, Franchesca is not sure she was equipped to handle the sudden success. The popularity she achieved was overwhelming. But after the Hollywood TV pilot flaked out, the book never materialized, and the college touring stopped, Franchesca didn't know what was next.

Back then there was no playbook for success in the digital age. There wasn't a blueprint for how to capitalize on the moment when your viral video popped online. Now, if a creator reaches a huge career milestone, they can do like others have before them and come out with new merchandise to sell, or collab with other YouTube creators on a trip to LA, or create a regular content schedule. Back then it was more the Wild West, so if your video popped it was kind of a crapshoot to figure out your longer-term strategy.

Even though Franchesca wasn't sure how she would maintain her success, ultimately she just kept making videos on YouTube. Her hard work and comedic timing paid off—in 2015, MTV, the same company which featured her "Shit White Girls Say to Black Girls" on their homepage, hired her to create the YouTube show *Decoded*, where she mixes her sensibilities on social issues and humor to continue to explore difficult issues. Over time, Franchesca took the long view toward her YouTube career and she not only enjoys creating videos ("the biggest thing is doing the work because I love it," she told me), she puts in the hard work that a lot of people don't ever commit to. And she offered this perspective: "It can be really hard to stay motivated because in creative fields, you hear 'no' a lot. It takes a long time for people to get on board with what you're doing. You have to believe in yourself, and a big part of that is enjoying the work."

Looking back after all that viral success and the work that went into her career afterwards, she is calm and cool about it all. As she told me, "I ended up where I needed to be. I'm exactly where I am supposed to be." And where is that? In 2016, she began working as a writer/contributor to Comedy Central's *The Nightly Show with Larry Wilmore*, which hired her for her varied and creative background.

Ultimately Franchesca wasn't chasing fame or money like some succumb to when they reach a critical moment of online success. It can be tempting to chase superficial rewards. Franchesca was grounded, and she told me that as a kid, she aspired to be honest, smart, and funny. Ultimately her career landed where it needed to be and those values ring true. She captured her lightning in a bottle after taking the long view with her work, and now she thrives in the digital age.

Lesson 3: Step Up Your Collaboration Game

Coffee is no longer just for closers. It's all about collaboration in the digital era. Stop asking to buy someone you look up a cup of coffee to "pick their brain," or ask for "career advice." Instead, you need to show that you have something to offer *them* as well, and that they should want to participate alongside you as a partner.

We've already talked a lot about how teaming with others is the path to thriving in the Influencer Economy. When lightning strikes, you need to make it easy for people who want to collaborate with you to connect with you. Are you giving people a venue to collaborate? As web video impresario Shira Lazar told me, in this era it's all about having an "on-demand" channel. People need to look you up and understand what your point of view is toward the world. When someone visits your platform, they need to get a feel for what moves you, makes you, and, more importantly, what makes them want to collaborate with you. When someone googles your name or idea, give them something awesome to see that makes them want to join your movement. The spotlight's on you now; this is your time to thrive.

When you experience your lightning in a bottle moment, it will be much easier for you to collaborate with others. By collaborating with fellow YouTubers like Hannah Hart and Grace Helbig and with various personalities in his *Auto Tunes* bits, Flula was ultimately able to reach celebrities like Will Ferrell and Paul Rudd and create fun "techno banger" remix videos around their movie press junkets. The collaboration was a two-way street, because these actors were seen with a popular YouTuber who was on the cutting edge of Internet culture.

The Reverse Oprah Effect

When you collab with well-known influencers, you can draft off their success by sharing the insights you learned from them. Whether it's posting an interview on a blog or podcast or simply writing a summary of conversations you've had with people whom you look up to, it's up to you to share your collabs with the world.

I love a concept commonly known as the Oprah Effect. The theory is that when a business or person appeared on *The Oprah Winfrey Show*, Oprah's endorsement very often accelerated their influence and success. A great example of this was when the founders of Twitter appeared on her show. After she signed up for Twitter, a network effect occurred and the app experienced a massive surge in popularity. This has also happened with her Book Club and her year-end "Oprah's Favorite Things" shows where she gave away products to the audience. Oprah's network TV show was extremely popular back in the day, and her platform was big enough to help others grow their influence when they appeared on her show. She had power and could effectively anoint kings and queens of business and industry based just on them appearing on her show.

But there's also something that I call the Reverse Oprah Effect. It starts when a more influential or famous person in your field collabs with you on your chosen platform, accelerating your visibility, influence, and success. In the digital age, when someone like Will Ferrell appeared in Flula's YouTube video, it gave Flula a bump in more mainstream credibility. But it cut both ways: when Ferrell appeared in Flula's video, it gave his movie some street cred in the YouTube community. When you collab with a larger influencer, remember that you too can offer them a new type of credibility. Even if your platform is relatively small, be confident in your work, and realize that you can add value to influencers as much as they can help you gain influence.

Actions to Step Up Your Collaboration Game

1. Identify and reach out to bigger influencers you can collaborate with now that you have captured lightning in a bottle. Consider more mainstream influencers as well, like Flula did when he reached out to Will Ferrell and Paul Rudd. Build a road map to reach your ultra-influencers now that you have a degree of notoriety to exploit.

2. Send an e-mail or make content asking your micro-community who they think you should collaborate with. Remember, these are your heart-and-soul community members. You should listen to them.

.

Step 3: Thrive

The leaders of the Influencer Economy have all launched their ideas, shared them with the world, and thrived. They have thrived because Step 3 is all about doing just that—opening doors for other people, making and meeting friends IRL (in real life), and giving your community ownership of your idea. This is a more sophisticated step because the mechanics start to kick in once your community is more evolved.

Once you've achieved a degree of success in the digital age, you need to lead by giving to others. By opening doors and giving to others without expecting anything in return, you reap all sorts of benefits. Nearly 100 percent of my podcast guests are givers and more specifically, they give to both their peers and their community. Treating your peers and community with respect and being generous with them is paramount to your success.

To thrive in the Influencer Economy, you also need to transcend your online relationships and transfer them into bigger in real life (IRL) friendships. Sure, these days everyone is accessible via e-mail, social media, or other digital connections, but it's important to connect IRL to forge deeper connections. Hop in your car to meet that client face-to-face, get on an airplane to attend the conference in your business category, put yourself out there to shake people's hands to say hi. There's nothing better than looking someone in the eye to make a meaningful connection. And once you meet others in your field, make friends with them. Making friends is more important than "building relationships." We all want to work with people whom we like, so you need to build these partnerships IRL. Finally, to thrive, leaders give their community ownership of their idea.

With my podcast I have worked hard to open doors for others and give first to help people get what they want. I also make intros and connections to help serve others simply for the sake of doing so. I also focus on hosting meet-ups when I travel to new cities, and love connecting with community members IRL. When you give to your community, amazing things will happen.

Chapter 8

Open Doors for Others

"You can have everything you want in life
if you just help enough people get what
they want in life."

—Zig Ziglar

Chapter Playbook

There is something that I call "the System." It's based on the premise that helping people and expecting nothing in return is the best business model for life. Without question, the successes that I've had in life come from helping other people achieve their goals. The process of helping others is what makes me succeed. That in itself is rewarding. When you provide something of value, like knowledge or an introduction to someone, and? ?you accept that you will get *nothing* in return, you're just doing it. Why? Because that's what good people do.

It's amazing how one introduction can change everything for someone's business. All it takes is you opening one door and from that single opportunity, 10 more doors will open. When you meet with people, focus on long-term relationships and friendships rather than quick deals. And always look for opportunities to help others along the way, just for the sake of it. That includes not only your peers but the people in your community. After all, they're the ones who got you to where you are in the first place.

There is general advice that I follow: on average I should make at least two introductions a week to like-minded people. Why? When you help others connect to become friends or do business together, you not only strengthen your connection with those people, but it generally feels good to help others. When thinking about making intros for people in both business or in life, consider if the people you're helping can add value to the other person's life. And don't ask for anything in return after making the intro. It took me a few years to accept this, but it's been one of the best choices I've made for my career.

There's an Austin-based digital production studio run by a guy who believes in the System and treats his community like gold along the way.

Burnie Burns

I got pretty lucky when Burnie Burns agreed to chat with me on my podcast in December of 2013. He was literally my first guest, and it would have been understandable if he had put me off until I was more seasoned as a podcaster. But that's not Burnie. He knew that I had once worked in the YouTube and gaming industry, which has been very good to him for the past dozen years. He's also someone who really grasps the importance of growing his audience by helping others to do the same thing. We spoke at the YouTube Space in Los Angeles—in a hallway where I could set up my microphone recorder and talk to Burnie about Rooster Teeth Productions, the Austin-based home of his pioneering digital studio. The event was Shira Lazar's Tube-A-Thon fundraiser for a homeless shelter in LA and featured numerous YouTube and online video stars who rallied together for a good cause.

Much of Burnie's success as creative director, writer, and actor is due to a groundbreaking web series known as *Red vs. Blue*. One of the largest fan-fiction projects of all time, *Red vs. Blue* is part of a slate of animation and gaming-related content on RoosterTeeth.com, a site with 1.6 million registered users. The company's YouTube channels—which Burnie and his team mainly use to syndicate their series programming, podcasts, news shows, live-action shorts, and instructional "Let's Play" videos—has more than 16 million subscribers and 3 billion views.

In this book, I talk about how old notions of coddled celebrities rarely mingling with their audience don't apply to people like Burnie Burns or Rooster Teeth. As with other leading influencers, at online video events or gatherings like Comic-Con and E3, Burnie gets a lot of love. He comes off as a broad-shouldered teddy bear with a scruffy beard and welcoming smile. At VidCon, the annual YouTube and online video convention at the Anaheim Conference Center, he tweeted his location and was soon mobbed by friendly fans wanting his autograph or a selfie with him.

Burnie knows that opening doors for others is paramount to success. At the Tube-A-Thon, he went out of his way to introduce me to the event's host, Shira Lazar of *What's Trending* on YouTube. Shira ended up being my guest on another episode of my podcast, as did Freddie Wong, who Burnie also introduced me to at the YouTube Space. You could argue that Rooster Teeth paved the way for Freddie and his company, RocketJump Studios, so it was very cool and generous of Burnie to bring me around to these other well-established folks. Remember, this was before I even had a podcast and years before my book was published. But Burnie didn't care. At the Tube-a-Thon event, I also ran into an old friend, Khail Anonymous, who connected me with Taryn Southern and Flula Borg, all of whom were guests on my up-and-coming podcast.

Burnie and I joked about the irony of being at a YouTube event, a platform that wasn't even around when Rooster Teeth launched its *Red vs. Blue* series back in 2003. Burnie had been a computer science major at the University of Texas and was still living in Austin, running a tech support company called teleNetwork Partners. He was also a gamer and part-time filmmaker.

Together with office mates Geoff Ramsey and Gus Sorola, Burnie filmed a parody video calling out Apple for not having fun built-in games in its computers. "There are a lot of great games on the Mac, like *Warcraft 3* and . . . that puzzle game with the Apple logo," says Sorola in the video.[1] Gus told me that the video worked because "at the time Mac was an easy punching bag and everybody had a friend who used a Mac that they wanted to make fun of." The trio hosted the parody on their short-lived website Drunkgamers.com. Their website was largely an excuse to solicit free games from publishers in exchange for reviews. After the Mac video went viral, Burnie and his Drunk Gamer friends had another idea.

They were all fans of a game called *Halo: Combat Evolved* on Microsoft's industry-leading Xbox platform. *Halo* is a first-person shooter game set in the future in which the player assumes the role of a cyber super-soldier battling aliens on a mysterious new world. Burnie saw the potential to do something different with the game's characters by using machinima, an animation technique referring to machine + cinema. He described the process as "putting dialogue and story to characters in video games. When you play video games, they are intended to be played a certain way, and we worked out a way to play them differently. We took the game of *Halo* and created a new story that we thought was funny. And it took off."

In Burnie's series, the soldiers borrowed from *Halo* wander that game's strange planet in red and blue teams that are ostensibly meant to destroy each other. But the soldiers are openly confused about why they are on this space rock, how their tank works, and the intentions of a Spanish-speaking robot—to name a few of the show's deadpan bits. Burnie and his collaborators voiced the characters themselves and hosted *Red vs. Blue* on their new RoosterTeeth.com website. The first video received 25,000 views. A week later, the next episode reached an audience of 50,000. As word spread, more than 100,000 fans of *Halo* and others curious about this bizarre machinima project viewed the new shorts.

Monetize by Giving People Exclusive Access

"I think it's really flattering and I think it's something that helped Rooster Teeth grow to what it is today," Burnie said of finding his true fans early on. He made content that was personally entertaining and also a slam dunk with this new audience. Burnie's theory for creating videos is to "make content that you'd want to watch and you'd want your friends to watch." When he launched *Red vs. Blue,* he had faith that "there were enough people out there with the same sensibilities."

Burnie wasn't the only one using machinima to tell stories, but he was savvy in his use of online video distribution, which itself was still a niche industry in 2003. By going online, he didn't need film distributors or the Sundance Film Festival, which had actually turned down a feature-length movie that he and Rooster Teeth collaborators Matt Hullum and Joel Heyman had made while they were in college together. Major film festival gatekeepers and other industry middlemen weren't needed any longer, and are even less relevant today. If you want to create content to share with people, you can use your own channels online and through social media to seek a like-minded audience.

Burnie was a computer science major and IT professional with an edge on other web creators because he knew how to encode, host, and spread his own videos to friends via the web. Of course this isn't easy, and it came with a cost, too. When the *Red vs. Blue* soldiers first appeared on RoosterTeeth.com, there were no video ad networks to support online video hosting. Or as Burnie put it, "The ad truck wasn't showing up at your door with a pile of cash." Hosting video was also expensive back then: "There was no way to host or encode a video like there is now. No push-button way to drag or drop videos online. If you had a two-minute video, it was 80 megs, and your location hosting bills were incrementally increasing every time someone else viewed your video." In other words, the more people watched *Red vs. Blue*, the more fees Burnie had to pay. Getting seen or going viral was great for building an audience but bad for the bottom line. And a potentially much bigger problem loomed as the *Red vs. Blue* series grabbed a worldwide following: Was it legal?

Microsoft owns Bungie Inc., the company that makes *Halo*, and had learned of Rooster Teeth's appropriation of its laser-toting characters. A case could be made that the filmmakers were stealing intellectual property and that the video links circulating on the Internet were an unfair use of a game intended only for Xbox consoles. But Burnie told me that the Bungie folks became fans, and stakeholders at Microsoft also had a permissive attitude. "This is something that's different. We don't really get it. But we do know that a lot of people seem to like this" was how Burnie described Microsoft's position. "And we are a company that values innovation. So let's put our money where our mouth is and say that this is an innovative thing and try to support it." Microsoft commissioned an episode of *Red vs. Blue* that premiered at a software-development conference and otherwise got out of Rooster Teeth's way while the production company went on to amass billions of views on the Internet.

Advertising opportunities eventually kicked in on Rooster-Teeth.com, but the company has its dedicated audience to thank for ultimately becoming profitable. Burnie and his team created an annual $30 sponsorship program for advertisement-free access to exclusive content and live streams—all released before the general public can take a look. Just like Amex, membership has its privileges. Sponsors get a star next to their profile names, can purchase Rooster Teeth merch at a discount, and have the satisfaction of knowing that their special relationship with team RT has helped to keep *Red vs. Blue* going for 13 seasons, making it the longest-running web series ever. Other shows on their network include a hugely popular anime series called *Rwby,* the official *RT Podcast,* and *Achievement Hunter,* which has its own website dedicated to "Let's Play" and other gaming videos.

Recruit Your Team from the Community

Barbara Dunkelman, the community manager for Rooster Teeth and a voice actor on *Rwby,* started out as a fan of *Red vs. Blue* who wanted to hang out online with other fans. I also interviewed her for the podcast, and she spoke about member support along with solid friendships that many develop in the world of Rooster Teeth. "I have friends to this day that I made on that community site in October of 2004. Two friends who actually met on the site started dating and got married. I was a bridesmaid at their wedding and now they have a baby. It's stuff like that that just shows the strength of the community relationships people create."

Originally from Montreal, Canada, Barbara knows that relocating to Texas for her dream job isn't a career path that other fans can easily follow. She tends to encourage people to start their own websites or make content that they enjoy rather than hope to rise as she did through Rooster Teeth fandom. "I'm a really bad example," she admits. But her current role is still an inspiring story for those who support RT and spend time in the chat groups and on other member pages.

Like Barbara, virtually everyone who voices characters in the animated shows or appears in live-action videos also holds down a behind-the-scenes job at the company. Barbara's includes serving as codirector of the RTX festival, which is an Austin-based

IRL gaming culture convention that Rooster Teeth created for its fans. When it started in 2011, about 500 people attended *Red vs. Blue* screenings at the Alamo Draft House and found their way to a pool party. The next year, Rooster Teeth moved the conference to the Austin Convention Center to accommodate 4,000 people. By 2014, roughly 30,000 fans came to Texas to meet Barbara, Burnie, Gus Sorola, and the other 90-odd employees of Rooster Teeth. Gus said Rooster Teeth appreciates live events "because they really allow creators to directly connect with their audience." Early on in Rooster Teeth's history Gus said, "we used to attend every event we would hear of in order to try and meet people in order to show them our videos and hope that they'd enjoy them and show their friends." They have taken that spirit to RTX and the event has exploded in popularity.

While it's true that Fullscreen, a massive multichannel network on YouTube, has acquired Rooster Teeth, Burnie and his team have always used their own website as a main hub and continue to make content on their own terms. In a statement on behalf of Matt Hullum, who is now the Rooster Teeth CEO, Burnie emphasized their longstanding creative freedom. "With Fullscreen, we look forward to continuing that tradition in even bigger and better ways. Matt and I are excited about the opportunities this alliance will present for our creators and all the amazing content it will empower them to produce for our audience."[2]

One of Rooster Teeth's smartest moves within this space has been to recruit top talent from other channels. In early 2015, Adam Kovic, Bruce Greene, and several of their colleagues left Machinima's *Inside Gaming*, a popular news show on YouTube, and began covering the same gaming world on a new Rooster Teeth channel called Funhaus. They are two of my former coworkers, and Kovic told me that Burnie is "the pioneer we all look up to. His team is dedicated to the brand of Rooster Teeth, and people love them for it." While years ago, Rooster Teeth brought on the internet-famous creator of Webby nominated "The Slo Mo Guys," Gavin Free from the U.K. to Austin, TX. Gavin, Daniel Gruchy, and their friends star in "The Slow Mo Guys" videos in which they do a lot of crazy stunts, where sometimes they will stick their tongues in mousetraps, other times people will get tasered. It's all in slow motion and the Internet eats up their videos.

It's also true that this Influencer Economy principle continues to drive Rooster Teeth projects. In 2014, Burnie and his team raised over $2.5 million in crowdfunding from fans for the feature-length *Lazer Team*, a live-action sci-fi comedy. Their goal had only been $650,000, which they reached in half a day. By the end of their month-long campaign, more than 37,000 backers helped Rooster Teeth set a crowdfunding record for a film project on Indiegogo. Geoff Ramsey, one of the founders of Rooster Teeth, told me a key to their crowdfunding success was that Rooster "has built up a tremendous amount of goodwill with our audience this last decade or so . . . at least I think we have." And jokes that "it's also possible we just appeal to an audience of really financially irresponsible consumers." Either way, the Rooster Teeth fans know that they won't get taken for granted.

It's no accident that this funding success and Rooster Teeth's goodwill with its audience has all the elements of a creative movement. Burnie is very aware of what can be produced just by finding your "first follower" and treating him or her as an equal—a kind of partner in search of something great that is made collectively.

Treat Your Community as Equals

One of Burnie's favorite videos is from a Derek Sivers' TED Talk on the topic of starting a movement and uses footage showing a shirtless guy enticing a vast group of people to join him dancing in a field. At first, he's alone and looking kind of silly, but one by one, people get up to dance alongside him. What's so striking is that the crazy dancer dude makes a point of acknowledging and appreciating his first follower, which seems to empower that person to invite more folks out to dance.[3] Burnie agrees with Derek's reading of that moment as critical to any movement—when the leader and initial follower are on equal footing, good things happen. And Derek knows a thing or two about building movements, as he started his independent music sales company, CD Baby, in 1998 for $500. After growing it into a $100 million in sales and working with over 150,000 musicians, the company was acquired in 2008 for $22 million. Derek told me that he ultimately gave the acquisition proceeds to a charitable music trust, which aims to create movements for future generations. Similarly if Rooster Teeth's community feels like it's involved in something of a shared undertaking, it's because that spirit of inclusion carries over into their programming.

One example is the *Rooster Teeth Podcast*, which is sometimes recorded in front of a live audience. The show keeps things light but adds a personal touch and behind-the-scenes vibe to what Burnie and Rooster Teeth are up to in Austin, or when they're attending conventions in other cities. Fans learn what the production team thinks about "robot sex" and airport security measures, along with 300 and counting other topics. "We've always kept a very open dialogue with our fans, especially using the podcast," Barbara Dunkelman told me. She is frequently on the show herself and is open to wherever the conversation may go. "We are real people. We want [our audience] to know the real us. We don't want to put on these fake facades and this fake personality. I think our fans really connect with us on a personal level that way."

For the most part, critics and the wider creative community have also been won over. Rooster Teeth's popularity even took a surprising turn as early as 2005 when the Film Society of Lincoln Center chose to screen *Red vs. Blue*. There was highbrow praise for the series. "The literary analog is absurdist drama," said Graham Leggat, former director of communications at the film society and a videogame critic. "It's truly as sophisticated as Samuel Beckett." Even the Sundance Film Festival came around, inviting Burnie and Rooster Teeth to demo their approach to machinima on a panel. While discussing his trip to Sundance with me at the YouTube Space, Burnie said it was a "weird experience" and observed that a lot of the excitement around this style of animation was based on gamers using the characters to literally discuss gameplay. "Commentary over the top of it. It's less become about narrative content, which I really like." Burnie's interest in storytelling uses of computer graphics has earned his company numerous awards, including several from the Academy of Machinima Arts and Sciences, a body that credits Rooster Teeth with taking machinima to a new mass audience.

So, from niche can come great things. Rooster Teeth may not have created machinima, but Burnie Burns and his friends were big and early in the category. In fact, a dozen years ago, gaming itself was thought of as a limited-market pastime for the shy and introverted. That's all changed. An innovative animation idea led to content that made its mark on pop culture and helped to redefine what was possible for the gaming industry. Burnie was out front of a new generation of creators who also started off doing one thing so well that it quickly caught on with an audience. As I've pointed out, Freddie Wong's career owes much to what Rooster Teeth has pulled off. Freddie called Burnie Burns an "OG [original gangster] and the true pioneer in the world of online video and film studios in the web era."

That rooster with its chattering teeth belongs on the Mount Rushmore of the Influencer Economy movement. Burnie himself is a key figure, but he knows he couldn't have gotten to where he is alone. Cofounders Geoff Ramsey, Matt Hullum, Joel Heyman, Gus Sorola, and everyone who shows up for work each day in the Rooster Teeth fold are all creating something that helps to enrich the lives of their fans. And all the gratitude that Rooster Teeth receives started with a series *Red vs. Blue* that Geoff told me "was created to 'hopefully' make our friends laugh. When it spread totally by word of mouth, so quickly, we learned we had a hell of a lot more friends than we thought." In the digital age Rooster Teeth thrives by opening up worlds to friends around the globe.

Influencer School Lessons: What Burnie Burns Can Teach You About Opening Doors for Others

Lesson 1: Make Time to Open Doors for Others

"The System" is when you accept that you will get nothing in return when helping people out. You're just doing it because you believe that you should help others.

Once you build your community, it's important, if not a requisite, to help others to grow their communities and to give them a bigger platform to share their ideas. In reality, it is a powerful way to make someone else's career or life thrive. There is a great TED Talk about the zero sum game model. The zero sum theory is that we can all be winners, and that because I win doesn't mean you lose. Very few of us actually compete directly with one another in business. Oftentimes, pooling resources and building teams like we talked about in chapter 3, "Book Your Own Gigs," can be a win/win for everyone.

From your friend list backing your crowdfunding project, to your high school buddy introducing you to the CEO of the company for your next gig, to the friends you see once a year at SXSW who always test your alpha product—it's all collaborating. With the Internet, social media, and mobile phones we collaborate globally, all the time. We need door openers, and we need to open doors for others?—?it's how the world operates.

After I recorded the podcast with Burnie in a hallway at the YouTube Space LA, Burnie said, "Let me know if you want to meet anyone here for your book and I'll make the introduction." That night Burnie introduced me to my guests for episode 2, Shira Lazar, and episode 7, Flula Borg, who later went on to create my podcast music. At that event, I also ran into an old friend, Khail Anonymous, who I worked with at Machinima.com. He introduced me to my guest for episode 3, Taryn Southern, and later Khail appeared on episode 40. Eventually, Barbara Dunkelman from Rooster Teeth and Adam Kovic and Bruce Greene, who now work at Rooster Teeth, came on the show.

That one event was transformational for my podcast. I went from having zero guests to suddenly having my first shows booked. And then when I shared the first episode on Twitter, Burnie of course tweeted it to his followers. My podcast didn't event exist when I interviewed him; it was merely an idea. And Burnie helped tremendously with the execution of it.

The moral of the story? Make introductions to help people. Add value and do something for the other person. Give time to others who are not as successful as you. Pay it back. It certainly helps them, and it always helps you.

Actions to Open Doors for Others

1. Determine how you can help other people. Make a goal to introduce one person a week to another person who may be able to help them. Think about the like-minded people in your network who can get value from an introduction, and make it happen. Don't worry about if you get credit for the introduction. But don't just

introduce people for the sake of introducing people—make it count.

2. Determine who—if anyone—in your network can help you with an introduction. Now, don't ask for that introduction yet. Make an offer to help them first, before asking them for any help. Some of the most sophisticated people I know just start helping people well in advance of when they may actually need help themselves.

Lesson 2: Monetize by Giving People Exclusive Access

Burnie talks about the Economy of First, which is in essence rewarding the people who support you first by giving them more of the stuff they love. These are the people who are the first to support your crowdfunding campaign, buy your new products, or attend your fan meet-ups. And these community members need to be rewarded for being there for you.

Burnie and Rooster Teeth support these folks with a program for what they call "sponsors." These members pay a sponsorship fee ($15 for six months) to get advertising-free access and exclusive content from Rooster Teeth. Sponsors also get a star next to their name on their online RoosterTeeth.com profile and discounts in the Rooster Teeth merch store.

But most importantly, sponsors know that the exclusive access and perks they are buying is their way to support Rooster Teeth to keep making stuff they love. Sure, getting discounts and stars on your profile is cool, but joining the sponsor program is about helping and supporting Rooster Teeth. In the eyes of the Rooster Teeth fan, Rooster Teeth has made some amazing and cool stuff for the community, and most of it's free to view on the web. Thus it's a win/win for a sponsor to get some cool stuff in advance of anyone else. And you feel a deeper kinship with Rooster Teeth as a sponsor than if you're an ordinary fan. It's like you're keeping their business growing in addition to just consuming their content.

Burnie rewards the top members of the Rooster Teeth audience in other ways. When fans backed Rooster Teeth's crowdfunding campaign for *Lazer Team*, they were given exclusive access to the creative process during the film's preproduction. Burnie calls that group his true influencers, and those top 37,000 fans who backed his crowdfunding project are yet another segment of the super-fans that Rooster Teeth creates for. Oftentimes your super-fans are the ones most likely to share your videos and content on social media, appreciate perks, and want to give back to you.

When you have worked hard to build a community, turning around and asking its members to pay for products or services can be scary. You don't want to literally "bite the hand that feeds you" by annoying people with advertisements or persistently cramming products down their throats. There's a delicate balance to making a living from an amazing community, and often this brand of exclusive access or knowledge is a win/win to get people to gladly support you.

Actions to Monetize by Giving People Exclusive Access

1. Determine if you can give people something exclusive to help support your business. For example, if you're a businessperson, can you give exclusive coaching? Or if you're a creator like Burnie, can you sell ad-free content? Or if you built a product, can you sell limited product offerings?

2. Determine if your idea has the makings to be a full-blown company. Consider that Pinterest and Facebook

are social networks, but also businesses. Rooster Teeth is an online production studio, but it is also a 90-person company. It helps to keep assessing if your idea is or should soon become a company, because you may need to hire employees, pay benefits, and create an office at some point. Creating a company may not align with your community goal, but you need to define who and what you are in the business-building universe if monetization is at all a possibility for your idea.

3. Create a tab on your website for your exclusive-service offerings. When you offer to coach, perform, host, speak, consult, give ad-free content, or whatever, add a tab at the top of your website to start marketing it. Once you start charging people for exclusivity, give them a clear way to see the opportunity on your site.

Lesson 3: Treat Your Community as Equals

In the Influencer Economy, there are three types of people:

* ❖ *The Influencers*—The 1 percent who are creating content and influence online.

* ❖ *The Curators*—The 10 percent who curate and share influencers' content to their networks.

* ❖ *The Consumers*—Everyone else who consumes and reacts to the content.

You want to treat your consumers with appreciation and respect, of course, but you *really* want to find and reward that 10 percent, the curators, because that audience is responsible for spreading your message to the world. Like Derek Sivers said, you need followers to create a movement, and oftentimes the first follower is the true leader. Barbara Dunkelman was initially a fan of *Red vs. Blue* and joined its online community to connect with other fans. She is now the marketing and community manager at Rooster Teeth and codirector of the company's massive RTX gaming and Internet convention. That is a powerful testament to treating a community member as an equal.

Barbara Dunkelman was a rare case where a fan was hired to work for Rooster Teeth. Burnie has also hired fellow influencers to join the full-time staff. My old colleagues Adam Kovic and Bruce Greene, who were also on my podcast, were seasoned video game hosts and producers at Machinima who chose to work with Burnie because of his vision and dedication to his audience. Adam and Bruce already had built-in followings and respect in the industry. Hiring them was a shrewd and smart move because they were already fans of the company and respected Burnie and his team.

Actions to Treat Your Community as Equals

1. Identify the top members of your community and determine how you can partner with them. For example, is there a job that you can fill with someone from the community? Can you give certain members exclusive access to help moderate a forum, or can you mentor them with advice and opportunity?

2. Identify peers, colleagues, even competitors in your field who seem like they would be a good fit in your enterprise. If you have a slot they might be able to fill, reach out to them. Don't look at this as typical corporate headhunting; it should be more collegial in spirit, done with a sense of camaraderie.

When Breaking Down Doors Helps You Open Doors

Anthony Saleh is a music talent manager, start-up investor, entre-preneur . . . you can hyphenate his job titles, because there are so many. In addition to managing the careers of world famous hip-hop artists such as Nas and Future, he collaborates with Nas to invest in start-up ventures with their group at QueensBridge Venture Part-ners. His world is squarely in the middle of music and hip-hop. His day-to-day work has varied from helping Nas produce his biographi-cal documentary, *Nas: Time Is Illmatic*, to guiding QueensBridge into investing in start-ups like Lyft and Dropbox. He straddles the line between the music and tech industries and has built an awesome portfolio of artists and investments. Anthony brings a hip-hop men-tality to tech, and a tech mentality to hip-hop.

In the Influencer Economy, most everyone I have spoken with believes that opening doors for others has led them to greater successes in business and life, and Anthony falls squarely in that camp. "I think one of the bigger lessons I learned pretty early is number one: there's no reward in life for being a jerk," he told me. "You don't get a gold medal for being a jerk." Across both tech and music, Anthony believes in giving to others as a core element to business and his life. He has always believed in playing the long game with his work relationships.

One of his most enduring partnerships has been with Nas, whose own values reinforce and guide Anthony's work. As he told me: "I really admire the way Nas approaches music. He speaks from his heart and he fucking writes his ass off and tells these stories and creates these vivid pictures for you. I appreciate his art. Very similarly to how I appreciate the way a VC approaches how they analyze deals right."

In fact, Anthony said that Nas would "give you the shirt off his back," and that his enormous success comes from helping others. Outside of being one of the top rappers of his generation, Nas is extremely loyal. Nas and Anthony named their investment firm QueensBridge Venture Partners, after Queensbridge Houses, the largest housing project in North America where Nas grew up. Queensbridge is in Long Island City in the borough of Queens, New York, and was rampant with crime and drugs when Nas was a youth. Years later, he continues to give back to the community, including making *Time Is Illmatic* with Anthony, which gives a lot of love to the area.

Anthony was born in Oakland and raised in the Inglewood and Carson neighborhoods of Los Angeles. "I carry a lot of my morals and values in business that I learned as a child when I grew up here in LA," he told me. In his late teens, Anthony moved to New York. His family and friends wanted him to stay on the West Coast, but he enrolled at SUNY Binghamton, a state college in upstate New York. After attending SUNY for a year, he decided to drop out and start to "pursue what felt right."

Anthony met Nas through Nas's former manager, whose relationship with the rapper was winding down. Anthony and Nas connected immediately. Investing in start-ups and managing hip-hop artists has opened many doors for Anthony. He's seen the world and is connected to some high-power circles in tech and entertainment. Now he's all about doing the same for others. On the podcast, we talked about the world of African American entrepreneurship and how he is shaking things up in Silicon Valley. In the technology industry, there are very few entrepreneurs and venture capitalists representing the African American community. QueensBridge is one of his avenues to change that. Similar to many American industries, which are dominated by white males and a club of insiders, Anthony takes an attitude about tech that Nas and other rappers took to music culture in the 1990s: "I think we're going to help redefine the good old boy network."

He passionately believes that the tech industry in Silicon Valley is "going to be bottom up, [with] people coming out of nowhere." When asked about what the traditional VC community thinks about his "bottom up" theory, he told me, "One thing I always tell people, you can have all the power in the world and all the money in the world. When you have heart, I mean it's very hard to keep someone down. And I feel like a lot of us younger venture [investors]—and by the way I mean [that] when I think of minorities, I think about women, I think about African Americans, Latinos, to some extent Asian and gay people, anyone. I think we can fucking accomplish anything."

It's hard not to get into what he's saying. People like Anthony are not only opening doors for people, they are breaking down doors and barriers to help others. Part of his vibe is also that there's an obligation to help others that come after you. The tech world is going to be more diverse and look a lot different in the coming years. He's doing it by opening doors—which benefited him—and which he is now doing to benefit others.

Chapter 9

Meet People In
Real Life (IRL)

"I've learned that people will forget what you said, people will forget what you did, but people will never forget how you made them feel."

—Maya Angelou

Chapter Playbook

I love global conferences like SXSW and VidCon. Why? Because you get to meet people you consider heroes in your field, take your online communities offline, and make friends with people in real life (IRL). In addition to the main event, I also like the smaller and more intimate events that often occur around big conferences. Attending influencer dinners, grabbing serendipitous lunches with new friends, and taking part in community meet-ups can be extremely rewarding. The thought of attending a major conference may be daunting, but it's important to navigate through the noise of a big event and make an effort to build bridges to both your community of fans, customers, or subscribers and to peers and colleagues in your field.

I can't stand a lot of "networking" in the modern digital age. Why? Too many people focus on building short-term "relationships" instead forming long-term friendships. Taking the long view when meeting people is a key to success in the Influencer Economy. You need to not just meet your peers but also make friends with them. If you connect with people whom you actually

209

enjoy being around, in the long run you will naturally find ways to support one another.

I often find the most success at conferences like Comic-Con and SXSW when I don't buy a ticket, or if I do, I avoid all of the crowds and talks. I know it sounds counter-intuitive but I'll weigh if I attend a conference based on whether or not I have organized a lunch or was invited to an important influencer dinner. Often that's when the real deals happen, away from the noise of the larger event.

Two podcasters who are the talent behind Sword & Laser and a YouTube creator who calls herself a "charming idiot" all understand the power of making friends IRL.

Veronica Belmont and Tom Merritt

For about a week in March each year, over 30,000 people flock to Austin, Texas, for South by Southwest (SXSW), an interactive, music, and film conference that seems to have something for everyone. The interactive portion of the conference is where the tech community comes to share their ideas with the world while washing down lots of BBQ brisket with Lone Star beer.

The conference does have its share of haters. A common complaint is that SXSW has grown too big and has sold out to corporate interests. Sure, there are big brands sponsoring events these days, but I've been going for years now and still can't think of a better media and tech conference to meet up with your friends or make new ones. And the food and music continue to be awesome.

The parties and general air of good times at SXSW means that most people have their guards down and are approachable. Don't get me wrong, there is certainly a lot of deal-making and big-talking at SXSW, but in general people come with the goal of hanging out in Austin with an attitude to take the conference as it comes. At the 2015 conference, while walking past the Driskill Hotel, I ran into Veronica Belmont and Tom Merritt, cohosts of the *Sword & Laser* podcast, standing on the sidewalk and eating greasy Texas pizza while chugging waters to stay hydrated. *Sword & Laser* (or *S&L*) started in 2007 as a science fiction and fantasy book club, soon adding a podcast, video show, and most recently a publishing imprint. I had already spoken with Tom on my podcast and was glad to meet Veronica and invite her on as a guest. Rather than being some sort of formal meeting, it was just as I portrayed it: a casual, coincidental meeting in front of a pizza joint.

Meet Your Community IRL

Tom and Veronica first met 10 years ago while working at the tech website CNET, and they embody how making friends in real life can not only bring fulfillment to your personal life, but that working with friends can bring similar fulfillment to your professional life. Most years at SXSW, Veronica and Tom host a meet-up along with the Diamond Club group (known on the Internet for its symbol), who are the most loyal members of their community. Their meet-ups feel like a reunion of sorts, where friends, listeners, and fellow hosts play Jenga and hang out on the rooftop while they talk books and grab a beer.

"We're more used to it now," Veronica told me regarding the meet-ups. "I mean, it was the same way with my guild members for *World of Warcraft*. When you play [fantasy] games with people for 10 years, it's not weird to meet up in person. It feels very natural. When we met in person, it's just like, 'Oh, there's Roger.'" Veronica was referring to the massive online multiplayer game, but that familiar feeling applies equally to the *Sword & Laser* community. The audience for the podcast is very much involved with each episode, recommending segment topics and offering feedback via e-mail or posts on the book social network Goodreads. Author hangouts with the likes of Adam Christopher (*The Machine Awakes*) and Brian McClellan (*The Powder Mage Trilogy*) are always popular, but the real draws for fans of the show are Veronica and Tom themselves.

Whether you are watching Veronica on video with Tom or just listening to their podcast, it's clear that their chemistry can't be faked or bought. Why? Because they are friends in real life. They are not playing roles. They are being themselves. They collaborate like musicians or a comedy duo who have worked together for years and are able to improv like jazz virtuosos.

Their community members appreciate this authenticity even more when they have a chance to meet and mingle with the pair IRL. Besides downloading the podcast, if you can't get enough of Veronica and Tom catching up with them in Austin during SXSW, you'll find an in-person community based in San Francisco and occasional meet-ups elsewhere during tech, gaming, or sci-fi and fantasy fiction conferences. Veronica and Tom have shared both a sense of humor and passion for their favorite genres with their fans for over eight years, developing a bond with their audience that sometimes offers more than just a discussion about books.

Make Friends with People You Want to Work with

In the digital age, we have more power and choice in who we work with than ever before. We are more empowered to choose our projects and jobs based on our terms, and often that includes partnering with people whom we like to work with. That's definitely the case with Veronica and Tom.

On their show, Veronica is the *Sword* to Tom's *Laser*. She is well versed in fantasy, while Tom knows science fiction cold. They each give off an attractive, geek chic vibe—Veronica with her dark bangs and Tom rocking salt and pepper stubble. In fact, the show had been a video podcast during its affiliation with Veronica's good friend Felicia Day's Geek & Sundry YouTube channel, though the hosts are now "proud members" of the Frogpants Studios network of artists and podcasters.

Starting off the show, they often have a drink in hand.

"Why is it slightly sour?" Tom asks Veronica regarding her wine choice during they're "What Are We Drinking?" bit.

"It's seen better days."

"Why are you drinking it then?"

"Because it's open."

After the cocktail chatter at the start of each podcast, the hosts report "Quick Burns" sci-fi and fantasy news items, such as updates on the next *Star Wars* book or the winner of a Ray Bradbury Award. They credit their audience with each of these stories because it is the show's fans who post the information on Goodreads hoping to get it on air. The *Sword & Laser* "Book Check In" is a progress report on whatever Veronica and Tom may be reading at the time. Listeners weigh in on the authors or other topics by e-mail and with those Goodreads comments during the "Bare Your Sword" portion of each episode. There are interactive book-of-the-month discussions and author spotlights. It's a lot of professional time together, riffing off each other and their listeners' input, and it simply would not be possible if Tom and Veronica didn't genuinely like each other. Their friendship is the foundation of their success.

Play the Long Game with Professional Friendships

It took years for all the pieces of that friendship to coalesce in their professional lives. Tom and Veronica's flagship *Sword & Laser* actually got its start way back in 2007 when Veronica was leaving her job at the tech news website CNET, one of the first online media companies to cover the tech industry with blogging, videos, and podcasts. A communications major, Veronica is part of the Emerson College "mafia," which we joked about. It's a humorous way to describe the large network of Emerson graduates working in entertainment, and how tight-knit the community is. Veronica actually moved out to San Francisco with five other Emerson alumni prior to working her way up at CNET. She started as an audio production intern and then became a producer on podcasts and video shows such as *MP3 Insider* and *Crave*. After her boss invited her on air for the tech roundup podcast *Buzz Out Loud*, she easily transitioned from editor and producer to cohost.

Veronica told me, "*Buzz Out Loud* really was what kicked everything off for me because I had never been someone to talk on the other side of the board. I had never turned my own microphone on, as it were. So being able to do that and realizing that people were interested in what I had to say . . . it was a little kick in the butt that made me think, 'Oh, I could do this. This is something I can do.'" Tom was also on the show and wanted to continue collaborating with Veronica after she eventually left CNET.

"I don't think I've ever said this out loud before, so this is pretty funny," Veronica said to me. "It's a strange memory that I have. I was in the car with my mom when I was very young, talking about what I wanted to do for a living. I said, 'I want to be the expert at something . . . I want to be the person they call to talk about a topic on a show.'" She seems to have gotten her wish. To many people, Veronica is respected for her knowledge of consumer technology products and geek culture. But others specifically love her expertise around genre fiction. Branching out from *Sword & Laser*, she has cocreated the *Vaginal Fantasy Book Club* to indulge her fondness for romance as well as fantasy novels. The title of the monthly podcast does create its share of one-off downloads. "I explain the show. I do that in the intro. 'This is what we do and this is what we're not.' But some teenage boys think this sounds awesome. Then they get in, and they're like, 'Wait a second, I don't want to read a book.'"

In the bigger picture of her career, Veronica has an even harder time explaining what she does for a living. She is an entrepreneur at her core, and her work has included podcasting, jobs with corporate clients, and serving as an emcee, voice actor, and start-up advisor.

When developing *Sword & Laser*, the cohosts weighed those interests and decided that since Veronica is more of a fantasy fan and Tom is more of a sci-fi guy, on the show they would educate the other person on the opposite genre. They first launched a fan community on a social network platform called Ning.com, building a group page and an online forum where they could talk about books. The forum naturally evolved. "We went in the podcast direction because we were both into podcasting and enjoyed doing shows together," Veronica said. "It just made sense. We were pretty OG." Meaning she was an early adopter of the platform. She had even worked out of the Odeo office way back in 2006— the company that would eventually become Twitter but started as a podcasting platform.

Tom, meanwhile, had combined his journalism major from the University of Illinois with his early love for computers and consumer tech. He had five years at TechTV in San Francisco before joining CNET. "That's where I really got the podcasting bug," Tom told me. "That's when I started *Sword & Laser* and started doing a lot of ancillary projects." That roster has included podcasts on everything from real tech stories and "really shaky analysis" (*Daily Tech News Show*) to discussions about classic TV pilots and streaming series (*AutoPilot, Cordkillers*). *Current Geek* takes on pop culture and "the geeky things you care about." *East Meets West* and *It's a Thing* also rummage through pop culture, though the latter is more about trend spotting and reunites Tom with Molly Wood, the co-creator of CNET's *Buzz Out Loud*.

Tom is also funny and accessible in person, a fact that I discovered when we first met on a panel about podcasting in the Santa Monica neighborhood of Los Angeles. Tom also joined a SXSW panel that I moderated on podcasting in 2016, where we both riffed off the cuff about creating audio shows down in Austin. He actually Skypes to create the audio for *S&L*, as Veronica still lives up in San Francisco. Tom had left CNET in 2010 to join the podcast network TWiT.tv, which was founded by his former TechTV colleague Leo Laporte. "I went independent in 2014," he told me. "I had a couple of shows like *Sword & Laser* that I was already doing, and I decided to try new shows that would tie in the things that I already love to do every day. Some were versions of previous shows that I've done—a daily tech show and one on cord cutting, but I was able to make them work."

Treat Your Community as a Partner and Friend

The audience itself often helps with that focus for *Sword & Laser* and other shows that look to their communities for suggestions and content. "I feel like the audience is the third host," Tom said. "I'll have a guest and the audience is telling me things in the chat room live while recording—helping me get perspective. They're submitting story ideas, saying 'Hey, we're really interested in *this*.' I'm taking e-mails from expert people who work in different industries from law enforcement to agriculture. Again, perspectives that I would never have. And it just makes my shows better."

"We got a really nice e-mail recently from a woman who had moved and not yet made a lot of friends in her new town," Veronica told me. "She said it was nice to be able to turn on *Sword & Laser* and feel like she had some sense of comfort or community. She's like, 'I was listening to you guys talking and just felt really good. It felt like I had friends that I could relax with for a little while and not feel so stressed out by being in a new place.'" This was great for Veronica and Tom to hear, proof that they were creating a kind of home. "Even if that home is virtual," Veronica said. "And we're just voices in her earbuds—not sitting with her at the cafe. But it's enough and feels good to have that community."

It's also true that there are a lot more podcasts and YouTube channels today than when *Sword & Laser* first launched. It may not be as easy to get noticed, but if you look at creating content as a way of connecting your interests with even a small group of like-minded souls, chances are you will find and build your own audience. When I started what I originally called *The Influencer Economy* podcast, I didn't have Veronica and Tom's level of audio production and editing skills—I still don't. But you're reading this book because I wanted to have and record conversations that some would find helpful or inspiring. As stories on a podcast or a website, my informing and hopefully entertaining people began as something I cared about and made time for every week.

Instead of focusing on the increased competition for attention, consider this a content golden age in the sense that it's easier for me and anyone else to create stuff, and there are more people worldwide willing and able to check it out. There's a greater awareness about these platforms, which means a rising tide of downloaders, subscribers, and streamers. It's about finding that first fan and testing the power of your idea.

"They are as passionate as we are, if not more passionate about these worlds" was how Veronica described *Sword & Laser*'s Goodreads community and other enthusiasts. "Maybe they don't have the desire to speak into the mic or to make a video on YouTube, but they are the heart and soul of what we do as podcasters. Without the audience, we would just be talking into a void. It's the audience interaction that drives us and feeds us and sustains us throughout the years. They literally make it possible by supporting us financially and emotionally."

Grace Helbig

A self-described "charming idiot," Grace Helbig is a video creator with a slightly different story about how her community has shown its appreciation. Grace had been a very popular vlogger for Mydamnchannel.com, a comedy multichannel network that once used Grace to promote shows on their website and create more of a dialogue with their audience. She was thrilled to land this job back in 2008 when she was trying to get her acting and comedy career off the ground in New York City. Until YouTube came along, folks like Grace mainly leveled up their comedy game by doing stand-up at clubs or joining Upright Citizens Brigade or other improv and sketch comedy groups that serve as farm teams for television gigs. Grace had taken classes at the Peoples Improv Theater (The PIT) and originally wanted to be a writer like her hero, Tina Fey. Then she started to play around with video.

If You Build It, They Will Come

"As a complete and utter hobby, I was making these things called vlogs," Grace told the VidCon audience in her 2014 keynote address.[1] I've said this throughout the book, but VidCon is a conference celebrating online video, where video creators like Grace give keynotes and talks, and bigger companies and brands attend to stay on the cutting edge of online video trends all the while fans get to hang out and see their favorite online video creators like Grace up close and personal. I tell the story of the Vlogbrothers in chapter 1: Find Your Big Vision, and go into more detail about VidCon there. Overall there's really no shortage of creators at this conference who have embraced digital media as an alternative to old-school entertainment platforms. But one VidCon talk that particularly stuck out for me was Grace Helbig's keynote presentation in 2014.

"My roommate and I would hang out with each other, drink a glass of wine, and talk about our days. But we'd talk about them to a camera."[2] Grace had taken editing classes in college and knew how to post her videos to YouTube, where they were soon discovered by My Damn Channel.

It's worth mentioning that the doors didn't open for Grace because she waited for *Saturday Night Live* to call or for one of her sitcom auditions to finally work out. Without censoring or discouraging herself, she made her own content and uploaded it to the Internet. Grace created her own opportunities by making and sharing work instead of waiting on casting directors and other entertainment industry middlemen to pass her upstream. And just like other creators in the Influencer Economy, she built her own audience from the ground up, brick by brick.

Her vlogging and improv skills did land her at My Damn Channel, which proved to be a mixed blessing. On the one hand, Grace thrived at the website and developed her voice as a video creator while amassing even more fans. Her employers also moved her *DailyGrace* vlogs to a YouTube channel in 2010, paying her to develop content that went on to attract a hefty 2.2 million subscribers. Grace and YouTube were a perfect fit, and she has been a fixture at VidCon since the beginning, counting the Green brothers, Hannah Hart, and other YouTubers as good friends.

The devotion of her fans also became critical for her in 2013 when she and My Damn Channel failed to come to terms on a contract renegotiation. Her bosses weren't willing to pay her what she was worth, and Grace decided to go independent. She stood to make more money through advertising on her own YouTube channel as long as her fans stuck with her. "I started engaging in the YouTube community," she told the crowd at VidCon. "I realized that ownership of your content is a thing that exists. I didn't have it at the time and I felt really bummed."[3]

Of course it was a big gamble going dark on over two million subscribers and hoping they would sign up to it'sGrace, the new channel she brought out in January of 2014. She was leaving behind over 1,000 videos and 200 million total video views, while the company that owned her content was free to syndicate reruns without compensating her. But despite not being able to promote the new channel while under her old contract, or even publicly discuss the reasons why she was, in a sense, starting from scratch, Grace went to work again as her own boss and discovered a breathtaking amount of support from her subscribers and the entire YouTube community.

Get Help from Your Friends

"Here's the lesson," John Green wrote on his Tumblr page to salute Grace's new YouTube channel. "Many corporations think that by owning YouTube channels, they'll have something valuable. But the value is not in the channel or in the number of subscribers. On You-Tube, despite the corporatization of everything, the value is in people. I'm not a *DailyGrace* fan. I'm a Grace Helbig fan. And at least on You-Tube, the individual still has more power than the corporation."[4]

Among other encouragements on Tumblr, Hank wrote, "Daily Grace is dead. Long live Grace."[5] When I asked him about how he and other YouTubers had helped Grace to finally own her work, he explained that many creators on this platform have each other's backs. "We're friends. We had all known for a year that Grace was in this situation. From my perspective, the idea that my YouTube channel would not be where I am anymore, and I'd have to try to move my entire audience—it's like having a piece of you ripped out. Knowing that was going to happen to Grace was infuriating and definitely mobilized me to want to help."

You've heard the word *collab* a lot in this book, but the YouTube family's generosity toward Grace somehow transcends talk of principles and Influencer Economy stats. A dozen other YouTubers appeared in the debut episode on it'sGrace and also drove a ton of viewers to the channel by inviting Grace to collab on their own shows. Thanks to them and Grace's fans, it took her less than three weeks to reach over one million subscribers. Today the number exceeds where she left off with My Damn Channel. In her keynote at VidCon, Grace told folks that this outcome "made me realize the power of community, the power of collaboration, and the power of being honest with other human beings."[6]

Building Friend Bases Rather Than Fan Bases

Jim Louderback is the editorial director for the Industry Track at VidCon and is the former CEO of Revision3, a pioneering media company acquired in 2012 by Discovery Digital Networks. Jim has a deep understanding of creators, their fans, and the communities that spring up around them, as his observations about VidCon attest.

"VidCon started out as a YouTube thing," he said, "but it's much bigger than that . . . this year we had Snapchat, Facebook, Twitter, Periscope, Meerkat, YouNow . . . and all these different places where people are building audiences and friend bases." His use of *friend* where you typically hear *fan* is no accident. Jim is aware of those barriers in traditional television that separate actors and onscreen personalities from audiences. Teleprompters and PR teams or other handlers have nothing in common with the vlogger's usual experience of looking into a camera to speak honestly and directly to viewers. Web-based video feels more like a conversation or friend-to-friend connection, which is fully realized at VidCon or other meet-ups throughout the year.

But to hear Jim Louderback explain it, the fun of VidCon is also in the audience interactions. "Online video is a very community-driven thing. It's not just being able to see, touch, and hear your favorite creators, but also the audience around it. So if you're a fan of the Vlogbrothers, or if you're a fan of Grace [Helbig] and Hannah [Hart], you can hang out with other fans of the same stars and connect with them. That connection of the audience to each other is as important as connecting with the creators themselves."

Influencer Economy Lessons: What Veronica Belmont, Tom Merritt, and Grace Helbig Can Teach You About Meeting People IRL

Lesson 1: Meet Your Online Community Offline

No matter what your field or industry, it's paramount to your success that you meet fans, customers, and community members IRL. Meeting them IRL only enhances and deepens your connection with them. By creating opportunities to hang out, meet up, or chat, you build partnerships with your audience. They become your teammates.

Tom and Veronica do a wonderful job meeting their community IRL. They host a smaller gathering each year at SXSW in order to meet their friends and broader community. SXSW is noisy, and Tom and Veronica understand the value of meeting people in more intimate and personal environments.

Industry trade shows can be expensive to attend and are often overwhelming. When you attend a conference like SXSW, over 20,000 people are hustling around the city of Austin, shaking hands, looking for deals, and networking their faces off. *Networking* is an annoying word, because it can imply being fake or selling yourself to other people in order to capture their interest and/or attention. But getting out on foot and meeting people in your community and business is important. In fact, I recommend people attend industry-specific conferences before they even launch their idea. Even if your project is in its early development, it helps to build your community and make productive connections in advance of its launch. Spend time at local meet-ups chatting with folks in your industry who you can learn from, and find and mingle with your audience—whether existing or potential members—at every opportunity.

I get it: meeting people face-to-face isn't always easy. Talking to people can be awkward and strange, especially if you don't know them from anyone. But conference networking is different than any other. People attend conferences specifically to chat up others. You've got to believe me on this: conferences are fantastic ways to meet new people, find friends, and build your community.

If you are hesitating to drive or jump in a plane to attend a conference with thousands of other people, maybe this reality will change your mind: people enjoy working with people that they *like*. And the better people know you and especially if you make an effort to get to know them, they will be more likely to hire you, recommend you for other work, or join your community. That is how the world works. You refer people who you know IRL and who you trust. And often the personal connections you make at one event can lead to unforeseen opportunities years later. Attending events is about the long game, not the short-term gain.

If you have the talent or desire for it, I always recommend speaking at conferences. When you speak, it obviously gives you a platform to meet others, but it also gives you an edge, because people will come talk to *you* when you speak rather than you having to seek out them. You need to be eloquent and smart, but as long as you are your authentic self and look at it as another way to connect with your audience just as you already do with your chosen platform, you'll do fine.

Attending new and up-and-coming conferences before they get super popular is also a good strategy. If you're an early adopter of platforms that are the focus of certain conferences, when the platforms get bigger and more well known, you will already know the lay of the land. And you'll understand who the key players are, you'll have met the organizers, and you'll increase your chances to speak and expand your profile even further.

So conferences are a biggie for IRL opportunities, but they are only one way to connect with peers and community members. Hosting webinars, live streams, and online chats are also excellent ways to meet with peers and community members. Anytime you can get a group together to make them laugh, become smarter, or engage around a subject they are passionate about, live online group events can be an excellent resource. And they are a lot of fun. It's a great way to connect the dots with your community in advance of meeting them IRL.

Actions to Meet Your Online Community Offline

1. Identify the top 10 biggest or most appropriate conferences in your field. In a spreadsheet, write the date, location, and most importantly the budget for you to attend these events. Think local or global, depending on your goals. Create a pathway for you to attend at least one of these conferences

2. Think of ways to meet with your community of fans, subscribers, or community members IRL. Determine if you want to host a meet-up such as an informal gathering at a bar, or partner with other influencers to host something for your audience. Make it easy for people to find you, and share it a couple of weeks in advance of the event.

3. Study the conference promotional materials, identify the speakers and other attendees you'd like to collab with, and come up with a plan to meet them. It could be by attending one of their scheduled events, arranging for an introduction through a mutual contact, or cold e-mailing them prior to the event to see if they'd have some time to meet and chat. Don't ask the speaker for a favor or make them exert a lot of effort to connect. Make it easy for the person to say yes to your collab idea.

4. If you're interested in becoming a speaker, list the conferences at which you would like to speak over the next three years. Write out a road map for how you'll get there. Sometimes the best strategy to get your foot in the door is to apply to speak on a panel rather than as a solo speaker.

5. Determine if your community wants to have a webinar, online video chat, or group hangout with you. If you don't have the time or budget to attend a conference, you can host these from your living room. If you even get two people to show up at your online event, it's well worth it. Getting your reps and practice is also important here, as this is often a bridge to speaking at conferences.

Lesson 2: Make Friends with Peers and Colleagues in Your Community IRL

When Grace Helbig came to a crossroads in her career and got out of a bad deal with My Damn Channel, she had to start rebuilding her community from scratch. Fortunately, she already was friends with fellow YouTubers like Hank and John Green and Hannah Hart, and many others were part of her early community when they collab'ed with her on her YouTube channel. This YouTube community of friends was incredibly supportive and helped her accelerate the launch of her channel and reestablish her subscriber base.

When communities come together like that it's a powerful thing, and conferences are often the most logical and convenient places to cement these bonds. Events like VidCon are often a reunion for friends to get together every year. Our lives get busy, and we often miss chances to see former colleagues and collaborators. At conferences, you can actually become friends with people rather than just build relationships. That's a big distinction. Friends are the people who will collaborate with you in the future, recommend you for work, and help open doors for you along the way to success. And events are where you can often meet friends IRL from around the word.

I'll share a secret with you. A key to making new friends at big conferences is to pair down the event into smaller pieces. Focused meet-ups like what Tom and Veronica put together for *Sword & Laser* are a good example. It makes the conference seem smaller and thus more manageable. You can actually speak with people that you have something in common with rather than chat with random folks who you will never see again. Meet-ups make conferences more efficient.

I recommend planning lunches, small dinners, get-togethers for drinks, and similar meet-ups at conferences. Planning smaller, more low-key events gives people a chance to take a break from the circus of the main convention hall and wind down a little. I've met close friends at lunches and dinners when attending conferences because it's where and when you can relax. Smaller gatherings allow you to recharge your batteries and are less about selling people on your idea and more about getting to know people.

Actions to Make Friends IRL

1. Plan a lunch, host a group dinner, or organize a meet-up at the conferences you attend. Pick a date, time, and the guest or guests. Think about a group of 5 to 10 people you'd like to invite to a low-key lunch/dinner. You don't have to pick up the tab, and it can be as simple as pizza and beer. As an organizer, you will get more value than you will ever realize.

2. Create a list of 10 people in your field whom you want to collaborate with. Think of the influencers whom you will be able to hopefully meet at different events IRL. Put it out in the universe that you'd like to collaborate with these 10 people and make it happen.

228

Chapter 10

Give Your Community Ownership

"Service to others is the rent you pay for your room here on earth."

—Muhammad Ali

Chapter Playbook

Giving your community ownership of your ideas means handing over your identity and brand to your audience. Your community members are your teammates—they will help you shape your idea and in the long run help your business grow. They will support your work because they believe in you. And you can never thank your audience enough for that support. So express gratitude for your community's contributions early and often. Givers succeed when they hand over ownership of their idea, because people want to support people who they emotionally invest in.

A main element of giving ownership is helping an under-served part of your community that needs a voice. Give these people what they want, and listen to their ideas about what will make them feel valued. With my podcast, I have recorded episodes on my own battles with depression, and how people can cope with their own depressed feelings. I believe that not enough people talk openly and freely about depression, and I want to represent that underserved community. It's important.

Turning your idea into a business or company is a challenge. You have to balance the push and pull of giving, while also thinking about bigger projects to make money or, at the very least, keep you breaking even. In the digital age we give away free advice, video content, and blogs to people, because we want to help others. However, finding creative ways to make bigger projects can serve you well. When I launched my book tour, it was a way to add value to my book and podcast. You always want to over-deliver with your community, and live events do that for me and my community. After giving out years of free podcasts and business advice to my community; my speaking gigs, business talks and live podcasts help deliver something that I can make part of my living.

In the end, creating value is all about giving people products they care about. One YouTube creator gives to her community in several ways and receives nothing but hearts back.

Hannah Hart

Hannah Hart usually speaks to her audience with a glass of wine in hand, and it's all in the name of entertainment, food, and good times. Back in 2011, Hannah was a recent UC Berkeley graduate working as a Japanese language translator and proofreader in New York City. She made the first *My Drunk Kitchen* video for a friend she missed who was still living in San Francisco.[1] Sipping wine in her sister's Brooklyn kitchen, Hannah more or less makes a grilled cheese sandwich. "It's important for you to remember when cooking . . . to use food" was one piece of advice.

Because she wasn't sure how else to send the large video file, Hannah uploaded it to YouTube, where the reaction was surprisingly widespread and positive. The online audience on YouTube wanted more. She didn't realize that the world of YouTube existed or that people called "YouTubers" made their videos for their "subscribers." All she knew was that YouTube commenters wanted more videos.

Hannah recognized this as her lightning in a bottle moment, so she felt encouraged to take a risk. Though she was poised to move to Japan for her job, she decided to quit working full-time altogether and couch surf from New York to Los Angeles in an effort to pursue making videos her primary focus. After six or seven more episodes in which she ties on a buzz and whips up meals, Hannah moved out to Los Angeles and was thrilled when Reddit and blogs started picking up the *My Drunk Kitchen* phenomenon. Soon, even mainstream news sources like *Time* magazine, *The Huffington Post*, and *Good Morning America* were covering her videos.

What began as a happy accident has evolved into a YouTube channel with over two million subscribers, international comedy tours, a best-selling parody cookbook, and feature films starring Hannah and fellow YouTubers Mamrie Hart (no relation) and Grace Helbig. For someone who had no ambition to become a YouTube creator, "Harto," as she's known from her Japanese translator days, has grown an impressive online audience and consistently gives to her community, which helps fuel her success.

Give to Your Community

The next stop on Hannah's road map literally took her on the road. The "Hello, Harto!" tour was Hannah's effort to give something to her fans, but it did require money to make it work. Hannah had been doing *My Drunk Kitchen* on YouTube for almost two years and wanted to meet her fans across the country. Hoping to avoid brand sponsorships, she explained her goal directly to her audience through the crowdfunding website Indiegogo. She promised her tour would be one part vlog, with "musings and karaoke," from a rented RV taking her to meet-ups in various cities. As a crowdsourced travel show, Hannah intended to ask for the zip code of each person who donated and base her route on cities with the highest concentration of "Hartosexuals," as she playfully calls her fans. She would also shoot an episode of *My Drunk Kitchen* in every city she and her crew traveled to. "Which leads me to ask," Harto wrote on Indiegogo, "Can I get drunk in your kitchen? Each person who donates gets their name thrown in the hat as a potential kitchen host. When we roll into town, we'll pick a person at random, call that brave person, and have a respectful culinary experience together."[2]

Adam Grant, a professor at the Wharton School of Business and the best-selling author of *Give and Take: Why Helping Others Drives Your Success*, was a guest on my podcast who spoke about "takers" as the people you'd want to weed out of your professional and personal circle. "Matchers," on the other hand, give you things that have value but expect stuff in return. They tend to keep score and have a transactional attitude about business dealings and beyond. "'Givers' are not just philanthropists or volunteers," Adam explained, referring to the third type in his framework, "but people who enjoy helping others and often do it with no strings attached." Grant explained to me that givers have the greatest opportunity to both succeed in business *and* to fail—often givers can be taken advantage of—yet the most successful givers thrive when they have their own self-interests aligned with giving.

I would put Hannah Hart in that giver category, as her entire motivation for Hello, Harto was to give her community a tour, something they had been collectively asking for. Hannah asked for $50,000 at the initial launch and reached that goal in less than six hours, ultimately raising $223,007 from her fans. In return for Hannah putting together what they wanted, her community gave back to her, funding over four times the amount of money she requested.

Hannah's mission is largely about giving back to her audience and recognizing that they have made her success possible. The

Hello, Harto tour was one way of expressing that gratitude. Even before she hit the road in her RV, she followed up her crowdfunding campaign with a 12-hour live stream "Thank-a-Thon." By having coffee with Harto in the morning, then enjoying a "crafts" session, live kitchen antics, and hours more programming, backers of the tour felt like they were spending the day with their friend and favorite chef. Of course, hard work, luck, and talent are important to Hannah's success, but the fact that she is a genuine giver is one of the major tenants of that success.

Sarah Weichel, Hannah's former business/talent manager, told me how the tour gave back in multiple ways: "It was her attempt at meeting her audience around the world. And you know, she held a meet-up in every city at a local food bank. So the idea was for her to be able to meet her fans, and for them to do something good for the community." That aspect of the tour was called Have a Hart Day, a volunteer program that continues throughout the country as a way of mobilizing Hartosexuals who share Hannah's desire to help the less fortunate. At these meet-ups, her fans could meet her and other online community members while giving something back to the cities in which they lived.

Give a Voice to Underserved Communities

Life prior to *My Drunk Kitchen* also reflected issues to which some of Hannah's fans could relate. Harto's parents were divorced when she and her sister were both very young. Her father was a Jehovah's Witness who had occasional visitation rights. "They have this thing called the District Convention, which is 12 hours of service," Hannah recounted on an episode of the podcast *Ear Biscuits*, hosted by fellow YouTubers Rhett and Link. "I remember if we had a dad visit on the District Convention, I would lay awake weeks knowing that it was coming. It was brutal. Having to go and sit still and be preached at for 12 hours. I couldn't doodle or write stories. I had to literally sit and listen and follow along in the book. It was hell."[3]

You wonder if all the fun of her 12-hour live stream Thank-a-Thon was also a kind of rebuttal to those early religious marathons. But there were even harder challenges. "I grew up in poverty and my mom is schizophrenic," Hannah said on Rhett and Link's podcast, explaining why she was a candidate for UC Berkeley's Educational Opportunity Program. "I was emancipated when I was 15 and my little sister went into foster care . . . I think at some point in my life I'd like to speak at length about mental health stigma. With an illness like schizophrenia, it's a psychosis." Her mother periodically heard voices and experienced other hallucinations, never accepting medication or treatment. She got pregnant when Hannah was 11, leading Hannah to ask her mom, whose condition had deteriorated, to consider aborting the baby. "And then she had the baby [Maggie], and that was like the best thing that happened to me," Hannah said. "Maggie totally saved my life. I one-hundred percent could have become that kid that does drugs and runs away from home and all that stuff. But Maggie was this smiling, loving baby . . . All you have to do for a baby is love it. And it loves you back. It was a good, pure thing."[4]

What makes YouTube a special place is that you will discover creators like Hannah that you wouldn't easily find on television or in films. As an openly gay performer and author, she is particularly loved by an LGBT community that appreciates her raucous focus on the good in life. Petite and a bundle of energy, with an occasional shaved-side hairstyle, Harto jump-cuts around her kitchen set, spouting puns and barely remembering to check her oven. She talks candidly about her sexuality, and people are comfortable responding with equal candor. She said her number one question from her fans is, "How do you know you're gay?"[5]

Talking About Depression

In crafting this book, I am regularly inspired by the people whom I am writing about. I have learned a ton from these teachers, and Hannah Hart is no different. When I watched her videos touching on difficult topics like sexuality (e.g., "How to ask a girl if she's gay"), I was inspired to speak about a subject that was personal to me: depression.

In my early and mid-twenties, I struggled with serious bouts of depression. I had a lot of days where I never left my apartment, slept through all hours, and generally avoided the outside world. In 2016, after two years of podcasting, I decided to open up about my depression and tell the story of my struggle. There is a stigma around depression, and I had friends at the time who thought I was "weak" or "not dealing" when I told them how badly I felt. It was hard to explain what I was going through, and I didn't really know how bad it was until a couple years later. I met my wife toward the end of this period and no longer struggle with the condition. But depression is still a part of my past.

I still think depression is an under-covered topic in the business world, and the stigma that depressed people are somehow weak can have negative repercussions on someone's career. I wish that I had understood my own depression, so I hoped to start a conversation on it and hopefully help others get through their depressed state.

My first podcast guest on the topic was Rand Fishkin, an entrepreneur and founder of the website and software company Moz. Moz is a thriving company and considered by many as their go-to resource for online marketing and analytics. Rand started the company with his mom in 2004 and was its CEO from 2007 to 2013.

Rand had written an online article about how he went through depression as a start-up founder. In the post, titled "A Long, Ugly Year of Depression That's Finally Fading," he shared his story in a public format. Depression is a serious topic, and Rand was open and honest about his personal and professional struggles. It was raw.

He admitted failures in different business decisions that he made, what he learned from it, and how that led to his depression. He too wanted to start a dialogue around depression and anxiety. We talked about how depression isn't a stigma and that people need to look for support when they are feeling anxious or bummed out.

I didn't talk about depression in my first 80 episodes; I waited until I had gained the trust of my community. Only then did I feel I could take a risk and talk about a topic many don't want to talk about. I am no longer crippled by the depression of my twenties, but it definitely has shaped me as a person and entrepreneur. The jobs of start-up entrepreneurs are stressful and, as such, these people are prone to get depressed. I don't want anyone else to have to go through my situation, and hopefully giving a voice to this topic will help others along the way. If I reach at least one person who is depressed, assuring them that, like me, they'll get through it, then it was a worthwhile endeavor.

Give First and People Will Pay to Support Your Other Projects

Hannah Hart's 2013 comedy tour, No Filter, was a collaboration with YouTube stars Grace Helbig and Mamrie Hart. The show premiered at NerdMelt in Los Angeles and was actually designed to be "pirated," in that the audience was encouraged to record and upload it to YouTube, Tumblr, and so forth. They were giving away content for free, which is always a good idea within the Influencer Economy model. By also doing a road version of No Filter, Harto added IRL meet-up opportunities for Hartosexuals as well as her collaborators' audiences. Hannah and her team were doing everything right, from crowdfunding with awesome fan perks to booking Harto's own gigs and meeting her community throughout the country—as well as Dublin, London, and elsewhere overseas. She really embraces the Influencer Economy and is accessible in real life for her fans.

That same year, Hannah, Grace, and Mamrie, three best friends in real life, also starred in their first movie, *Camp Takota*, about three women who are reunited at their old summer camp. But the group was in uncharted waters. With *Camp Takota*, the women were stretching well past their normal five-minute You-Tube video length and asking their audience to pay to download a feature-length movie from a new website.

Jamie Wilkinson, founder of the website Know Your Meme as well as VHX, the digital distributor that finally powered the movie, was also a guest on my podcast. He described how his company's drag-and-drop technology was well suited to *Camp Takota*'s offerings. "They had a variety of packages for sale on their site—just the film, or the film and the documentary. They had merch that they were selling . . . Because the nature of our platform is flexible, they had a lot more control and access, but they still distributed everywhere else, too. And it's been hanging out on the top 10 list of iTunes for quite a while, and I'm sure will go elsewhere too, which is good. The goal is more people seeing your movie all over the world."

But the gut check for creators who use a website like VHX is its pay-per-download system. The three creators charged people for the movie, which they weren't used to doing; their YouTube videos, of course, were available for free. But it was a phenomenal success, making back its money within 24 hours.

Meanwhile, the book publishing world is also starting to gamble on the communities built by YouTubers and other digital content creators. In 2014, Dey Street Books, an imprint of the "big pub" house HarperCollins, brought out Hannah's book, *My Drunk Kitchen: A Guide to Eating, Drinking, and Going with Your Gut*. At the time, HarperCollins still wasn't sure if Hartosexuals would line up to buy the cookbook, which was a self-help parody with recipes like the Hartwich and Latke Shotkes. But the book did turn up on the *New York Times* best-seller list, where it remained for six weeks.

"The Harto," as you might call harnessing the momentum of a post that goes viral, is worthy of analysis. Is there a way to increase your chances of catching lightning in a bottle like Hannah did? And if you are lucky enough to get linked to on Reddit of *The Huffington Post*, how do you work your ass off to become a longer-term success? Who knows where exactly *My Drunk Kitchen* will lead. It is true that unpredictability is a strangely reliable ingredient on the show. On one Valentine's Day episode, Harto attempts to make a chocolate soufflé. It doesn't rise as planned, but by adding a few orange slices, she ends up making something equally delicious. And in the end it doesn't matter, because Hannah's community feels ownership in her idea, and they're equal partners in whatever she is making.

Influencer Economy Lessons: What Hannah Hart Can Teach You About Giving Your Community Ownership

Lesson 1: Give to Your Community

My wonderful Mom Williams, like many parents, worked hard to reinforce certain values in me at a young age. Often those values came down in the form of advice on how to treat people. She wanted me to always say please and thank you and show people similar gestures of respect. She also wanted me to be generous and share with others. She helped create habits in me that I still aim to keep to this day.

In the digital age, influencers like Hannah Hart say please and thank you all the time, and they do it by constantly giving to their communities. In the Influencer Economy, prioritizing your community over making money is a natural, even strategic move.

As John Green said at VidCon one year, "What's good for your community is good for your business. What's bad for your community is bad for your business." Not all of us will grow a global YouTube audience like Hannah. But all of us can learn a lesson about how she was a giver to her community. That appeal is universal.

Hannah knew her community wanted a tour and to meet her face-to-face, so she engineered a way to give that to them. Crowd-funding is a fantastic way to galvanize your community around your idea, and Hannah's community gave back to her as she reached her goal of $50,000 in *less than 24 hours*, with over 10,000 backers from not only the United States but countries like Canada, England, Australia, and New Zealand.

Hannah also had some amazing perks, giving her community simple things that went a long way to engender their appreciation and loyalty. She had a $1 perk that, according to her, would be a "wistful sigh as I gaze gracefully into the ether." For $250, she gave a "Personal Thank You Video" where she e-mailed you a video "directly to your face." She also gave people a chance at 30 minutes of Google Hangout time for $250 called a "Thank You Fun Time Cuddle Sesh." And for $500, a backer got "Whatever You Want on the Phone." Hannah's personal touch and connections were giving people fun, simple rewards that they wanted.

Hannah also created a single event just to thank people. She called it a Thank-A-Thon, an event where she thanked her community for helping support her Hello, Harto tour. She threw a party online, and her YouTube buddies Mamrie Hart, Grace Helbig, and Tyler Oakley stopped by to take part in the fun. It was part drunk kitchen, part jokes, and part spotlighting her community backers. She even put up fan pictures from the Twitter accounts of people who backed Hello, Harto, giving them shout-outs and acknowledgments on the live stream.

When you are accessible, you are in a better position to listen to your audience and react based on what they want. Oftentimes you may think they need something else, but they tell you otherwise. Hannah has taken this principle to heart. She is a giver, and she delivers to her community in ways that all of us can learn from.

Actions to Give to Your Community

1. Come up with a big-ticket item that you want to give to your community. Even if it's something that you sell, as long as it has clear mutual value, it's a win/win for everyone. Consider if writing a book, going on a tour, or creating a live show is something that gives value back to your community.

2. Determine if you are expressing enough gratitude to your community. Among other ways, Hannah gave her community a dedicated Thank-A-Thon. Write out equally creative ways to thank and show love to your audience. They won't forget it.

Lesson 2: Give First and People Will Pay to Support Your Work

We've established how Hannah is a master at giving back to her community. During the Hello, Harto tour, she shot an episode of *My Drunk Kitchen* in people's kitchens in each city she visited. She attended community charity meet-ups with her fans, volunteering her time at a local food kitchen and inviting her community to pledge their time alongside her. In the end, 95,000 people were served 114,584 pounds of food on the tour. Hello, Harto was literally a DIY tour, completely planned by the Hartosexual community. Hannah served up the structure and made it easy for people to participate. This is about as collaborative as it gets.

But her giving goes even deeper than that. We have talked about how everyone on the Internet has a home, and with Hannah she gives people a sense of belonging—a place online to forget about their worries and laugh in her drunk kitchen. It's authentic. It's fun. And as a result, her community loves her and is receptive to any other project she may conceive.

Like Hannah, learn to listen to your community and stay adaptive. Collaboration is key in the Influencer Economy, and Hannah adapted along with the needs and wants of her community, which resulted in the Hello, Harto and No Filter tours and ultimately her *Camp Takota* movie. More importantly, she integrated them into the conversation of her idea.

Branding your own terms and language is an important component of this integration. Hannah gives her community ownership of her name, which provides her audience a great sense of belonging. Harto is her nickname. *My Drunk Kitchen* is the name of her YouTube series and book. Hartosexuals are what her community members are called. Hello, Harto was the name of her first tour. Have a Hart Day is the name of her day dedicated to giving back. Thank-A-Thon is her marathon live stream to show personal appreciation for her community. A lot of other Influencer Economy communities have similar insider lingo and, like Dead Heads, Phish Heads, and other fans of cult-like bands, it gives people a sense of ownership over your brand.

When you give stuff away for free, when do you start charging for other stuff? Harto was used to giving away content for free. This is a modern strategy that a lot of people in the Influencer Economy have used to acquire devout followings. But it's not easy to build up an authentic community and then turn around and expect your crowd to start paying for things. It takes trust. But if you give to people first, and always remember to give more along the way, then great things will happen. Your community will gladly pay to support your other projects.

Actions to Give First and Get People to Pay to Support Your Projects

1. Determine if you're ready to start charging people for stuff you make. When you transition from giving things out for free to starting to charge your audience, it's a big move. Think about the longer-term products you'd like to sell or make, and determine if it's realistic to expect people to buy them from you at this stage in your journey.

2. If you think you're ready to begin selling things, make a list of logistical matters that need to be in place. Turning your idea into a business includes setting up a business LLC or corporation, building a shopping section on your website, setting up a PayPal or Patreon account, and keeping track of your inventory. You need to treat your business seriously, which even includes hiring people to help you fulfill your business objectives.

3. Come up with ways to brand specific terms for your community to give it an identity. Hannah is known as Harto, her community members are Hartosexuals, and she hosted a Have-a-Hart Day. Think about consistent branding that is easy to remember and helps people feel involved in your idea.

Lesson 3: Give a Voice to Underserved Communities

YouTube is a unique network because you will discover creators like Hannah that you wouldn't easily find on television or in films. As an openly gay creator, author, and performer, she is particularly loved by the LGBT community. Being gay is not the main focus of her videos and community, and she is a lot of different things to different types of people. But to some she is a leader in the gay community, demonstrating how it's okay to embrace your personality in the digital age and explore parts of yourself that are perhaps underrepresented in the mainstream world.

Hannah talks candidly about her sexuality on her YouTube channel. People e-mail her asking for advice about things like coming out of the closet, and she answers these questions directly and honestly. When you gain that level of trust after growing your community, it's important to think inward about certain things you care about. For some, that might mean creating a charitable cause or volunteering movement like Hannah's Have a Hart Day. For others, it may be giving back to your community by talking about serious problems you've gone through in life. For myself, it was having a real conversation about depression on my podcast and hoping to help others understand how painful it can be, but telling them that there's hope.

Think about ways your community can be better served if you give them a voice. It's important to give back when you reach a certain level of success. By doing so, your community will galvanize behind you.

Actions to Give a Voice to Underserved Communities

1. Now that you have a community, determine how you can help others. What part of your voice, personal story, or concerns could help other people along the way?

2. Determine if there's a cause that you strongly believe in, and a charity or nonprofit attached to it. Consider if you can give back by organizing a volunteer movement, setting up an online fundraiser, or raising awareness for this cause via your community.

Acknowledgments

Crowd-editors

My crowd-editors were gracious enough to read chapters in advance and give me amazing and helpful feedback. These are podcast listeners and friends who lent me their time and who undoubtedly made the book 100% better.

The Editors: Ian Beckman, Anna Boyette, Emily Boyette, Andre Briggs, Kara Dake, Christy Pool DeHaven, David DeHaven, Jr., Aaron Dodez, Elsie Dortelus, Susan Fesperman, Grant Garlock, Hunter Gilden, Sam Glassnap, Edie Gonzalez, Sarah Hubbell, Carol Kaffenberger, Jeff Kaloski, Neel Ketkar, Zal Kumar, Cody Lindabury, Matt Perez, Jeb Quaid, Akeel Qureshi, Saiqa Qureshi, Hanes Roberts, Anup Shah, Ryan Stoner, Mike Woalleger, Katherine Williams, and Audrey Wu.

Friends and family who inspired me along the way or helped to make intros to guests on the podcast: Timon Birkhofer, Rachel Bullock, Paul Bullock, Andres Buritica, Lisa Clark, Espree Devora, Annie Duncan, John Duncan, Mike Duncan, Harry Duran, Brett Erlich, Coleman Greene, Charlene Jimenez, Josh Jordison, Jonas Koffler, Ron Lin, the Moores, Meghan Murphy, Scott Perry, Chad Pugh, Miki Reynolds, Rachel Romero, Meghan Sette, Adam Sachs, Cody Simms, Tim Street, David Tyndall, Michael Williams, and Patrick Vlaskovits.

Thanks to all the folks who helped this book get published: my awesome editor Jon Ford, my amazing writing collaborator David Neipris, the inspiring book cover designer Erin Taylor, my clever book designer Jon Peck and detailed proofreader Carole Quandt.

My Family: Mom, Dad, Stephen, Michael, Katy, Justine, Henry, Elliott, and Emmie.

Thanks to all my podcast guests who comprise the DNA of the book.

Burnie Burns	Bernie Su
Shira Lazar	Brian Koppelman
Taryn Southern	Ryan Ford
Flula Borg	Caleb Bacon
Jeff Ullrich	Justin Jackson
Andy Baio	Lance Ulanoff
Jamie Wilkinson	Willie Geist
Adam Kovic	Troy Carter
Bruce Green	Alan Sepinwall
Freddie Wong	Jonah Keri
Mike Wolf	Nir Eyal
Adam Grant	Jayson Gaignard
Michael Goldfine	Dan Pashman
Ty Hildenbrandt	Jordan Harbinger
Barbara Dunkelman	Paul Jarvis
Sloane Davidson	Tucker Max
Hunter Walk	Ezra Cooperstein
Brendan Mulligan	Sarah Weichel
Harrison Barnes	Khail Anonymous

Dan Casey

DeStorm Power

Bryan Alvarez

Tom Merritt

Anthony Saleh

A.J. Jacobs

Veronica Belmont

Greg Goodfried

Jemele Hill

John Corcoran

James Altucher

Cenk Uygur

Tom Scharpling

Meredith Walker

Scott Belsky

Brendan McDonald

Jim Louderback

Omar Zenhom

Adam Rymer

Brad Feld

Farbod Shoroka

Chris Morrow

Chris Yeh

Derek Sivers

Jen Yamato

Jay Samit

David Nihill

Rand Fishkin

Franceshca Ramsey

Hank Green

Hrishikesh Hirway

Seth Godin

Brent Bushnell

Max Joseph

Kevin Kelly

Keith Bullock

Endnotes

Chapter 1

1. Reddit, Nerdfighter Community https://www.reddit.com/r/ nerdfighters/comments/3e60tz/eight_years_since_accio _deathly_hallows/

2. Joshua Cohen, "The Vlogbrothers' Project For Awesome Raises Over $1.2 Million To Decrease Worldsuck," *Tubefilter*, December 14, 2014,

3. http://www.tubefilter.com/2014/12/17/ project-for-awesome-p4a-vlogbrothers-million-charity/

4. Sam Gutelle, 2015 Edition Of Vlogbrothers' Project For Awesome Raises $1,546,384, *Tubefilter*, December 28, 2015.

5. http://www.tubefilter.com/2015/12/28/ vlogbrothers-project-for-awesome-2015-results/

6. Don't Forget to be Awesome website, http://store.dftba.com/pages /mission-statement

7. Hank Green website, http://hankgreen.com/

Chapter 2

1. Chris Hardwick, *The Nerdist Way: How to Reach the Next Level (In Real Life)*, (New York: Berkley Publishing Group, 2012), Addiction-Ary Chapter.

2. Eric Deggans, Revenge of the 'Nerdist,' Chris Hardwick Takes Over Your TV, *NPR*, January 9, 2014. http://www.npr.org/2014/01/09 /261050616/revenge-of-the-nerdist-chris-hardwick-takes-over -your-tv

3. Chris Hardwick, Self-Help for Nerds: Advice from Comedian Chris Hardwick, Wired Magazine, October 21, 2001. http://www.wired. com/2011/10/mf_hardwickexcerpt/

4. Nerdist About Page, http://nerdist.com/about/

5. John Patrick Pullen, Inside Nerdist's Media Empire for the Digital Age, *Entrepreneur Magazine*, August 21, 2013, http://www. entrepreneur.com/article/227443

6. Farhad Manjoo, Podcasting Blossoms but in Slow Motion, *New York Times*, June 17, 2015 http://www.nytimes.com/2015/06/18/technology/personaltech/podcasting-blossoms-but-in-slow-motion.html?_r=0

Chapter 3

1. Nir Eyal, Hooked: How to Build Habit Forming Products, (Portfolio Publishing, November 4, 2014), http://www.nirandfar.com/hooked

2. Andrew Leonard, Amazon's Scorched Earth Campaign: Why the Internet Giant Started a War, *Salon*, June 1, 2014 http://www.salon.com/2014/06/01/amazons_scorched_earth_campaign_why_the_internet_giant_started_a_war/

3. Michiko Kakutani, Television That's Worth Dissecting, *New York Times*, December 3, 2012. http://www.nytimes.com/2012/12/04/books/the-revolution-was-televised-by-alan-sepinwall.html?_r=0

4. Ibid.

Chapter 4

1. Kickstarter Projects, Freddie Wong, https://www.kickstarter.com/projects/freddiew/video-game-high-school

2. James Altucher, *Choose Yourself*, (Amazon Digital Services, June 3, 2013)

3. Chapter 5

4. Billy Procida, A look Back as Marc Maron's Podcast Reaches 100 Million Downloads, *LaughSpin*, December 12, 2013, http://www.laughspin.com/2013/12/12/a-look-back-as-marc-marons -podcast-reaches-100-million-downloads/

5. Marc Maron, WTF Flashback Episode 1, July 25, 2012, http://www.wtfpod.com/podcast/episodes/wtf_flashback_-_episode_1

6. Patrick Freyne, Marc Maron: the First 100 Episodes are Me Asking Celebrities for Help, *Irish Times*, August 31, 2015, http://www.irishtimes.com/culture/tv-radio-web/marc-maron-the-first-100-episodes-are-me-asking-celebrities-for-help-1.2332476

7. Marc Maron, I Have Work to Do on Myself, WTF Podcast, October 14, 2013, http://www.wtfpod.com/dispatches/entries/i_have_work_to_do_on_myself

8. Andrew Clark, Revelations: Marc Maron, *Bostonia*, Winter/Spring 2013, http://www.bu.edu/bostonia/winter-spring13/marc-maron/

9. Hideout Theater, What is Improv, Hideout Theater, http://www.hideouttheatre.com/about/what-is-improv

Chapter 6

1. B.S. Report with Bill Simmons, Wesley Morris, Grantland Podcasts, April 4, 2015, http://espn.go.com/espnradio/grantland/player?id=12612977

2. Ibid.

3. Ibid.

4. Ibid.

5. College of Holy Cross, June 1, 2001, HollyCross.org, http://news.holycross.edu/blog/2001/06/01/bill-simmons-92-is-bostons-sports-guy/

6. B.S. Report with Bill Simmons, Wesley Morris, Grantland Podcasts, April 4, 2015, http://espn.go.com/espnradio/grantland/player?id=12612977

7. Seth Godin, The Dip, (Portfolio, May 10, 2007).

8. Ibid.

9. Barry Petchesky, The Sports Guy Before ESPN: A 2000 Bill Simmons Column Unearthed, Deadspin, January 19, 2012, http://deadspin.com/5877536/the-sports-guy-before-espn-a-2000-bill-simmons-column-is-unearthed

10. Bill Simmons, Is Clemens the Antichrist, ESPN Page 2, http://proxy.espn.go.com/espn/page2/story?id=1206543

11. Barry Petchesky, John Walsh the Godfather of ESPN Will Step Down, Deadspin, January 22, 2015, http://deadspin.com/john-walsh-the-godfather-of-espn-will-step-down-1681228088

12. B.S. Report with Bill Simmons, Wesley Morris, Grantland Podcasts, April 4, 2015, http://espn.go.com/espnradio/grantland/player?id =12612977

13. Bill Simmons, Growing Queasy in the Big Easy, ESPN Page 2, http://proxy.espn.go.com/espn/page2/story?page=simmons/020129

14. Sam Laird, Free Simmons: NFL Crisis Illuminates ESPN's Complicated Duality, Mashable, September 14, 2015, http://mashable.com/2014/09/25/free-simmons-espn-nfl-goodell /#m1_b7xlVHaqa

15. Bill Simmons, In the NBA and Life it's All About Getting Your Reps, ESPN Page 2, November 26, 2008, http://espn.go.com/espn /page2/story?page=simmons/081126

16. Peter Kafka, Sports Guy Bill Simmons Helped Make Podcasts a Thing. Next Up: Business, ReCode, http://recode.net/2014/01/03/ sports-guy-bill-simmons-helped-make-podcasts-a-thing-next-up-a -business/

17. Seth Godin, The Dip, (Portfolio, May 10, 2007).

18. Michael Vitez, From West Philly to GaGaland, Philly.com, February 25, 2015, http://articles.philly.com/2013-02-25/news/37271823_1 _lady-gaga-troy-carter-bus-fare

Chapter 7

1. Kevin Kelly, 1,000 True Fans, KK.org, May 4, 2008, http://kk.org/thetechnium/1000-true-fans/

2. Flula, *Flula Makes Techno Banger* w/ Will Ferrell & *Anchorman 2* Cast,

3. December 19, 2013, https://www.youtube.com/ watch?v=WxHrRM8Asx8

4. MyHarto, MY DRUNK KITCHEN: Spätzle! (ft. Flula!), October 10, 2013, https://www.youtube.com/watch?v=9eNFjX4UHfo

Chapter 8

1. YouTube user: Jamespoppy22, Gamer Apple Switch, featuring Rooster Teeth, YouTube, March 17, 2006 https://www.youtube.com /watch?v=xo4BpgfWiBE

2. Todd Spangler, YouTube Network Fullscreen Acquires Digital Studio Rooster Teeth, Variety, November 10, 2014, http://variety.com /2014/

digital/news/youtube-network-fullscreen-acquires-digital-studio
-rooster-teeth-1201352394/

3. Derek Sivers, How to Start a Movement, TED, February, 2010,
http://www.ted.com/talks/derek_sivers_how_to_start_a
_movement?language=en

Chapter 9

1. Grace Helbig Keynote - "Where the Value Lies" (VidCon 2014),
November 12, 2014, https://www.youtube.com/watch?v
=Gb-zYIz3s1w

2. Ibid.

3. Ibid.

4. John Green, So For Those Unfamiliar with the Situation Grace,
Fishing Boats Proceeds Tumblr, January 2, 2014,
http://fishingboatproceeds.tumblr.com/post/72148332379/
so-for-those-unfamiliar-with-the-situation-grace

5. Hank Green, Daily Grace is Dead – Long Live Grace, Edward
Spoon Hands Tumblr, January 1, 2014, http://edwardspoonhands.
com/post/71918119174/daily-grace-is-dead-long-live-grace

6. Grace Helbig Keynote - "Where the Value Lies" (VidCon 2014),
November 12, 2014, https://www.youtube.com/
watch?v=Gb-zYIz3s1w

Chapter 10

1. Taylor, My Drunk Kitchen's Hannah Hart: The Autostraddle
Interview, Autostraddle, August 29, 2011. http://www.autostraddle.
com/my-drunk-kitchens-hannah-hart-my-favorite-color-is-plaid
-the-autostraddle-interview-107414/

2. Hello Harto, IndieGoGo Page, https://www.indiegogo.com/
projects/hello-harto#/story

3. Ear Biscuits with Rhett and Link, Episode 5 with Hannah Hart,
SoundCloud, October 25, 2013, https://soundcloud.com/
earbiscuits/ep-5-hannah-hart-ear-biscuits

4. Ibid.

5. Ibid.

Books I Love

Business books:

James Altucher's *Choose Yourself!: Be Happy, Make Millions, Live the Dream*

Scott Belsky's *Making Ideas Happen: Overcoming the Obstacles Between Vision and Reality*

Nir Eyal's *Hooked: How to Build Habit-Forming Products*

Brad Feld's *Do More Faster: TechStars Lessons to Accelerate Your Startup*

Kevin Kelly's *The Inevitable: Understanding the 12 Technological Forces That Will Shape Our Future*

Jayson Gaignard's *Mastermind Dinners: Build Lifelong Relationships by Connecting Experts, Influencers and Linchpins*

Seth Godin's *The Dip: A Little Book That Teaches You When to Quit*

David Nihill's *Do You Talk Funny?: 7 Comedy Habits to Become a Better (& Funnier) Public Speaker*

Jay Samit's *Disrupt You!: Master Personal Transformation, Seize Opportunity, and Thrive in the Era of Endless Innovation*

Derek Sivers' *Anything You Want: 40 Lessons for a New Kind of Entrepreneur*

Reid Hoffman, Ben Casnocha, and Chris Yeh's *The Alliance: Managing Talent in the Networked Age*

General Non-Fiction

A.J. Jacobs' *The Year of Living Biblically: One Man's Humble Quest to Follow the Bible as Literally as Possible*

Jonah Keri's *The Extra 2%: How Wall Street Strategies Took a Major League Baseball Team from Worst to First*

Dan Pashman's *Eat More Better: How to Make Every Bite More Delicious*

Alan Sepinwall's *The Revolution Was Televised: The Cops, Crooks, Slingers, and Slayers Who Changed TV*

Willie and Bill Geist's *Good Talk Dad: The Birds and The Bees...and Other Conversations We Forgot to Have*

About the Author

Ryan Williams is an entrepreneur, writer, podcast host, and former stand-up comedian. He helps people and companies build their platforms and launch their ideas to the world.

He is the founder of Ryno Lab, a collaborative influence-based studio that helps brands and entrepreneurs develop and scale their platforms. Ryan's professional experience includes 12 years in marketing, business development, and entertainment. He has been a pioneer in the social media industry, overseeing online go-to-market launches for companies such as Disney, Microsoft, Activision, and Warner Bros. He was also an early team member at the venture-backed startups DigiSynd (acquired by Disney), Machinima.com, and State.com.

When Ryan isn't working with clients, he hosts the podcast Stories from the Influencer Economy, featured on Apple's "New and Noteworthy" list in 2015.

Ryan received his B.A. in Human and Organizational Development from Vanderbilt University and attended secondary school at Choate Rosemary Hall. He currently lives in Los Angeles, CA with his amazing wife and two daughters.

Made in the USA
Charleston, SC
30 September 2016